Politics, Disability, and Education Reform in the South

Politics, Disability, and Education Reform in the South

The Work of John Eldred Swearingen

Edward Janak

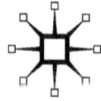

POLITICS, DISABILITY, AND EDUCATION REFORM IN THE SOUTH
Copyright © Edward Janak, 2014.

All rights reserved.

First published in 2014 by
PALGRAVE MACMILLAN®
in the United States—a division of St. Martin's Press LLC,
175 Fifth Avenue, New York, NY 10010.

Where this book is distributed in the UK, Europe and the rest of the world, this is by Palgrave Macmillan, a division of Macmillan Publishers Limited, registered in England, company number 785998, of Houndmills, Basingstoke, Hampshire RG21 6XS.

Palgrave Macmillan is the global academic imprint of the above companies and has companies and representatives throughout the world.

Palgrave® and Macmillan® are registered trademarks in the United States, the United Kingdom, Europe and other countries.

ISBN: 978–1–137–48405–5

Library of Congress Cataloging-in-Publication Data is available from the Library of Congress.

A catalogue record of the book is available from the British Library.

Design by Newgen Knowledge Works (P) Ltd., Chennai, India.

First edition: December 2014

10 9 8 7 6 5 4 3 2 1

Transferred to Digital Printing in 2015

Contents

List of Figures	vii
List of Tables	ix
Acknowledgments	xi
Permissions	xiii
Introduction	1
1 South Carolina, Populism, and the "New South," 1865–1908	15
2 Fighting the Good Fight, 1907–1915	53
3 Political Triptych: Swearingen, Blease, and Tillman, 1911–1915	87
4 Swept Up in Progressivism, 1915–1919	123
5 Robert Cooper and the Final Battle, 1919–1957	161
6 Conclusion: Not the Windows but the Occupant Looking Through	201
Notes	213
References	243
Index	253

Figures

1.1	John Cloud Swearingen with sons, John and George	32
1.2	Anna Tillman Swearingen	34
1.3	John E. Swearingen, student at South Carolina College	39
1.4	John E. Swearingen, South Carolina College Graduation	42
1.5	John E. Swearingen, candidate for state superintendent of education	49
3.1	Tillman on Blease, *Anderson Daily Mail*	101
5.1	Textbook advertisement, *The State*	184
5.2	George Swearingen, South Carolina's "Cotton King"	191
5.3	George Van Swearingen, West Point Graduation	195
5.4	Mary Douglas Swearingen	196
5.5	John E. Swearingen, Jr.	197
5.6	Mary Hough Swearingen, Mother of the Year	198

Tables

2.1	Course units recommended for accreditation	57
2.2	Course descriptions recommended for accreditation	57
2.3	Growth of secondary education in South Carolina, 1906–1910	63
2.4	National comparisons of high schools	64
2.5	Further analysis of national comparisons of high schools	64
2.6	Selected per capita expenditure according to enrollment, 1908–1909	65
2.7	High school enrollment in the Southern states	66
2.8	African American high schools in South Carolina, 1911	67
2.9	Facts for sample cities with populations above 2,500	83
3.1	ASCPS guidelines for high school classification	117
4.1	Chronology of enactment of compulsory education laws	127
4.2	Revised notation of high school accreditation, 1915	130
4.3	Mills enacting compulsory attendance regulations, 1916	139
5.1	Illiterates over the age of ten in South Carolina	168

Acknowledgments

This work has been more than 12 years in the making; in that time, there are multiple debts of gratitude I must acknowledge from the outset. I was a high school teacher throughout my graduate career; thank you to the faculty, staff, administration, and students of Swansea (South Carolina) High School, 1995–2002. During my time at the University of Wyoming, I have been fortunate enough to get two internal grants that supported my work on this project: first, the Mary Garland Early Career Fellowship, which allowed me to return to the Palmetto State and conduct the necessary research to fill in many of the blanks that I had encountered early on; to Mary Garland and all on the Fellowship Board, I thank you. Second, I was awarded the inaugural Patricia McClurg Education Faculty Fellowship; to my former dean, Pat McClurg, and all on the selection committee, I thank you. And to Kay Persichitte, my dean who supported my work above and beyond the call, words cannot express my thanks.

Of course this work would never have been completed without my access to materials in various archives. I am eminently grateful for the patience and courtesies shown to me by the archivists and staff at the South Caroliniana Library, University of South Carolina; the South Carolina Department of Archives and History; Special Collections at the Strom Thurmond Institute, Clemson University; and the Rockefeller Archives, Sleepy Hollow, NY.

To the members of the Swearingen family: posthumous gratitude to John E. Swearingen, Jr.; deepest gratitude to Mary Van Ehrlich for assisting me and offering words of support through the years; and thank you to Marcia Pfeeger and Linda Arnold for the kind words and support in the final stages. To a biographer, the support of the subject's family means everything. Finally, to Sarah Nathan and Mara Berkoff at Palgrave: you are both due for canonization for putting up with me in the final push.

Permissions

Cover photo of John Swearingen's 1932 Campaign Flyer, "Progress Without Extravagance," courtesy of the South Caroliniana Library, University of South Carolina, Columbia, SC.

Chapter 1 photos of John Swearingen, student at the South Carolina College, and John Swearingen's 1908 Campaign Flyer courtesy of the South Caroliniana Library, University of South Carolina, Columbia, SC. All three photos taken from the John E. Swearingen Papers, South Caroliniana Library.

Photos of John Cloud Swearingen with twins, George and Sophie; Anna Tillman Swearingen; John E. Swearingen at South Carolina College Graduation; Mary Hough Swearingen, on their wedding day; George Swearingen as South Carolina's "Cotton King"; George Van Swearingen at West Point Graduation; Mary Douglas Swearingen; John E. Swearingen, Jr.; and Mary Hough Swearingen as Mother of the Year courtesy of the John E. Swearingen, Jr. family scrapbook; permission granted by Marcia S. Pfeeger and Linda Swearingen Arnold.

Photo excerpts from the *Anderson Daily Mail* and *The State* newspapers accessed via Coe Library, Media Collections, University of Wyoming.

The story told in this work has been excerpted in the following:

Janak, E. (2010). Adventitiously blind, advantageously political: John Eldred Swearingen and social definitions of disability in Progressive-Era South Carolina. *Vitae Scholasticae*, *27*(1), 5–25 (reprinted as Janak, E. (2014). Adventitiously blind, advantageously political: John Eldred Swearingen and social definitions of disability in Progressive-Era South Carolina. In Morice, L. C. & Puchner, L. (Eds.). *Life stories: Exploring issues in educational history through biography*. New York: Information Age).

Janak, E. & Moran, P. (October 2010). Unlikely crusader: John Eldred Swearingen and African-American education in South Carolina. *Educational Studies, 46*(2), 224–249.

Janak, E. (December 2009). "'Lordy Miss, That's a Man': John Eldred Swearingen and the Office of State Superintendent of Education in South Carolina." *Research in Higher Education Journal,* (5), 42–57.

Introduction

Sonnet XIX: When I Consider How My Light Is Spent

In the 1650s, John Milton was one of the most educated and revered literary figures in England. He was also going blind. As he came to terms with his blindness, he crafted "Sonnet XIX: When I Consider How My Light Is Spent," sometimes referred to as "On His Blindness." The questions posed by Milton throughout the sonnet exemplify the career of one remarkable teacher, husband, father, grandfather, farmer, and politician who would come almost three hundred years later. When Milton wrote, "Doth God exact day-labor, light denied?" John Eldred Swearingen would answer gruffly and humorously in the affirmative. Swearingen's remarkable career is a fine reminder of those who, in Milton's lines "Bear his mild yoke, they serve him best... / thousands at his bidding speed, / And post o'er land and ocean without rest; / They also serve who only stand and wait."[1] Indeed, John Swearingen is the model of one who served for good cause.

In the present day in the capital city of a state that reveres its history almost above all others, it is remarkable that there exists no monument to John Eldred Swearingen. Short of two endowed positions in the college of education at the University of South Carolina (USC)—the John E. Swearingen Professor of Literacy Education and the John E. Swearingen Professor of Education—a portrait hanging among many others in a hidden conference room on the eighth floor of the State Department of Education, and the dust-covered annual reports in USC's Thomas Cooper Library, there are few reminders of his career. There isn't even a Wikipedia entry to commemorate his legacy. This is remarkable as it seems you cannot go more than a few miles in any direction in South Carolina without coming across a historical monument, marker, or house of some sort. In many cases, the roads themselves are tributes to the past, with various miles marked with the legacy of some financial or historic shaper of the state's story.

The lack of tributes does not mean that Swearingen's career was inconsequential; in fact, he was one of the most influential educators in South

Carolina's history. Serving as state superintendent of education from 1909 through 1922, Swearingen directly oversaw major reform efforts at both state and national levels; he tried to make South Carolina's schools perform on average, if not above regional standards; he made education an ongoing priority for the state legislature; and, most remarkably, he actively campaigned for equal educational opportunities for disenfranchised populations such as mill workers' children and African Americans. The fact that he worked toward these amazing personal and academic goals while adventitiously blind (someone who becomes blind during their life as opposed to someone born blind) makes his story all the more remarkable.[2]

In contemporary educational studies circles in the United States, knowledge of the history of education is no longer trendy. Knowledge of the people who paved the road for contemporary thinkers is at best an afterthought, at worst nonexistent. In light of the contemporary climate of schooling being that obsessively concerned with meeting standards, following a core curriculum, and "scientifically proven" teaching methods, colleges of education have shifted their focus away from foundations toward a more direct, pedagogical approach to training preservice teachers. Even the flagship journal of the field, the *American Educational Research Journal*, chose in 2013 to move to strictly empirical studies in print, eliminating publication of foundational or theoretical work.

This focus on the current in lieu of, instead of combined with, the historical and the philosophical is wrong: it leaves teachers asking the question of "what happened," without having any answer. In spite of this anti-foundational approach, every once in a while, educators come across a figure—or the story of someone's life, for example—reminding them that there is value in such knowledge, lessons to be learned. These figures do not always come with a name such as Dewey or Mann—often they are found buried in the annals of local lore or state documents. This is one such life story.

Swearingen's life proves a fascinating study for many reasons. First, it provides a fascinating analysis of how society treated people with disabilities—and what can happen when someone doesn't subscribe to these societal definitions of disability. Second, Swearingen was reforming the public schools during one of the most interesting, oversimplified, and overlooked periods in their history. At the beginning of the Progressive Era, Swearingen proves that progressivism did not just take place in Chicago and New York, and that the definition of progressive is bound not just to temporality but also to regionalism. Indeed, Swearingen's term in office incorporated many of the fundamental battles of the Progressive Era: "Efficiency versus democracy, freedom versus control, respect for labor versus power for the capitalist: these were the many conflicts that citizens confronted on the shop floor as well as in the local neighborhood school."[3]

Here it must be noted that throughout this work, the word "progressive" is used frequently, and in many contexts. Historically it signifies the Progressive Era, the time approximately between the years 1880 and 1920, in which the United States undertook significant social and political reform in multiple arenas. Educationally it signifies progressive education, the movement that began in the nineteenth century and sought to improve schooling by many means, pedagogically (child-centered progressives) and bureaucratically (administrative progressives). Philosophically it signifies progressivism, a value matrix, those who possess a forward-thinking orientation in their beliefs. In this text three terms will be used as signifiers: Progressive Era, progressive education, and progressive. The third reason Swearingen's life is worthy of study is that his political career is both a model and a cautionary tale. Never one to let politics get in the way of doing his job, yet ultimately undone by opposing machinations, Swearingen's career proves particularly poignant in today's political climate. Indeed, echoes of Arend Flick's description of the life of James Joyce, as that of "an inherently interesting life ... a nearly unbroken sequence of highly charged experiences punctuated by moments of great drama," resound in Swearingen's life story.[4] Fourth and finally, in addition to his contribution to the field of education in South Carolina, Swearingen's life can serve as a model for people with disabilities in today's society, demonstrating what can happen when someone refuses to accept societal expectations.

In spite of these reasons, only two biographies have been published. The first, *A Gallant Journey: Mr. Swearingen and His Family*, was written by his wife, Mary, in 1950.[5] Similar to much earlier works by Lucy Hutchinson and Margaret Cavendish, this almost hagiographic memoir of Swearingen serves as a good introduction to the personal life of the man, as well as provides extensive family history. While Mary provides some details about how Swearingen ran his office and the struggles within his society, she provides neither context nor long-term analysis of her husband's efforts.

The second, *John Eldred Swearingen: Superintendent of Education 1909–1922*, was written by James Dreyfuss in 1997.[6] This monograph summarizes Swearingen's legacy in the field of education and provides a scholarly depiction not only of Swearingen's life, but also of his contributions to the field of education then and now. It provides much of the legalities and numbers missing from Mary's work; however, it does so at the expense of any significant detail about Swearingen's life and daily operations, let alone the political battles Swearingen chose to fight.

When taken together, these two works provide an almost complete portrait of Swearingen—informing readers of both his personal and his professional life. However, even when considered jointly, they do not nearly do justice either to the remarkable nature of Swearingen's life, or to the sociopolitical legacy he left. Neither work explores the remarkable relationship between the state superintendent and his "Uncle Bennie," US Senator Benjamin "Pitchfork Ben" Tillman. Both works tend to gloss over Swearingen's hyper-politicized, ultra-contentious dealings with South Carolina Governor Coleman Blease—a relationship that had a tremendous impact on his career.

This work seeks to redress and combine what has come before. It not only addresses the best of both previous works, but also seeks to expand on what is missing. Additionally, reading both previous works leaves the reader asking a series of "why's?" Why did Swearingen take stances so opposed to those of the family and society in which he was raised? Why did he work so actively to reform the schools of South Carolina? Why did he so actively oppose groups that could further his causes? While avoiding psychoanalytic analysis, this work does attempt to address these questions, exploring how intersectionality—in this case, the intersections of race, class, disability, and masculinity—impacted Swearingen's life and career. It is easy to say, for example, "Swearingen did so because as a man who was blind he felt sympathy with other marginalized populations"; this work hopes to problematize and add complexity to this view.

Swearingen's Life as Narrative

The "thrilling narrative" that was Swearingen's life was not just an apt description of his political career, but rather of his personal life as well. Blinded in a hunting accident in 1888, Swearingen never allowed himself the luxury of self-pity or doubt. His academic life began with that year spent in the Georgia Academy for the Blind. There Swearingen mastered a set of coping skills, then moved on to become a student at the Cedar Springs Institute for the Deaf and Blind of South Carolina, which he attended from 1890 through 1893. Swearingen then had an outstanding career as a student at the South Carolina College from 1895 to 1899.[7] Upon graduation, Swearingen became a teacher at the Cedar Springs Institute for the Deaf and Blind. Persuaded by friends and family, Swearingen ran for the office of State Superintendent of Education after eight years of teaching.

Throughout his public and his private life, Swearingen kept his love for his home state first. As such, he was concomitantly shaped by and helped shape his home state, truly reflecting the notion of a Southern gentleman. In terms of performing masculinity, while Swearingen could not serve his state in a martial capacity, at least he could serve it in the political. As in many other aspects of Southern society, Swearingen was a man of contradictions.[8] He maintained some antebellum philosophy while simultaneously embracing a more progressive stance in his beliefs. Proud to be a farmer in the Populist-Tillman notion of the word and a member of a long-standing cotton-growing family, Swearingen effectively ran the schools of South Carolina and lived in the capitol city, Columbia, while maintaining both the family plantation located near Trenton in Edgefield County and an additional lumber farm in Florida.[9]

However, the most powerful contradiction of Swearingen's career is observed in his attitude toward race. A social traditionalist, Swearingen received letters from home discussing the performance of "your darkies."[10] However, he also encouraged the colored schools of South Carolina more so than any previous state superintendent. As noted by Dreyfuss in his monograph:

> Swearingen ultimately believed, in the broadest sense, that education should be equitably provided, funded, and available to all citizens, regardless of class, race, or gender. Even though guided by the precepts of *Plessy vs Ferguson* (1896), Swearingen's writings proves his commitment and dedication, time and again, to the provision of educational opportunity for both races.[11]

Swearingen's significance cannot be understated. John Garraty presents a three-tiered paradigm regarding biographical subjects. In short, biographical subjects are sorted based on the writer's "over-all view of the importance of individual intelligence and character in determining the course of events." There are three types of significant subjects: those who are "significant only because of the times in which they live make them so"; those "forceful individuals" who have "change[d] the trend of events"; and those who are not controlled by themselves or their times, but rather by an outside force such as luck, chance, or destiny.[12]

Within this paradigm, Swearingen is most definitely a forceful figure who worked to change the society in which he lived. Swearingen was unafraid to take on any and all challengers to his vision. During his term, he came into political and professional conflict with textbook vendors, state legislators, the governor, the General Education Board, and even the Ku Klux Klan. However, nothing deterred Swearingen from doing his utmost to improve his beloved state's schools for all students, regardless of race, ethnicity, or income. He was in a position determined on Election Day, but worked to improve the state whether it made him popular or not. If opinion polls had existed at the time, many of Swearingen's decisions would have ranked in the cellar; he would have made the same decisions regardless.

Discovering Swearingen

In spite of and because of these contradictions in his life, and the fact that he overcame great odds to achieve much success, Swearingen serves as a wonderful biographical figure. Finding his life story is a good example of the experience described by biographer Jane Maher, that if a biographer "is willing to devote the time, energy, and resources to subjects who are not particularly prominent or popular, it is not all that difficult to find extraordinary people whose lives most certainly deserve to be recorded."[13] Indeed, in light of the constant bombardment of negative, partisan political messages that dominate mainstream media in the current-day United States, the reminder of Swearingen's story is fortuitous. It reminds us that politics has always been a turbulent career, but that the best of those who practice politics find ways of, if not transcending the worst, at the very least overcoming it.

In the decade between discovering Swearingen's story and focusing on getting it down on paper, one of the most common questions I get regarding the project is how I came to it. My pat response is a paraphrase of Stephen King, or Spider Robinson: "It is the story, not he who tells it." Swearingen's story is extraordinary enough to glean attention in its own right, and I deem myself fortunate to have discovered it. However, when pressed, I have to reluctantly admit that I met Mr. Swearingen entirely by accident.

I was in near-panic mode. I was fishing for a dissertation topic while preparing to move halfway across the country, from South Carolina to Wyoming, and needed to get a topic nailed down and at least initial research conducted in less than six months. I was sitting down with a graduate student who had a position at the South Caroliniana Library, lamenting my topic-less state, when he mentioned that they had got several rolls of microfilm in something education related, but it had not been catalogued yet. He said I was welcome to go through it as they were cataloguing to see if anything jumped out. The microfilm was correspondence with the state of South Carolina from the General Education Board, and I spent the better part of a week skimming reel after reel.

After thousands of pages of correspondence in tones that ranged from businesslike to deferential, the letters were beginning to blur together. And then, visually, one page stood out as the signatory signed his name like a seismograph—a series of jagged spikes that filled the entire bottom of the page. And like the tremor recorded on a seismograph, so too was my view shaken by Swearingen's correspondence. Gruff, demanding, and dismissive, he consistently informed the board that he didn't care about them personally or politically. His attitude caught my attention; after going through all the correspondence with the board, I was told that his family papers were in the Caroliniana if I was interested. I moved on to another library to examine his state superintendent annual reports, and found several intriguing items therein. From there, I read the two works written about him, and the beginning of not just a dissertation topic but also my initial line of research as an academic were set.

Swearingen and the Schools of South Carolina

This work is one attempt to present exactly how Swearingen's vision shaped the development of the public high school in South Carolina, mirroring what was happening in public high schools nationally, and what legacies of his tenure remain in today's schools. As described by USC Emeritus Dean of Faculty Francis W. Bradley, "The story of Mr. Swearingen's life is the history of education, especially primary and secondary education, through a critical time in this strategic field of activity." Swearingen's efforts in this position, while overlooked in the annals of South Carolina history, are significant. Indeed, "[Swearingen] laid the solid foundation for the much-needed growth and development out of the three-month school into the standardized nine-month schools we now have. Without his brilliant intellect, his iron will, and his unshakable faith the task could not have been accomplished."[14]

Education historians in the United States tend to examine specific periods in the development of public schools. The Colonial Period is necessary to study because of the deep roots put down during that era. Likewise, the Modern Era/Five E's is studied for its revolutionary impact on desegregation and integration in the United States. Of all the periods in between, however, one of the most influential in regard to the development of public schools is often overlooked. For example, when one thinks of a typical modern high school, the bulk of the curriculum, policies, and even physical plants are a direct extension of the turn of the twentieth century. Nationally, regionally, and in South Carolina, the first 25 years of the century was the period that had the most long-term effects in terms of the development of public schools; however, it is the least examined in terms of study. While the roots of the public schools extend through the Colonial and Early National Periods, the majority of the shaping of the modern schools was a direct result of the debates, laws, and policies crafted between 1900 and 1925.

It is fitting that Swearingen's career was of his time. During his career, Swearingen served in a variety of educational roles in his home state, culminating in that of state superintendent of education. Swearingen's was one of the first educational administrations to devote a significant amount of attention, time, and resources specifically on moving South Carolina's public high schools from the nineteenth century notion of the academy to the twentieth century notion of the public high school. After leaving this office, Swearingen never again worked for the public good, choosing instead to tend to his family farms and raising his children. In spite of serving only for 14 years, Swearingen's legacy as one of the most outstanding leaders of education in South Carolina is assured.

As state superintendent, Swearingen brought a unique blend of philosophical beliefs to his vision of public schools in order to make the educational transition from the nineteenth century notion of the private, elite academy to the twentieth century model of public schools. For example, in discussing the 1909 High School Act, Swearingen wrote that "the high school is the college of the people. It brings better educational advantages to every boy and girl in the district."[15] With his educational background in the classical curriculum, Swearingen was an essentialist, a firm supporter of the core academic curriculum as outlined by Harvard's Committee of Ten.[16] He would find common ground in contemporary movements such as the Coalition of Essential Schools and the Core Knowledge Foundation.

However, Swearingen was also a pragmatic; he shared the distinctly Southern notion that agriculture was the key to South Carolina's economic prosperity and, as such, vocational education should be fully funded in schools.[17] During his time, the implementation of the 1917 Smith-Hughes Act provided federal dollars in support of vocational and agricultural programs. Having South Carolina high schools fully prepared to accept this funding, Swearingen was able to greatly expand upon vocational education, not just in agriculture but also in a variety of high school courses such as domestic science, bookkeeping, commercial geography, manual training, and stenography and typesetting.[18] These courses fit Swearingen's philosophy of education, as he stated in a 1902 essay written for *The Bohemian* magazine: "All peoples have learned not only that education imparts a potential energy to the field of practical industry, but also that the best part of education comes not so merely from knowing, as applying knowledge in action."[19]

Through these course offerings, Swearingen tried to craft a tie between the schools and the industries of South Carolina—specifically the cotton mills. Swearingen attempted to begin to link education and industry in a commercial-educational impetus to benefit the state as a whole. Swearingen's office sponsored many educational efforts to improve the educational lot of the mill workers and their children. For all his work trying to make progress for historically marginalized cultures, he never fully won their political support. It cannot be forgotten that Swearingen was in a political position and, as such, subject to the whims of the electorate—and the cotton millworkers perceived reformers such as Swearingen as a threat more than an asset. In an ironic turn, in spite of this educational support for the industrial education that supported the mills of the state, Swearingen noted that "the cotton mill vote went against me about three to one. This was the strongest element in the opposition, so far as any one class of schools or voters was concerned."[20]

Swearingen and the Politics of the Period

In spite of all this positive work during his tenure in public service, Swearingen grappled with contradictory issues surrounding his career. Swearingen was the nephew of former South Carolina governor and US senator Benjamin Tillman, and his family was considered among the political elite in the upstate (northwestern) region of South Carolina. Swearingen was interested in studying politics, and had even applied to Columbia University in New York City to enter their political science department. However, he was denied the Rhodes Scholarship, and thus devoted himself to his career in teaching. With this political background—having seen the best and worst in South Carolina politics—and sensing the national trend to separate education and politics in light of the corruption of the period, Swearingen insisted on keeping his position as state superintendent as apolitical as possible. In an early statement to the press, Swearingen wrote:

> Politics is not my profession, but I have always cherished the ambition to serve my native state. My interest in public affairs has been second only to my interest in education, and for years I have tried to be an earnest student of both. I am therefore impelled by every consideration of taste and training to make the race. The office is one of honor and importance. It is educational rather than political, and affords to any man an inviting field of work and opportunity.[21]

This is not to say that politics did not affect Swearingen's tenure in office. Nationally, as described by Michael Kirst, political control was revolutionized during this period. Indeed, "The most significant changes [in educational governance] occurred during...1900–1920."[22] The wave of progressivism that swept across the entire nation did not crash on the mountainous shoals of the state's northwestern border; Swearingen's tenure was characteristic of Progressive Era politics that overhauled much in the state. Politicians in the state such as Coleman Blease, who vigorously opposed this progressive wave, came into direct conflict with Swearingen. Ironically again, it was the very politics that Swearingen vehemently tried to bar from education that provided the undoing of his career in public office: Swearingen's career was "a thrilling narrative" of "the turbid waters of politics, where some people forget conscience in the heat of the campaign and resort to calumny and slander."[23]

Methodology: Contextualizing the Life

When considering methodology, two distinct areas need to be addressed: writing and research. In the "Present Practice" section of *The Nature of Biography*, Robert Gittings details five areas of a subject's life to which the biographer must attend. While not using these five areas as a blueprint to this work—in fact, not all areas are particularly relevant—they do offer a helpful paradigm in contextualizing Swearingen's life. First, the biographer must include an analysis of their subject. While Gittings cautions that this psychoanalysis leads to many potential shortcomings, in Swearingen's case it is a risk well worth taking.[24] In this work, the question of "why" is the most frequently asked when listeners and readers come into contact with Swearingen's story.

This work utilizes multiple lenses through which Swearingen's life and actions can be viewed and analyzed. As previously stated, Swearingen is not merely a product of his historical context—but rather an advocate of issues years ahead of his time. While there are many reasons for his actions, for the sake of this work only the effects of societal notions of masculinity on his actions will serve as analysis: Gail Bederman's delineation of masculinity is used, a "historical, ideological process...the cultural process whereby concrete individuals are constituted as members of a preexisting social category—as men." In short, Swearingen was acting to prove his masculinity in the aftermath of a period during which "Northerners and Southerners also argued about what kind of men they were...the political and physical conflict over slavery's extension also spawned a rhetorical battle over the meanings of manhood."[25]

Returning to Gittings's paradigm, a second category of biographical analysis is the physical being of the subject. Indeed, as noted by the author, the "physical states of the subject of biography" definitely have "far-reaching historical consequences."[26] Swearingen's life proves an excellent example of this: another reason why Swearingen acted as progressively as he did was directly related to his disability. Swearingen was acting to reject what he had been taught he was capable of. Additionally, Swearingen knew via his disability what it was like to be seen as "different" and have society immediately categorize him based on physical appearance. In this light, Swearingen's actions to benefit African Americans via the schools are understandable.

The final area of Gittings's analysis is the political history of the subject and their times. This area most definitely shaped Swearingen's life and career. Swearingen had a strong love of his state, and an even stronger desire to provide some public service to it. In light of his disability, politics was his best hope at being of public worth. While his relationship with his uncle flavored his political views, much of what Swearingen attempted was in opposition to his uncle's racist beliefs; in fact, Swearingen began his most ardent efforts for African American education after Tillman's death.

As interesting as it is, however, writing Swearingen's life story is not the only purpose of this work. There is a pressing need to study not only the man, but also the context in which he functioned and the larger world he helped shape. Local scholarship tends toward the opposite extreme; most studies tend to be school specific. Also, much local scholarship tends to neglect the period before the progressive era influenced South Carolina's schools. Conversely, most contemporary national scholarship tends to be general, focusing on the more storied periods in school history—such as the common school era or the progressive movement, while none focuses in any depth on the period when both merged. Utilizing a variety of works of educational history and sociology, as well as works of general history, Swearingen's life is used as a lens through which to view the "big picture," the larger mosaic of national and state trends in history and education.

The second aspect of methodology is research. As previously noted, there are only two biographies of Swearingen, neither an overtly scholarly work. In spite of these gaps, there are several sources of information from which this work draws. In an attempt to overcome the limitations inherent in writing biography, this work uses as wide a variety of sources as possible.[27] In addition to the broader works surrounding public education of the period and in spite of the fact that his official papers consist of three documents, Swearingen's extensive personal papers are available at South Caroliniana Library. Additionally, Swearingen's correspondence with his uncle, political and personal, can be found scattered throughout the Tillman Papers located at Clemson University. Correspondence with the governors in office during his tenure is available via the governor's papers located at the South Carolina State Archive.

Swearingen's official papers while in office, unfortunately, have been either lost or destroyed; while the State Department of Education has relatively contemporary records, most of the previous records, before the move to their current building, are essentially nonexistent. To compensate, the annual reports of the state superintendent of education are public records. These reports, written specifically for the state legislature, serve both as strong documentation regarding Swearingen's challenges, attitudes, and visions regarding the public schools of South Carolina and as further documentation of the relationship with the legislature.

In addition to the formal annual reports issued by Swearingen's office, the reports drafted by Swearingen during his tenure regarding public schools serve as excellent documentation of his efforts while in office. He maintained a steady correspondence with the General Education Board of New York, all documented and microfilmed by the Rockefeller Foundation. Swearingen's correspondence with the General Education Board is not only on microfilm, but also complete with handwritten notes and interoffice interviews, archived at the Rockefeller Archive Center, Sleepy Hollow, New York. *The State* newspaper gave occasional press to educational issues and the comings and goings of the state superintendent. All in all, there is enough material that biographer Leon Edel's lessons of properly using archives must be used: to not bog down in trivia, to temporally shuttle back and forth among materials, and to treat archival data as raw material and not antiquarian possessions.[28]

General Overview

This work takes a fairly traditional view of biography, choosing to present Swearingen's life and times in near chronological order. The first chapter presents the sociopolitical environment that produced Swearingen. Beginning in Reconstruction, chapter 1 looks at how much South Carolina fit (and chose not to fit) into the New South paradigm. This chapter starts to explore the relationship between education and politics, also providing a bit of background on "Pitchfork Ben" Tillman, Swearingen's uncle and political mentor, and the populist movement in the United States. Additionally, the chapter looks at educational trends nationally and how the Palmetto State fared, particularly setting the stage regarding the education of African Americans. The chapter continues with the accident that left Swearingen adventitiously blind and the educational efforts of his family and the institutions to which he was sent. Furthering this educational trend, Swearingen's remarkable career at the South Carolina College (now the University of South Carolina at Columbia) and his early days as a teacher and principal are detailed. Finally, the chapter examines Swearingen's first campaign for state superintendent, where politics and education truly merge.

The bulk of the work examines Swearingen's years in office, including his efforts in service as well as major events from his personal life, all presented against the backdrop of national social, political, and educational movements. Keeping with the theme of the relationship between politics and education, chapters 2–5 focus on the relationships between Swearingen and the governors who held office. These men were remarkably different in their political philosophies, from reformers such as Martin Ansel (chapter 2) to progressives such as Richard Manning and Robert Cooper (chapters 4 and 5, respectively), and even a governor who served one day (Charles Smith, highlighted in chapter 3). As a nemesis both to Swearingen and to Tillman, Governor Coleman "Coley" Blease warrants detailed exploration. The intersecting careers of Swearingen, Blease, and Tillman form a fascinating political triptych (chapter 3). The work's climax is chapter 5, which summarizes the final electoral battle that drove Swearingen from politics, his post-retirement life including one more run for public office that he embarked upon in the 1930s, and the lives of Swearingen's wife and children during his retirement and after his death.

The conclusion puts Swearingen's life not in historic, but in contemporary, context. It explores where we are as a society regarding many of the positions Swearingen adopted on race, disability, and masculinity, and where Swearingen hoped we would be. It concludes by looking at Swearingen as a sort of "model politician," a reminder that even in times of extreme political conflict, those elected to office should never put their personal or political agendas in front of the needs—or the desires—of the electorate. It also serves as a reminder that sometimes politicians need to take risks because it is in the best interests of the people they serve and represent, even if politically inexpedient.

Overall, this work presents the life and career of Swearingen in light of his effects on the public high schools of South Carolina. In his book *South Carolina and the New Deal*, historian Jack Irby Hayes presents one of the most accurate, clear, and concise summaries of South Carolina history: understanding South Carolinians "is as simple as ABCD." The "A" is for ancestors, "who were worshiped with regularity" by the state's citizens. The "B" stands for blacks, booze, Blease, and Baptists. The "C" stands for contrasts, Confederacy, conservatism, and cotton. The "D" stands for Depression and Democracy. As noted by Hayes: These factors fostered a sense of civic duty, legitimated public officeholders, established the extent of political tolerance, and gave definition to terms such as equality, democracy, and liberty. They also set the precedent for how Carolinians assessed human predicaments, selected heroes, defined the role of government, viewed relations both human and holy, and grouped people into social classes.[29]

All of these "ABCDs" shaped Swearingen's life and molded his political career. His story is inspirational for his overcoming the challenges of being visually impaired; it serves as a powerful example of one person flying in the face of social tradition; it is truly representative of the best of South Carolina.

1

South Carolina, Populism, and the "New South," 1865-1908

Prologue: South Carolina as Seen by a Yankee[1]

South Carolina is a State of perpetual irritation, situated between Georgia and North Carolina, and some where [sic] between the Revolution and the War Between the States. It is the fighting State of the Union, and is the unsafest [sic] spot between the Atlantic and the Pacific in which to discuss politics or edit a newspaper.[2]

South Carolina is about as big as the frontyard [sic] of a Texas cattle king. It contains 30,000 square miles, is shaped like a five cent out of a pie, and has 1,500,000 people, including Republicans, Chinese and Indians not taxed. The population is almost equally divided between whites and negroes, but one white Carolinian, when he gnashes his teeth and draws his breath with a low hissing sound, can make one hundred colored residents go away in search of rest and a change of climate without waiting for the next train.

South Carolina was settled about 250 years ago, but has been unsettled ever since. It has always been noted for its nervous disposition, and its willingness to rise up and smite the universe on all occasions. The British were having an easy time in the Revolution when they struck South Carolina, but Gen. Marion soon made them look like a Republican who had criticized General Lee in Charleston. The State helped win the Revolution but threatened to take its doll things and go home in Jackson's administration and in 1861 it opened war between the States by seceding with a prodigious explosion. Later it contributed Tillman to the United States Senate and has listened to the uproarious results with pride ever since. South Carolina was severely shaken by earthquake in 1886, but did not secede at that time.

South Carolina raises rice and sweet potatoes and supplies turpentine and rosin to the world at large. It begins at the Atlantic Ocean in a modest way about six feet below high water, and for many miles inland is so moist that farmers keep life belts handy on their wagons. It has many fine old towns, full of polite and chivalrous citizens, but the population peters out in the mountains of Western Carolina, where the people eat clay instead of ice cream and lobsters, and empty the hook-worms out of their Sunday shoes by pounding the soles with a stick. There are three religions in the State, Protestant, Catholic, and States Rights. Between the Savannah and Pee Dee Rivers John C. Calhoun is still the greatest man in the world and history closed in 1865.

Charleston, a beautiful petrified city on the seacoast, is the metropolis of South Carolina.

Reconstruction, Red Shirts, and the Rise of the New South

The preceding passage, though comic in tone and considered impolitic by today's standards, summarizes the South Carolina of Swearingen's youth perfectly. A person's life is shaped by, whether through deference or resistance, the context in which they live; to fully understand a person one must understand their times. To say the period in which John Eldred Swearingen came of age in South Carolina was a time of turmoil is a gross understatement. While the late 1960s are viewed by popular society as a turbulent time in US history for civil rights, the 1870s were much more so; Reconstruction marked a hugely significant time in the history of the nation. The ocean of social consciousness was stormy, and Swearingen was navigating these rocky shoals without the benefit of sight.

The South presents an interesting study, particularly in the first part of the twentieth century. Educational historian John Hardin Best provides an apt description:

> Historians and other writers have described the South and its institutions in terms such as *different*, or on occasion *distinctive*, or even *unique*. The South has also been termed "aberrant" and its distinctive institutions, in the famous phrase of Jefferson, "peculiar." None of these descriptive terms is necessarily pejorative, but they do clearly indicate the departure of the South as a region from what has been claimed as the "mainstream" of America. The South as a regional culture has differed from the other regions of the United States from the seventeenth century to the present time.[3]

While not explicitly shaping Swearingen's acts, personal or professional—he was not out to prove his manhood explicitly—societal notions of masculinity did shape Swearingen's actions, both proactive and reactive. It can be argued that proving masculinity was one means of explaining both the groundwork of Swearingen's actions and the conflicts these actions entailed. Timothy Beneke explains that masculinity is a "multidetermined phenomena" shaped by material conditions, prevalence of war, changing women's roles, industrialization, and genetic predisposition; in Swearingen's case, all these contributed to his desire to prove masculinity.[4] Historically, the region as a whole was hypermasculinized; Swearingen sought to be of use as "a man" against this backdrop.

It must be noted that, particularly in the South at this time, white masculinity and black masculinity cannot be described in the same terms. As explained by Ronald Jackson, "Black masculinist scholarship cannot afford to accept, approve, and adopt the same cultural, social, and political agendas as traditional White masculinist scholarship. The two areas of gender theory share some commonalities, however, there is a distinction that emerges at the intersection where gender meets culture."[5] Of significant import was the fact that Black masculinity during Reconstruction was becoming defined into what Professor of Law Frank Rudy Cooper describes as a "bipolar identity" split between a "Bad Black Man who is crime-prone and hypersexual and a Good Black Man who distances himself from blackness and associates with white norms." Beginning in Reconstruction, but still arguably true through the twenty-first century, this led to a dominance-based "compensatory subjugation" that took the form of social incentive: "The threat of the Bad Black Man label provides heterosexual black men with an assimilationist incentive to perform...identities consistent with the Good Black Man image."[6]

While Black masculinity was being split, white masculinity was becoming complicated through domesticity and greater social events. White material culture dictated Swearingen act as "a man" in running the family farm. Swearingen's family and community were still recovering from the Civil War when World War I took place while he was in office. The South was transitioning from a mainly agricultural to a more industrial, textile-based economy. And there was Reconstruction. When a human limb breaks, the speed and quality of the healing process depend upon the nature of the break. A quick, clean break results in a sound, relatively painless healing process, while a jagged, distended break results in a slow, painful, sometimes incomplete healing. The Civil War was such a jagged, distended break, and Reconstruction was the subsequent attempt at healing. These years (1865–1877) in South Carolina were as politically damaging as the years of Civil War (1861–1865) were economically and socially damaging. Mary Swearingen, the descendant of a Confederate veteran, explained that in her grandfather's eyes, "Reconstruction necessitated a higher degree of grit and endurance than had been needed to face the enemy's gun."[7]

The very identity in which the antebellum South was completely wrapped obsessed over dated notions of honor and masculinity; as delineated by Craig Thompson Friend and Lorri Glover, "[h]onor was a set of expectations determined and perpetuated by the community, which differentiated men in the eyes of others through public rituals. Achieved by controlling households and commanding slaves, mastery was less scripted and more of a consequence to a man's self-identity."[8] If manhood was determined by ownership of land and slaves, Reconstruction's legacy of taking these ownerships away was a threat to the white-male-dominant society as a whole.

The South after the Civil War was a region that had more pressing concerns than the development of education. It had a large, newly freed, uneducated African American population. The white population reacted with surprise and fear to this new element of society owing to the widespread (albeit wholly inaccurate) belief that Blacks were inherently indolent, lazy, and prone to criminal tendencies without proper white supervision.[9] The whites were surprised that the former slaves would leave the plantations, not recognizing the inherent problems with a slave system; and they were afraid that the newly freed population would rise up en masse to (some would argue rightfully) claim property, by force if necessary.

Along with the destruction of the Southern social structure came the destruction of the Southern economic structure. Those fields unscarred by war lay fallow as there was no labor force to till them. The white Southern male population was decimated by war and the new freedmen were less than eager to engage in the same tasks they did during the Antebellum Period. This, in combination with inflation and the destruction wrought by Sherman's forces, made rebuilding the Southern economy a precarious event. Northern reformers swept into the South for reasons both pecuniary and philanthropic, and were looked upon with dread by native South Carolinians: those who moved south to cash in on the reform efforts were "carpetbaggers" and those locals who assisted them were "scalawags." Education reformers were part of this larger impulse, attempting to impose Northern ideas and models on the Southern culture, with no regard to the social and economic disarray of the postwar era.

Emblematic of Southern resistance to the changes wrought during Reconstruction was a group of resistors called the Red Shirt Riders. Called Red Shirts because of the red calico, flannel, or silk shirts they would all wear on rides, they were a group of men, including wealthy farmers, schoolteachers, and bankers, united and clear in their goals: white supremacy and rule by the Democratic Party. The Red Shirts staged torchlight processions, committed night raids against carpetbaggers, whipped politically active African Americans, and fired cannon during Republican rallies. They were similar to the Ku Klux Klan, with one notable difference: "Unlike the hooded Klansmen, the Red Shirts wanted Republicans, Populists, blacks, and the entire white population to know who they were and what they stood for."[10]

Red Shirt Riders did not hide behind masks or hoods for many possible reasons. First, as the power structures in their respective towns, they existed above and within the law; there would be no repercussions. Second, to most of the populace, they represented the last spirit of the Old South, a spirit that remains popular in particular among poor whites in the South to this day. Third, if Reconstruction was an attack on Southern manhood, then these riders were returning masculinity to the South.[11] They represented, to use Cheng's term, hegemonic masculinity, "constructed in relation to femininities and subordinated and marginalized masculinities" and "characterized by numerous attributes such as domination, aggressiveness, competitiveness, athletic prowess, stoicism, and control."[12]

Two proud Red Shirt Riders were Swearingen's father and Uncle Ben Tillman. As a result of Red Shirt efforts, political power returned to the white elites across the South: as John Hope Franklin aptly explained, "The Confederacy was beaten but refused to die. The spirit of the South and the principles underlying it were very much alive." Explaining the defeat of Reconstruction, he writes, "Those who had fought against the Union were in control, pursuing most of their prewar policies as though there had never been a war. This was reconstruction, Confederate style!"[13] This period led to the formation of the "New South," for better or for worse.[14]

The Emergence and Development of Public Schools

Just as Reconstruction shaped and affected all aspects of Southern society, so too did politics play a role in the reformation of public schools. Historically, the South had a two-tier system of schooling. Children of well-to-do parents sent their children to private schools or to Europe for the best education money could afford; it was a social status symbol. Children of lower classes, particularly after 1811, attended any of a wide variety of public schools. Southern African American students were educated in the same way as poor white students until the slave revolts of the 1820s caused most Southern states to outlaw the education of slaves. Philanthropic groups such as The Society for the Propagation of the Gospel often set up schools for marginalized populations such as African

Americans and American Indians. Unfortunately, the Civil War halted school development in the region. The then predominantly male teaching force served in the armies by volunteerism, draft, or conscription. Schools were converted for martial use, serving as barracks and makeshift army hospitals. Male students of age were in the fight, and female students were often busy keeping the home front as intact as possible.

One Reconstruction gain that lasted, however, was schooling reemerging in importance. Of particular importance was the question of what to do with the newly freed slaves of the time. Many saw the passage of the Fourteenth Amendment in 1868 as legal grounds to equalize the schools; however, as is commonly known, it took almost a hundred years before the amendment would be applied specifically to the schools. With Reconstruction in the South came new state constitutions, all of which exhibited Northern influence by calling for a statewide system of public education for all children. Once again, South Carolina was emblematic of the region during this period. The 1868 Constitution of South Carolina, like constitutions of most southern states, called for education of all its children. Specific features of the constitution included the creation of the offices of state superintendent and county commissioners, the creation of a uniform system of public schools for all children, the setting of the school year at a six-month minimum, the stipulation that all children should receive at the least 24 months of education, and the poll tax reserved for the schools. Another trait South Carolina shared with its regional counterparts was the fact that most educational provisions were never implemented.

For the next 28 years, the state would grapple with how to educate children of marginalized populations. In some extremely rare cases, schools became desegregated. More common were schools such as those in Charleston, which opened "Negro Schools" that operated with the same budgets as white schools and were staffed by white teachers. Both cases frustrated the white-dominant population of the time, and, more often than not, local officials chose to remain defiant of the new laws, proved incompetent at educating a diverse population, pled ignorance at inclusivity, or some combination thereof. By 1878, the South Carolina legislature passed a school law banning desegregated schools, but featuring funding to train African American teachers. All of this indecision led to the general failure of the schools of the period.

Not all schools were failures: African Americans were quietly exercising their post-Reconstruction powers and opening their own schools—hosting community fund-raising drives, volunteering to donate time and materials, and even enduring double taxation in order to promote education within their community. However quietly ex-slaves opened schools across the South, there was an overt hostility toward educating freedmen and their descendants by white society. As noted by John Hope Franklin, this hostility was part of a scheme to keep whites superior. African American schools were destroyed, razed, or burned. White teachers who worked with the African American population were ostracized by the community. African Americans were prevented from attending school by all means necessary. In Franklin's words, "Already the pattern was emerging: bitter resentment of 'outside interference' that would contaminate the Negroes and yet no effort by white Southerners to improve conditions."[15]

Swearingen's family, like most white families of the period, was extremely racist. This was the norm; racism was everywhere at the time. Considering the endemic racism of the region, it is easy to become dismissive when discussing Southern education. Stereotypes come to mind of a people and a region long resistant to formal education. There is some validity to this belief; as laid out by Irving Gershenberg:

> Most students of southern history have concluded that the people of the South cared little for education...While public education was well advanced in the North and West before 1860, the South provided very little in the way of educational opportunities for the mass of its population before the twentieth century...While every Northern state could, at that date, claim to have established a creditable public school system, only five of the Southern states had even begun to do so. In 1880, the average school age child in the South received only 23.6 days of schooling while his Northern counterpart received 72 days and as late as 1930, the comparative statistics were 95.9 and 1209.[16]

Lack of public interest and reinforcement of the stereotype of the backward Southern rural person would be the easiest, and also erroneous, assumption. As further explained by Gershenberg, a wide variety of hypotheses have emerged to explain poor performance. These range from poverty to limited urbanization to "the burden, both financial and psychological, of having to educate black as well as white children," and white resistance: "Southern whites felt public education had a leveling tendency and as such objected to its extension, even if education was provided for the races in separate schools." Also, in working to preserve their antebellum way of life, many Southerners actively sought to "discourage human mobility and creativity" and, as such, actively discouraged education. Whether this emerged from a sense of *noblesse oblige* of the upper classes or outright racism among the lower classes, many Southerners "championed human inequality, accepted the static state as ideal, and discouraged progress."[17]

Another theory, laid out by Swearingen monographist James Dreyfuss, comes in two parts. First, South Carolina schools took an extremely hard blow during the Civil War. Sherman's march destroyed buildings, led to serious financial inequity, and caused looting. According to Dreyfuss, as unlikely as it may seem to contemporary readers, many of the books from South Carolina schools and libraries were carried by Sherman's troops back north. Second, the Reconstruction constitution itself led to the schools being behind. Since very few citizens were allowed to participate in the process—particularly few native whites—there was a large distrust for the document as a whole. Since the office of state superintendent—indeed, all state control—was reestablished in the constitution, the people of the state tended to look askance upon state-sponsored schools until the rise of the New South.[18]

For a variety of reasons, the birth of public schools in South Carolina was as tumultuous and stormy as any other event throughout this period in the state's history. By the time Reconstruction hit the South, public schooling had become *de rigeur* in the majority of Northern states. The rhetoric of common school advocates such as Massachusetts State Superintendent Horace Mann had become a national outcry: public schools were essential to the very being of the nation. A good example of Mann's rhetoric can be found from an "Introduction" to his *Common School Journal*, in which he wrote:

> *The common school is the greatest discovery ever made by man*...Let the Common School be expanded to its capabilities, let it be worked with the efficiency of which it is susceptible, and nine-tenths of the crime in the penal code would become obsolete; the long catalog of human ills would be abridged; men would walk more safely by day; every pillow would be more inviolable by night; property, life, and character held by a stronger tenure; all rational hopes respecting the future brightened.[19]

Schools came to be seen as the means to right all social ills and create the strongest nation on earth. Accordingly, most states in the North had public schooling written into their state constitutions; those that didn't soon amended accordingly.

It logically followed that when Northern reformers swept into the South during Reconstruction, they brought with them this great value placed on public schools. The rhetoric of the time was similar to that of the founding fathers: for democracy to be successful, participants in a democracy must be educated. In light of this belief, many state constitutions written during Reconstruction cited public education as important a cause as universal suffrage. In fact, each Southern state wrote a clause into its constitution calling for free public education for all children of school age, usually defined as between the ages of 5 and 21; however, the debate whether this would mean mixed or segregated education was too hotly discussed to be resolved.[20]

South Carolina's constitution was no exception. Article X established a system of public schools that would be tax-exempt institutions. It divided the state into uniform free school districts and called for each county to elect a commissioner (or superintendent) of education, who in turn would sit on the State Board of Education. These schools would be free, supported by land grants and a poll tax of $1, and open to all without regard to race or color. In fact, the document called for compulsory education of all children between the ages of 6 and 16. Teachers would be produced by a state normal school and would instruct in all areas except religion, all overseen by the state superintendent.[21] Hugh S. Thompson, the first state superintendent of education, set to work reorganizing and desegregating the public schools.

The call for public education and establishment of state superintendent of education were all but ignored for the next 27 years. As noted by State Department of Education employee C. J. Martin, "During this period the state school system was an utter failure."[22] The populace was angered by the notion of mixed schools, taxation was levied at the whim of the voters, and school officials were often ignorant, incompetent, or just defiant of the new system. Whites in South Carolina often refused to support public schools, stigmatizing them as "pauper schools."[23] In spite of this, public schools quietly came into existence across the state for both black and white residents. Noted educational historian James Anderson explains that ex-slaves contributed money and labor to open schools in the towns of Camden, Sumter, Marion, Darlington, Simmonsville, Florence, Kingstree, Chetau, Bennettsville, and Timmonsville.[24] An 1870 law created 469 districts within South Carolina; those districts housed 630 public schools.

When South Carolina finally ended its attempts at Reconstruction and drafted a new constitution, much of the education article was taken directly from the old one. The article called for a state board of education comprised of representatives from judicial districts, rather than each county; a state superintendent of education was still included. The constitution even provided for "the maintenance and support of a system of free public schools open to all children in the State...as may be desirable."[25] Before this, public school expenditures for blacks and whites had been nearly equal.[26] After this, however, the public schools became seen as another threatening reform, and South Carolina followed the trend of many southern states by rejecting public education. According to William Reese:

> Southern leaders necessarily viewed education differently. They lived in a society built on the backs of enslaved blacks and free poor whites. The northern ideology of free labor, individual merit, and social mobility through schooling hardly appealed to southern elites. Traditional southern attitudes toward education for whites and blacks did not disappear in the 1870's, when reformers supported the adoption of Yankee school systems. Some high schools opened, yet it took decades before the South invested seriously in a broad system of public instruction.[27]

The impact of this resistance on education was devastating. By 1890, 45 percent of the population of South Carolina was illiterate.[28] In 1900, the color barrier of education was beginning to show significantly in literacy rates across the state. The ratio of literate to illiterate men over the age of 21 was positive for white males (111,685 literate to 15,711 illiterate), implying an effective educational system. However, for black males (69,201 literate to 83,594 illiterate), the ratio was negative, implying a dearth of educational opportunities.[29] By 1897, the state was funding $1/pupil for black students; that cost was more than doubled for white students. Of the 1,776 black schools in South Carolina that year, 778 were privately owned; 403 were in log houses and 1,311 were in frame buildings.[30] This disparity is even more pronounced in regard to secondary education. In 1896 there were 85 secondary academies in South Carolina catering to the white population, 27 enrolling white females; there were just 7 black academies.[31]

By 1901, South Carolina passed a compulsory attendance law. Even this act of legislation, however, was not color-blind: whites in South Carolina, the social if not numeric majority, vehemently opposed expanding public education for blacks.[32] The effects of this law on secondary education for white students were tremendous. Following the national trend to include high schools into the common school model, public school systems now were sending students who normally could not afford more than a grade school education to private academies. In Charleston, for example, the compulsory education act forced both the creation of a free girls' high school and the public school system to pay the tuition of boys to the city academy.[33] However, many townships, in an effort to claim they were providing high schools for their students, were in fact only providing limited scholarship. William Hand, first high school inspector of South Carolina, cautioned against this practice:

> In like manner the village school of thirty-five pupils, ranging from beginners to first lessons in Algebra and Latin, is miscalled a high school. Often it has not a full high school course of even one year; often it has no regular

course at all. Schools of this class can be found by the score. They serve the fatal purpose of deceiving the people into believing that they have what in reality they have not.[34]

School enrollment during this period rose because of two major factors. First, with a rise in the economic prosperity of the nation came a concurrent rise in the desire for education among the citizenry of the United States. Second, with a decrease in child labor nationally came a need for those children to be off the streets—specifically in schools.[35] The notion that children needed to be out of the workplace and in school—a custodial purpose to schooling added to the purposes of religion, socialization, and politicalization—was given a more ominous note by Henry Perkinson. He writes that children, especially in urban areas, generated "both compassion and fear" in the populace at large, giving rise to compulsory attendance laws. Children, particularly of the poor, were "unkempt, uncared for, and untutored…in need of help." However, they were also "a threat to the working-man, a threat to social customs, mores, and institutions, and a threat to the future of American democracy. Partly from fear and partly from compassion, thirty-one states enacted some form of compulsory education law."[36]

There was societal conflict during this time as well, which created a need for public high schools. As explained by sociologist John Richardson, people in the United States living between the Civil War and World War I wanted to create a simple social majority. In the North, there was much labor strife as organized labor movements began to take form. Across the nation, but heavily in the Northeast, there was a widespread amount of ethnic diversity as new immigrant groups moved in from across Europe. Across the Southern states, the agrarian model was quickly being eclipsed by a move toward large-scale organizations. These social and economic difficulties created a strong desire for conformity, and schools were seen as the solution. Thus, a sociopolitical purpose for schooling was formalized.[37] High schools, public more so than private, met the needs of this demand, opening their doors to an ever-increasing enrollment. By 1910, the United States Bureau of Education reported that of the secondary schools reporting data, 85 percent were public high schools—up from 60 percent a mere 20 years before.[38] South Carolina echoed this national trend; the state reported 162 public high schools that year, an 81 percent gain from three years earlier.

Populism and Its Spread in South Carolina

Understanding the overall sociopolitical as well as educational climates of the period that produced Swearingen is important. If the New South was a hypermasculinized society, the politicians who represented it—the sons of privilege who held local, state, and national offices—were the ultimate extension of its vision. A perfect example of this notion is the incident that occurred on May 22, 1856. US Senator Charles Sumner (Republican—Massachusetts) had delivered two days of oration regarding his opposition to slavery in the entering state of Kansas; in the speech, Sumner took Southerners to task—specifically South Carolinians. Representative Preston Brooks (Democrat—South Carolina) took exception to being called out and brutally caned Senator Sumner on the floor of Congress.[39] While predating the period in question, it serves as apt foreshadowing of the post-Reconstruction politicians who followed.

Another aspect of Southern masculinity was the political force known as Populism, one of those terms that is frequently used but seldom discussed in regard to turn-of-the-century politicians. Depending on the source and context, to be populist might mean a wide variety of things, such as the following:

- One who practices a form of socialism when confronted with modernization;
- One who supports rural people who feel threatened by urban, industrial, and/or financial interests;
- One who supports traditional values in opposition to modernity;
- The belief that the true arbiters of society should be the common, everyday people and their collective cultures/traditions as opposed to an elected elite;
- The will of the people;
- A supporter of a political party that relies upon the support of the working classes, urban and rural, but does not specifically try to organize them into a power base;
- A member of what is arguably the last viable third party in US politics, which began as the Alliance and turned into the People's, or Populist, Party.

No matter what definition is used, however, populism as a movement comes down to three essential principles: more equitable distribution and production of money, use and control of land, and ownership and production of transportation. Many people use the term populist in any of the first six definitions given above when applying to South Carolina politics; and while many politicians of the period did embrace the essential principles of populism, it is incorrect to link them, owing to beliefs and temporality, to the People's Party. To fully appreciate the difference, the story must necessarily and briefly regress to Texas and Kansas in the late 1880s.

During Reconstruction, emissaries from the federal agricultural bureau traveled the South and realized the dire circumstances facing farmers. Knowing the distrust held for the North and federal government, and with backgrounds in fraternal organizations such as the Masons, they realized the way to help the farmers was through organizing, not legislating. They formed the "Patrons of Husbandry," otherwise known as the Grange. While the group caught on in the North and West, it never quite caught a foothold in the South. By 1873, the Grange had exploded its membership, but the economic panic of 1873 and the depression it caused led to a rapid decline in membership.

To fill the gap, a new group was formed in Texas and quickly spread throughout the region. Calling itself the Farmer's Alliance and Industrial Union, by 1890, its membership was 2,500,000. At its height in 1891, the Alliance included members from the Farmer's Alliance and Industrial Union, the National Farmer's Alliance, the Knights of Labor, the Colored National Farmer's Alliance, the Farmer's Mutual Benefit Association, and the National Citizen's Alliance. After the dissolution of the People's Party, members of the Alliance would later go on to found the Confederacy of Industrial Organizations (CIO) that would later famously merge with the American Federation of Labor (AFL) to become the AFL-CIO.

Alliance between Midwesterners and Southerners sounds a bit challenging, but at the time the two groups had much in common. Both groups, for example, believed in the politics of sectionalism: in the south, it was support of the "Lost Cause" of the Confederacy; in the west, it was "waving the bloody shirt" of political strife, Republican versus Democrat. Both groups argued for white supremacy; in the south, the Red Shirts and Klansmen worked explicitly in these areas; in the west, the political system (granted, often led by Klansmen) stripped blacks of the legal rights held in some cases since before the Civil War. As time progressed, political issues such as prohibition, the greenback monetary system, and bimetallic basis of currency/free silver all united southern and western politicians under the big tent that was Populism.

The People's Party, the political organization that came out of it, was not quite as successful. At its height it counted one senator who ran under its umbrella and two independent senators who declared their allegiance to the Party. Its standard-bearer was William Peffer, the People's Party senator from Kansas, who at one time was even viewed by some (with the full range of reactions, negative and positive) with an eye for the presidency. From his first term, Peffer broke political traditions; for example, at the time tradition held that freshmen senators did not speak on the senate floor; however, Peffer began voicing his opinion and raising specific legislative proposals weeks after taking office.

Many politicians on both sides of the aisle, republican and democrat, courted the support of the millions of Alliance members by adopting parts of the party's platform. However, they allowed party loyalty to trump all, and, no matter how much of the Alliance platform they would adopt, supported candidates only from their own parties. South Carolina had a long tradition of this; John Irby, Tillman's predecessor in Congress, was president of the South Carolina chapter of the Farmer's Alliance and ran on a straight Alliance platform; but once elected, he refused to bring forth any Alliance resolution, issue, or policy to the senate floor for discussion.

While the Farmer's Alliance caught on in the South, the People's Party was never able to trump the stranglehold of the Democratic Party. Populist Senator Peffer described it in very blunt terms, writing that it was "obvious—self evident" that in the "Southern States the antagonism was not only clearly manifest—it was deep-seated and to the extent of actual fighting." Peffer continues that "Populism was not in accord with Democracy on any essential point" and that the two parties "were at war."[40] It was this context during which Swearingen's uncle, Ben Tillman, a senator of the populist tradition but not a member of the People's Party, took office.

"Pitchfork Ben" Tillman

Benjamin Ryan Tillman's career can be oversimplified in one paragraph. Born near Trenton in Edgefield County on August 11, 1847, Tillman originally pursued college, but left school in 1864 to join the Confederate Army. Unfortunately he was stricken with a severe illness that he blamed on too much reading by too poor light as a student and lost his left eye; he never saw action on behalf of the Confederate States Army. Throughout his career he focused on the advancement of agricultural and educational pursuits; while governor of South Carolina (1890–1894), he established Clemson College and Winthrop College. Moving to national politics, Tillman was elected as a Democrat to the US Senate in 1894; a member of the state constitutional convention in 1895; reelected in 1901, 1907, and 1913; and served in the US Senate from March 4, 1895, until his death. While in the Senate, Tillman served as chairman of the Committee on Revolutionary Claims, Committee on Five Civilized Tribes of Indians, and Committee on Naval Affairs. He died in Washington, DC, on July 3, 1918.

These facts alone do not even come close to encapsulating the vulgar, racist, divisive alpha male that was Tillman. While he and his nephew "Johnnie" held deep respect and affection for each other and were both gentlemen farmers throughout their lives, Swearingen was quite a bit more forward thinking in many ways. Though they differed in several sociopolitical aspects, they both were shaped by masculinity and disability. In terms of proving masculinity, similar to Sumner's caning incident, Tillman was censured by the Senate in 1902 after assaulting another Senator on the Senate floor. During his years in the Senate, Tillman was known as "Pitchfork Ben" because of, as legend says, his threat against President Grover Cleveland that he would spit him on his pitchfork and hoist him around Congress.

Further demonstrating his racist streak, early in his career, Tillman took place in what he, and South Carolina history texts, called the "Hamburg Riot" that is now more accurately known as the "Hamburg Massacre." The town of Hamburg, South Carolina, first rose to prominence as the steam rail line that connected it, in the state's up-country, to Charleston in the low country was the first and at the time longest steam rail line in the United States. During Reconstruction, this rail hub was home to one of the many African American regiments of Union soldiers sent across the south to enforce the much-maligned federal reconstruction policies. Just as the name of the event depends on who you read, so too does the description of the events those days. *History, Stories, and Legends of South Carolina* (1927), a reader for school-age children, described it as a "clash between the white and black races." To author E. C. McCants, there was clear blame: "The trouble was begun by a company of negro soldiers who obstructed a highway and threatened some white men who were passing." McCants continues his rather one-sided narrative, saying that "a body of white men gathered and attacked the negroes. The negroes shot one white man, and then the infuriated whites brought up a small cannon, shelled the negroes out of their brick armory, and slew a number of them."[41] *Annals of Pride and Protest* (1957) describes it as a necessary military action. Acknowledging in the one paragraph devoted to the incident that "a good many were indicted for murderous roles," it quotes Tillman as saying, "Nothing but bloodshed and a good deal of it could answer the purpose of redeeming the state."[42] Another version, from D. D. Wallace's 1961 *South Carolina: A Short History*, prefaces the event by saying it came from "a series of outrages both by and against" African Americans and describing the town itself as having "long been disliked by whites as harboring disorderly Negroes." According to Wallace, a company of African American soldiers held a trial for two young white men, found them guilty, and threatened to lynch them when a white regiment marched in "to protect the two young men" and demanded both disbanding of the African American company and their immediate surrender of all weapons. When they refused, in the ensuing confusion, "a young white man fell dead. The Negroes fled from their armory. The whites killed one in fighting and that night three, or perhaps five, more as they were told to run."[43]

Even famed South Carolina historian Walter Edgar paints two different portraits of the event. In his seminal 1998 work, *South Carolina: A History*, Edgar explains that the *incident* (his terminology: not riot, not massacre) began when "the commander of the town's militia company harassed some white travelers...They filed charges against him, and he filed countercharges." However, the event turned violent as "hundreds of armed whites descended on Hamburg, and in the ensuing skirmish one white and one black were killed." Edgar was one of the first to widely acknowledge that six members of the militia were "murdered in cold blood" *after* they had surrendered.[44]

In a later work of which Edgar was principal editor, The *South Carolina Encyclopedia*, contributor Richard Zuczek provides a substantively different portrait of the massacre. Zuczek alludes to the fact that there existed much deeply entrenched "antagonism between whites and black militia units. The militia...was unacceptable to many whites. To them, an armed, nearly all-black force in the service of (in their eyes) an illegitimate state government brought animosity rather than security." Another not subtle detail mentioned in this account was that the militia had taken refuge not in their armory, but in a warehouse, at the trial judge's suggestion. That trial judge, former slave and veteran Prince Rivers, disappeared before the trial could conclude. The six executed were from a larger group of thirty, the unarmed remainder of whom was fired upon as they fled into the woods.[45]

However horrific those events, Tillman was one of the hundreds of armed whites laying siege and remained quite proud of what was the closest to military action for Tillman. He was always keen to recount the events; for example, in 1911 correspondence Tillman sounded almost melancholy that those days of terror and violence were gone: "That procession of men in white shirts smeared with poke berries and venetian red to imitate blood was certainly a unique and daring thing to do under the circumstances. But as you know we were all wrought up and expected to do some killing or be killed."[46]

Tillman was never afraid to speak his mind, whether against political foe or potential constituent. At one campaign stop, for example, a citizen of the state had been boasting that he intended to "burn him down." As soon as Tillman stood to deliver his speech, this man began to antagonize Tillman, saying he wanted to ask a question.

> Tillman replied, "My friend, you have the advantage of me; you know my name; I do not know yours. What is your name?" The man said his name was Calhoun. Then Tillman said: "Aw, hell! All the Calhouns I ever heard of who were worth a damn have been dead nearly fifty years!" Tillman continued his speech as if he had not been interrupted and the man who said he was going to "burn him down" jammed his hands into his trouser pockets and shuffled off to the outer rim of the crowd.[47]

Early in his career in state politics, Tillman was formally active in resisting Reconstruction, even when not wearing his Red Shirt. With the withdrawal of federal troops from the South, many of the Progressive Era reforms were also withdrawn. Most states quickly reverted to pre-Civil War policies, and the education of marginalized cultures was one of the first things to go. The election of Tillman as governor in 1890 almost ensured a call for a new constitutional convention. With blacks having the vote, Tillman had to campaign for both white and black voters—campaigning that could easily disenchant either group. As Walter Edgar explains, "In order to eliminate black voters, Tillman opted for rewriting the state's constitution. The statewide referendum on calling a constitutional convention passed by fewer than a thousand votes."[48] The new constitution was one that eliminated almost all of the progressive reforms written into that of the Reconstruction constitution. In a clause not unique to South Carolina, suffrage now came with a literacy test—a test specifically designed to disenfranchise black voters. With this disenfranchisement began the segregated schools and the problems created thereby that still plagues the South to this day.

The Swearingens of Edgefield County

In the midst of this political and educational turmoil was born Pitchfork Ben's nephew, the man who would have the most lasting impact on public education and public high schools than anyone else. John Eldred Swearingen was born on January 9, 1875, near the town of Trenton located in Edgefield County. When, in 1922, Swearingen was asked to describe himself and his family to a distant relative in Guthrie, Oklahoma, Swearingen created a brief family tree: "I am seventh in line from our immigrant ancestor as follows—Gerret, Zacharias, Samuel, Van, Moses,

John C., John E. My folk have been in Edgefield County, South Carolina since the Revolutionary War."⁴⁹

He was the son of John Cloud Swearingen, a confederate veteran and Red Shirt Rider, and Anna Tillman Swearingen, sister of Benjamin Tillman.⁵⁰ Though he was the second child, Swearingen was the oldest because his elder brother, Benjamin Eldred, died two years before John Eldred's birth. Two years separated John Eldred from his twin siblings, younger brother George and sister Sophia. The Swearingen family had a long legacy of being active defenders of the state. The family had first moved to South Carolina immediately before the American Revolution. Van Swearingen, John Eldred's great-grandfather, led an armed revolt against measures imposed by the British governor of South Carolina in 1768 and later fought for the colonies during the Revolution, even hosting General George Washington in their home. Moses Swearingen, John Eldred's grandfather, proudly fought alongside his father and brothers during the revolution (Figure 1.1).

With the outbreak of the Civil War, all of Moses's sons assumed the mantle of the military. Eldred M. Swearingen started in Company A, 7th SC Regiment, then enlisted in the 96 Riflemen, Edgefield, where

Figure 1.1   John Cloud Swearingen with sons, John and George

he served during 1861–1862 under Capt. Thomas Bacon. Eldred served the entire four years of the war; wounded once, he ultimately returned to Edgefield. William N. Swearingen served in the 3 Alabama Regiment Rhodes Brigade and the Army of Northern Virginia. He was killed in battle at Winchester, VA, while in Stonewall Jackson's Corps 25: "Leaping on the breastworks and shouting to comrades to 'follow or die like men' he was shot down almost instantly." Arthur "A. S." Swearingen served in Company A, 7th SC Volunteers, and the Army of Northern Virginia. He was wounded frequently: at Sharpsburg, he was shot all over his body; at Chicamunga, he was shot through the right elbow of his right arm; at Strassburg he was shot in the right knee "and has always been lame—bullet was never located." A. S. was promoted to 2nd Lieutenant to Charleston "there to Pole Cat," then to Virginia where he "fought in every battle that the Army was in except Fredericksburg." Corporal Ben "B. T." Swearingen served in Company D, 14th Regular Infantry South Carolina Volunteers. He went out with the 1st Company of Edgefield Riflemen under Cicero Adams and died of a fever in hospital at Charleston, SC, in 1862. The youngest, James "J. T." Swearingen, enlisted in Company D, 5th Calvary and returned home with no wounds.[51]

Like his brothers, John Cloud Swearingen (John Eldred's father) had a distinguished career in the Confederacy. The fifth of the six sons to enlist, he was among the first troops to leave Edgefield County. He served first in Company C, 1st Regiment SC Infantry for six months, then the 7th SC Volunteers on the South Carolina coast under Gregg; next, he transferred to Virginia Company A, 7th Regiment Kershaw's Brigade, McLaw's Division, Longstreet Corps, helping to lead the assault in Knoxville, Tennessee. John Cloud returned to Charleston for six months to lead the 1st Company of Edgefield Riflemen under Cicero Adams before joining the Army of Northern Virginia. In spite of sustaining injuries at Gettysburg (to the head), Lookout Mountain, and Cedar Run (through the elbow), John Cloud remained on active duty until the war's end. In fact, it was a matter of some pride that he could claim to have never returned home from the war's beginning until his 1865 parole in North Carolina.

Like many Southerners, just because Lee surrendered didn't mean the war was over to John Cloud. Upon returning home from the war's end, he was a charter member of Abner Perrin Camp, United Confederate Veterans. However, love of country was soon supplanted by a more romantic love; according to family history, John Cloud approached his future wife, Anna Tillman, on horseback and handed her a note of proposal. It read: "Dear Anna: From the first moment of my acquaintance with you, I felt that you were the one destined to make me happy or forever miserable. I hope not the latter."[52] This gift of brevity and wit would be passed down to their son.

Anna Tillman, daughter of Benjamin and Sophia Tillman, and sister to Pitchfork Ben, was a woman widely recognized for her exceptional intellect.[53] She hosted a private day school for her children and those of her neighbors. An avid reader, Anna loved poetry and literary classics. In addition, she was a skilled musician, needlewoman, homemaker, and planter's wife. The love of reading and the desire for learning would also be passed down to their son (Figure 1.2).

The family farm grew cotton and hosted a variety of domesticated animals, including goats, pigs, cows, horses, mules, chickens, turkeys, and hunting dogs. Swearingen grew up equal parts avid outdoorsman and student. Possessed of an athletic physique, he would hunt and fish, as well as play sports with his younger brother; this love of things physical would stay with him the rest of his life. He dreamed of continuing his family's military background by attending West Point and becoming a general in the US Army. He attended school with his mother, learning to write by filling his copybook with phrases that would become life lessons: "A soft answer turneth away wrath; Follow that which is good; Many birds of many kinds, many men of many minds; Kind words can never die."[54]

Ultimately it was Swearingen's mother who would have the most influence over Swearingen's life. His love of education and desire to serve the state both arose from his Tillman background. This was because of, at least in part, one of the most shocking events in Swearingen's life: his father

Figure 1.2 Anna Tillman Swearingen

was gunned down in broad daylight on April 24, 1895, over a property dispute, leaving Johnnie, along with his brother George, to become the patriarchs of his family estate. It also gave Swearingen a sour taste about those who put masculinity and "saving face" above human decency.

How My Light Is Spent: Swearingen's Blindness

Like many male children of planter families, Swearingen was taught to hunt at an early age. Whether this passion for hunting emerged owing to Swearingen's performing masculinity at a young age in terms of becoming a provider for the family, or whether it was owing to his performing social expectations, hunting became a primary interest to the young boy—as well as to the other men in his family. During his freshman year at the South Carolina College, he told the story of one of his last hunting trips with his father, uncle, and cousin. He explained how his cousin Pierce had been trapped under a falling tree. When he was revived, the first question from Pierce was, "Did you get the opossum?"[55]

Swearingen received his first shotgun, against his mother's wishes, for his thirteenth birthday. Like many children with a new toy, Swearingen took it with him on most of his outings. Less than a week after receiving his gift, Swearingen went out on a firewood hauling expedition with some of the field hands from the farm. Swearingen saw a dove, shot, and, excited to capture his kill, ran to pick up the fallen bird. A nearby bush tripped the trigger of the second barrel of his gun, discharging the entire load of bird shot through Swearingen's right hand. The shot entered at the little finger and exited at the base of the thumb, shattering every bone in the hand before settling into his forehead, face, and eyes.

Taken immediately back to the house by an African American worker, Swearingen insisted that the men carrying him cover his face with a handkerchief so his mother couldn't see how badly he was injured. His parents immediately called for a doctor and informed the extended family. Benjamin Tillman, two years before his career in state politics would begin, was one of the first to arrive. Tillman and the doctor soon began a heated argument. The doctor wanted to amputate Swearingen's injured hand; Tillman wouldn't stand for it. Benjamin Tillman knew of what he was speaking: being blind in one eye, Tillman knew the value of the tactile sense. Hearing the argument, the 13-year-old voiced his own opinion—he wanted to take the risk and keep his hand. Eventually, probably because of the enormous pressure from patient and family, the doctor relented— fortuitously, for even though Swearingen never recovered full strength in the injured extremity, it was the fingers of his right hand that became sensitive enough to learn to read Braille. In fact, Swearingen would refer to his right forefinger as "the educated one" or his "eyes," using that finger for tasks as delicate as feeling the texture of suits as to not get items confused.[56]

Initially, Swearingen's family hoped that his eyesight would return. He would recall scenes from the family house and property, and describe them as if seeing them. However, when his sight was tested by having him fetch a pail of water for the house, he became lost on the way, tripped, and hit his head on a tree. His mother, ever the educator, would not stand to see her son go on helplessly. She began a strict program of reeducation for him, beginning with having him relearn to perform simple household chores such as lighting stove fires, bringing in firewood, fetching water, and tending the extensive family garden. She advanced his training to include proper table manners, the techniques of which Swearingen would later use as a teacher of the blind. Swearingen was always athletically inclined, so next she had him relearn activities such as basic exercises, acrobatics, wrestling, and horseback riding. As Swearingen was re-mastering household duties and activities, his mother continued his education by reading to him.

There exists a "boy culture," as argued by E. Anthony Rotundo, which prepares boys to become masculinized. The culture formed by boys "helped to prepare them in many ways for life in the adult spheres they would inhabit." However, if performance in this culture is worthy of analysis, so too is its null: the lack of engagement in this culture cannot be neglected. Swearingen was not provided the opportunity to engage in much of the boy culture that existed at the time. Further, if boy culture is what taught boys to reject the notions of feminized domesticity, then it is likely that Swearingen' extended term in the household prepared him for what was determined by society of the time to be a feminized career in education.[57] Rotundo continues the argument that this break with domesticity and emergence of boy culture is what taught them "differences of ethnicity and social status." While Swearingen was most definitely exposed to a huge variety of other social structures that would reinforce social norms regarding the treatment of people who are "other," such as the disabled or those of another race, Swearingen would not have these patterns set in him via his teenage play. This might help explain the somewhat progressive social attitudes held by Swearingen throughout his career.[58]

While Swearingen was not engaging in boy culture, he continued convalescing and learning. The family brought in a variety of doctors to try and heal Swearingen's eyes. When all doctors failed, his family still hoped that he could learn to see; in September 1888 Swearingen's family sent him to the Georgia Academy for the Blind in Macon. He remained for one term, at the end of which the headmaster informed the family that there was no hope of his sight ever returning. Once the family accepted his permanent blindness, Swearingen attended the School for the Blind and Deaf at Cedar Springs, South Carolina, from 1889 to 1894.

Nature or nurture, whether the result of being Anna Tillman's son or learning her lessons, it quickly became apparent to the teachers at the school that Swearingen was more advanced than any other student they had. In order to keep their new student challenged, the faculty developed a new curriculum of courses for Swearingen, more advanced than anything previously offered. Swearingen majored in the literary course but also studied music, learning to play the piano, pipe organ, and violin. In fact, he often performed solo works and in groups at the school's graduation ceremonies. He learned to read and write, first using the Point Print method, then Braille.[59] While at Cedar Springs, Swearingen also developed his astute mind and memory; between listening to his mother's readings and working under a variety of teachers, Swearingen quickly developed an eidetic memory.

In spite of the best efforts of family and faculty, Swearingen was unhappy with the education provided to him at the school. He later wrote that owing to societal expectations of the disabled, the blind must do double the work of the sighted: "It is only by constant and dilligent [sic] application that he can surmount the difficulties that lie in his way."[60] Dismayed that he had to wait three years before entering college, Swearingen blamed, at least in part, the education available to him at Cedar Springs for this.

Upon his graduation from Cedar Springs, Swearingen was determined to continue his education. He applied to the South Carolina College, only to be rejected. It was his first taste of the discrimination society heaped upon the disabled of the time. In an effort to overcome the college's perception that he was intellectually incapable, Swearingen made a formal appeal to the president and board of trustees of the college, who granted him provisional admission: Swearingen had to provide his own guide and readers for his textbooks, and any sign that he could not keep up with the other students would result in his being asked to withdraw from the college.

Swearingen clearly anticipated his collegiate experience with much relish. Writing about his first days in an essay titled "First Impressions and Experiences at the College," Swearingen wrote in his English notebook:

> When on the morning of the 20th September I descended the steps of my home and with heavy heart bade farewell to mother and sister, it was to me the beginning of a new phase of boyish experience, the realization of

a long-cherished hope, for I was at last to enter college. This had for years been the dream of my ambition, and when at length an opportunity presented itself, I gladly availed myself of it. My attention had been so often called to the advantages offered by the S.C. College and the friends of the institution had been so loud in its praise that I had prepared myself for a deep draught of knowledge from the historic old font.[61]

As luck would have it, Swearingen's cousin, George Bunch, lived with his family near the college. The Bunch family was the primary doctors and caretakers of the South Carolina Institute for the Insane located on Bull Street, a simple ten-block walk from the college. George was entering the college that same year and agreed to act as Swearingen's guide and reader for the first couple of years, mirroring Swearingen's program of study. In a July 31, 1895, letter to Swearingen, George wrote, "I think Mama and Papa have fully decided to send me to the South Carolina College next fall or rather session and I write to know if you will not come up and join me in my studies. I want some company and I am satisfied that I could be of untold benefit to you."[62] In retrospect, Swearingen compared his time with Bunch in the same way as Helen Keller and Anne Sullivan.[63]

Much to the surprise of everyone involved (except Swearingen), he excelled in all of his coursework. The grading scale at the college was broken into divisions; division I meant marks between 80 and 100 percent down the scale to division IV that meant marks less than 40 percent. Swearingen was never marked out of division I. Within the division, a single star meant a mark between 90 and 95 percent; double stars signified 95–100 percent. Swearingen double-starred in all but three courses. The first single-star grade, in an English composition course, was because of a hired transcriber's spelling error in one of Swearingen's compositions. The second, in French, was because of Swearingen's inability to associate French sounds with their proper spelling. The third, in pedagogies, was because of a difference in opinion with Dr. Patterson Wardlaw (whom the USC's College of Education is now named) regarding school administration theory. While serving as state superintendent, Swearingen was asked about the particular theory. He responded, "I still believe in my theory, and so does Dr. Wardlaw—now."[64] Swearingen's academic excellence drew notice: president of the college James Woodrow wrote comments such as "Most excellent—I congratulate you" and "you deserve renewed congratulations" on many of Swearingen's grade reports.[65]

His blindness clearly did not hamper Swearingen in his studies or collegiate life.[66] An English assignment—a descriptive piece written in the form of a letter home to his mother—reveals much about how he got around campus. Rather than produce the usual "this looks like, that looks

Figure 1.3 John E. Swearingen, student at South Carolina College

like" Freshman English descriptive essay, Swearingen generated a truly multisensory description. For example, he incorporated touch by describing how long the walk was each day, and the comfort of the furniture; he incorporated sound by describing what he heard in his room.[67] This was indicative of the man Swearingen would become: unafraid to accomplish any task in his path and willing to seek out accommodations to achieve the task (Figure 1.3).

Swearingen's wife echoed such sentiments when she was presenting the John Eldred Swearingen Papers at the Annual Meeting of the South Caroliniana Society in Columbia on April 27, 1961. She related a story that occurred at the College:

> Mr. John McMahan told me a good story about Major Sloan, then the physics and astronomy teacher. When the time came for young Swearingen to enroll in his physics class, Major Sloan appeared before the faculty to say

that it was impossible for a blind student to pursue his course in physics because of the laboratory work. But with the usual proviso that a young man was prepared to withdraw at any time, the professor reluctantly admitted him to his classes. A few weeks later the Major reappeared before the faculty to report: "By George, young Swearingen is the best one I have in my class. He sees more in an experiment than those with two good eyes take in." While I am bragging, let me add that the young man in question also made "double stars" in the Major's astronomy class even though the laboratory was in the heavens.[68]

Much of Swearingen's work of the period demonstrated not only how powerful a hold social notions of disability had on his professors, but also how hostage to his times were many of Swearingen's own opinions. In a four-page paper titled "Reconstruction in South Carolina," Swearingen presents his thoughts that were very reflective of the Southern values in which he grew up. Beginning with the premise that Abraham Lincoln was "the only man who could have carried into effect his patriotic and statesmanlike plan," Swearingen then takes a characteristic negative view: describing Thaddeus Stevens as a "very vindictive leader" who perpetuated reconstruction based on "his desire for revenge, and a mad passion for Negro in franchise and equalization"; describing the Constitutional Convention of 1868 as "proceedings...characterized by many of the most flagrant abuses that ignorance and malice could invent." Politicians of that period, in Swearingen's estimation, tended to fall into two categories: "Yankee carpet-baggers" or "kinky-headed Solons." The ultimate result of the new constitution was that "bribery, theft, speculation, and every form of public dishonesty soon ran rampant in this state." To Swearingen, Reconstruction ultimately caused several things:

> Violence ran riot in every community. Taxation was so heavy that property holders could not possibly meet its exactions. Labor was thoroughly demoralized, and to thrash a Negro was to invite the severest punishment...The culmination came in the cool clocks trial, in the proclamation of President Grant of martial law in eight counties, and the riots at Hamburg and Ellington. T. J. Mackey, himself a Republican, declared that the white race had never been subjected to such humiliation since the Saxons wore the iron collar of the Normans. At last the white people could stand it no longer, and in the red shirt campaign of 70 – six, they drove out the Republican harpies, and vindicated the honor of South Carolina by placing Wade Hampton in the governor's chair.[69]

Whether Swearingen actually believed these things, was simply echoing what he had been taught since birth, or was writing what he knew his instructors wanted to hear to earn another double star is unknown. What is known is that within two years Swearingen had earned a reputation as being the most intelligent student on campus. As such, when Bunch separated from Swearingen in order to study pre-medicine after two years, many students willingly volunteered their time to serve as readers and transcribers for Swearingen because doing so would result in an automatic study partner. Even students Swearingen had experienced prior personal difficulties with on campus were more than willing to volunteer their time. When Swearingen wrote to fellow student Mason C. Brunson requesting his help as a reader, Brunson was effusive with his praise in his reply:

> I consider that you pay me quite a compliment in asking me to read to you. I have informed Father of your request, and he is delighted with your preference for me. He considers it an honor for me to be helpful to you in any way, having heard so much of the excellent stand you take in college. Believe me Swearingen, I will be delighted to help you in any way possible, and realize fully that this joint study will be very advantageous to me.[70]

Swearingen went from being "that blind student" to that student whose high standard all other students were measured by, often to their discouragement. For example, once a faculty member was upbraiding a student for their poor performance, saying, "He is blind and must depend entirely on the assistance of others for his knowledge. Yet he is leading you and you have two good eyes in your head." The student responded, "That's just it, it's dead easy for John. He can't see the balls on a billiard table, or the pretty girls either. It's a snap for him to be a grind."[71] Similar sentiments are echoed by Swearingen's son, John Jr., who recalls college friends of his father's visiting their house years after Swearingen had retired from public life: "As I was growing up, I observed many of them come by and shake hands with him, and say that 'I learned more from you than I ever learned from any one of our professors.'"[72]

It was during his years at South Carolina College that Swearingen's outspokenness and wont for political action began to show. In 1896, Swearingen was one of 42 students (including his cousin George Bunch and best friend/future congressman John J. McSwain) who signed a petition trying to shut down fraternities. The accusations included tampering with the election process of the literary societies (tantamount to threatening today's Division I football programs) and undermining the honor code by refusing to report cheating. The Greeks defended themselves, but the damage had been done. While the college's trustees debated the merits of the arguments, the state legislature passed a law in 1897 banning all Greek-letter fraternities in state-supported colleges (literary societies excepted).[73]

By the time Swearingen graduated from the college, he was amazing his fellow students with his feats. He could walk unassisted anywhere on campus, with no difficulty, and could identify all 200 students on campus by voice. He was so skilled in mathematics that he performed math recitations in front of the whole faculty and college president.[74] Returning to Rotundo's argument regarding boy culture, Swearingen probably was exposed to enough of it during these years to foster his competitive spirit. Since boys were taught via their culture to "seek each other's defeat and thus prove individual mastery," Swearingen probably strongly desired to prove his worth in the academic arena—the only one perceived to be open to a blind student of the time.[75]

When he graduated on June 17, 1899, Swearingen was the top graduate in the college (Figure 1.4). The Clariosophic Literary Society named him the top honors graduate. In a graduation address delivered by Edward S.

Figure 1.4 John E. Swearingen, South Carolina College Graduation

Joynes, Swearingen was lauded highly. Joynes stated that "on this occasion, I see something I have never seen before. I see a blind boy—one of those whose education is usually restricted by loss of sight to narrow and harmful limits—bearing away prizes, not only by the unanimous suffrage of the Faculty but with hearty sympathy and approval of all students."[76]

Swearingen's Teaching Career

Upon graduation, Swearingen returned to the Cedar Springs Institute as a teacher. In his first year, Swearingen was frustrated by the faculty and environment; these frustrations would help shape his campaign for state superintendent years later. Writing to his mother in 1900, Swearingen complained that the faculty did not work hard enough in their teaching, instead teaching "for rec reation [sic]." The location and populace were surprisingly too rural for Swearingen. He lamented that the blind students would never hear "something more than the ands and urrers of a onehorse [sic] country preacher."[77]

While making such laments privately, Swearingen's public life was beginning to take off in earnest. At one point, he was asked to address the Fairfield County Chamber of Commerce on his views of education. There is little doubt that the good gentlemen who extended the invitation had no idea of the powerful rhetoric they were in for. Swearingen used the opportunity to demonstrate his intellect and oratorical skill. Swearingen opened with a challenging series of questions: "Have you ever stopped to consider seriously what the schoolhouse stands for? How many of you patrons have ever formulated a creed of education for yourselves?" Swearingen urged his audience to "go another step further" and think about "how many of you can frame to yourselves your own reasons for favoring education, other than the general and vague reason that your neighbor sends his boy to school and your children need the same training?" He began answering his own questions immediately, saying, "Education is one of the serious problems of life. Those who possess it are the only lords of the earth, and constitute the only nobility among men."[78] Swearingen provided an extended metaphor for what, to him, education truly meant:

> Some years ago a mechanic was standing in the midst of the beautiful campus of one of our best colleges. Around him stretched the classic grounds where men of genius had wrought for the inculcation of learning. The splendid buildings presented a stately front, and the whole scene was worthy of the labor, and money that had been spent on it. As the man stood up he chanced to observe the president of the institution as he approached

along one of the walks. When the educator drew near the practical minded materialist [he] asked, what do you turn out here, when we have a plant like this we do something and have something to show for our work. The president thought for a moment then replied, "We turn out power." The mechanic could understand even though he could not appreciate the full import of the words. Power was to him the sine qua non of all action, the driving wheel of all activity...the mind like a plant dies the moment it ceases to acquire braoder [sic] and fresher life.[79]

Swearingen used the opportunity to address a variety of topics. He challenged social definitions of ability and disability, demonstrating through words and example that the blind are more than capable. He included a personal account to demonstrate. He had attended a music festival at Converse College when, at the conclusion of the performance, he "was making my way slowly to the door when some gentlemen seeing that I was blind ask [sic] if he could assist me. His heart was allright [sic], and though I did not need him I could not refuse."[80]

Having challenged notions of education and ability, Swearingen next took on popular culture in his speech. Swearingen lamented the shoddy state of the arts and the lack of quality reading among American youth, saying, "Americans are prone to spend too much time over newspapers and periodicals, and to neglect the substantial contents of books." He felt it completely wrong that "[a]s a nation we rank first as publishers of this fugitive literature, and only fifth as producers of books." Swearingen wanted a more enlightened approach: "Mere reading as a diversion is often a literary dissipation which destroys the mental powers as completely as does alcohol those of the will. The morbid appetite for novels is pervasive of all study and yet our printing presses fairly groan with their loads of fiction."[81]

After continuing on for some time, Swearingen included a surprising comparison. Knowing his family's military history, the comparison Swearingen made is highly surprising: "The trained mind and the trained hand are in greater demand than ever before, and men are recognizing that it is not a mark of true greatness to lead an army to victory over the mangled bodies of slain enemies." Whether he made that comment in response to the family and friends he lost to war is a matter of supposition; however, he immediately followed that statement with one honoring his agrarian roots: "But he does the best service who makes two stalks of corn and one cabbage where two jimson weeds and a thistle grew before."[82]

His public persona blossoming, during the first few years of his teaching career Swearingen intended to pursue a career in law, political science, or economics. Since he did not have the money for graduate school, he applied for a Rhodes Scholarship to pursue a degree at Columbia University, New York. To this end, he secured effusive letters of recommendation from almost every professor he had at the college, influential friends, and state-level professionals, as well as the political clout of his Uncle Ben, now a US senator. In spite of these efforts (and proving that discrimination against people with disabilities wasn't unique to the South), he was refused the scholarship because of his blindness.

Faced with this rejection, Swearingen threw himself into his teaching passionately. He quickly became principal of the blind department, earning a reputation as a tough, compassionate instructor. When one blind student refused to eat with silverware, Swearingen insisted on not allowing him to eat at all. He stated that when the student was hungry enough, he would remember where the proper utensils were. Primarily, Swearingen taught through example: he "never complained about the hardships and handicaps of blindness; his own practice and example inculcated similar attitudes in his blind friends." He urged his students "to participate in business and society and preached to them the therapy of work."[83]

Writing to his mother in 1908, Swearingen described his days at Cedar Springs: on a typical day he met visitors until lights out, then typed his letters to family and friends. Interestingly, while he made a practice of not sharing too much personal information in writing, this was one of the few times Swearingen lapsed, even half joking, into self-pity—which also demonstrated just how isolated and alone he felt while at Cedar Springs. When answering his mother's query about possible romantic interests, he wrote, "No other girl will have me, and when you leave me I shall cut a sorry figure as a lonely old bachelor?"[84] This comment comes in direct contrast to the reflections of some friend or part-time biographer, likely from around the time of Swearingen's first campaign (1908). Titled "Brief Sketch," the piece describes Swearingen the teacher:

> As a blind man and a teacher of the blind, he has always admitted the desirability of eyesight, but he has never complained about the hardships and handicaps of blindness. He has practiced and inculcated the widest activity and participation in business and society, and has preached the gospel of work... Music and higher education are the most available fields for service and self-support, but handicraft should be available in some form for all. This is more for occupation than for profit, but enforced idleness is to be prevented in every instance, if possible.[85]

In spite of his loneliness—or more likely because of it—just as quickly as he rose to principal, Swearingen became superintendent of Cedar Springs. However, this quick transition into administration didn't appease Swearingen's sense of duty or his intellect. He grew tired of the frustrations facing teachers of the time, specifically teachers of students with disabilities. For a variety of reasons Swearingen opted out of teaching and into a career that would combine his loves: politics, service, South Carolina, and education.

The First Campaign: Election 1908

While Swearingen was teaching, the state superintendent was a relatively ineffective man named O. B. Martin. Perhaps realizing that his intellectual shortsightedness was becoming a liability, O. B. Martin declined to run for reelection in 1908, and Swearingen decided to make a run for the office. Swearingen had continued moving into the public eye in the previous years; in 1905, for example, he was a featured speaker at a centennial celebration. In addition, he was being groomed at home by his Uncle Ben. Thus, it came as no real shock when Swearingen chose to enter the race for school superintendent. Swearingen wrote to a friend that some of his friends had requested him to make a run for the office. He believed himself qualified by taste and training, and wrote that even if he was to lose the election, he didn't "think I shall have occasion to regret the work put into the campaign."[86] Proving masculinity probably helped Swearingen decide on this course of action as well. As described by Friend and Glover, "As manifested through honor, civic identity shaped southern masculinity." While this masculine honor was most frequently expressed in military service—something Swearingen clearly desired to do but could not—serving the state in support of its schools was arguably an extension of this notion. If he couldn't carry a musket and bayonet to serve his state on the battlefield, he would carry his beliefs and efforts to serve his state in its capitol.[87]

Political campaigning during this period was long, grueling work. Reflecting on following her husband on later campaign trails, Mary Swearingen wrote that the process was "a grueling practice which may not be peculiar to South Carolina, but which is certainly peculiar."[88] Candidates had to speak in public debates held in the seat of every county in South Carolina, creating the need for much travel. To make the traveling uncomfortable, the campaigns were held in the intense heat of late summer. In addition, all traveling was done by coal-burning train, with its associated discomforts of coal smoke and hot cinders in the cars. Also, campaigning was not inexpensive, all too often making politics the sport of the wealthy. In his financial disclosure statements, Swearingen revealed he spent $518.22 on the first primary and $136.58 on the second—a total of $654.80. While that doesn't sound like much, when converted into contemporary dollars the amounts are a bit more striking. Using the consumer price index (CPI) as the measure, in 2012 dollars Swearingen spent $13,300 on the first primary and $3,520 on the second. Someone living on a teacher's salary could ill afford $16,820 to spend just on the primaries.[89]

During the whistle-stops of the primary campaign, Swearingen listened closely to his two competitors, Stiles R. Mellichamp and E. C. Elmore, who did not take the blind candidate seriously. Journalists at the time described the two opponents as "prominent, respected 'old-school' gentlemen, both of whom have been closely associated with educational work in South Carolina for many years." He realized two things: first, that he was not a politician and did not necessarily want to become one; and second, that his competition was rather pedantic. Both men viewed themselves as "the logical candidate for the high position" and both men "presented the candidacy of the other as a sort of unwarranted intrusion." In fact, "neither of the interested gentleman paid the slightest attention" to Swearingen's entry in the race; this oversight would be their undoing.[90] While never conceding that his effort should be taken seriously, Mellichamp and Elmore "extended Swearingen…unfailing courtesy." While Swearingen made a point of "treating his older opponents with extreme courtesy and deference," there was a limit to his patience.[91] After listening to one of his competitors deliver the same speech at every whistle-stop, Swearingen put his eidetic memory to humorous use. At the next stop, when Swearingen was slated to deliver his address first, Swearingen rose and recited one of his competitor's speeches verbatim—leaving the poor man, quite literally, speechless.

This is not to say that Swearingen was without rhetoric of his own. Reading Swearingen's stump speech reveals many aspects of his educational beliefs while also demonstrating the extremely convoluted beliefs that comprised the man. Swearingen tapped into the same populist notions championed by his Uncle Ben—agriculture and racism—while also being gender inclusive. His speech set forth the ideas that would come to shape his entire career—developing rural schools, fostering agricultural education, and expanding opportunities.

Tapping into the same farming culture (and their inherent racism) as his populist predecessors, Swearingen stated, "The demand of the hour is for intelligent labor on the farm and thanks to our Anglo-Saxon instinct for land-grabbing and land-holding, the soil of our state is still in possession of its native sons." Of course, the best use of this land must be taught in the schools: "Nature has given them the power and inclination to hold it, but modern agriculture has become a profession, and demands intelligence and efficiency of those who would be masters rather than possessors of the soil." Swearingen embraced, rather than resisted, the shifting cultural dynamics marked by the Industrial Revolution and attempted to reach out to the mill workers: "The industrial awakening that has stirred this country can be seen in the cotton field as well as in the cotton factory, and I for one believe that both these can be best developed by the white man."[92]

Shifting focus, Swearingen called for great expansion of the number of schools, particularly in rural areas: "To-day the boy or girl in town who grows up ignorant does so because he does not care for knowledge. But many a country boy or girl would take an education, if their schools could give it." Of course, more schools would mean more teachers, and Swearingen was on their side as well: "The great deficiency in teacher's salaries would keep many of our choice spirits out of the schoolroom, were it not for the fact that teaching has attractions and rewards of its own." Swearingen knew that salaries had to be increased to attract and retain the best teachers: "Under present conditions, the wonder is that our corps of teachers is so excellent. It is now constantly recruited by young men and women who use it merely as a stepping-stone to something else, and this reproach will last as long as salaries continue to be too low to maintain profession."[93] Whether proving masculinity, or simply demonstrating the sense of privilege experienced (if not totally understood) by wealthy white society, Swearingen ended his speech on what can only be described as a paternalistic note: "The schoolroom and the playground can be made the nursery of character, and it is the privilege of the State Superintendent to work for moral no less than for intellectual stamina."[94]

Continuing these themes, Swearingen's platform had multiple facets, most of which were highlighted in the broadside pamphlet printed for his campaign, which he mailed to business owners in the larger towns across South Carolina (Figure 1.5). In it, Swearingen didn't try and hide his blindness. On the broadside, a photograph fills the center of the page, taking up almost one-third of the document, with highlights of his life printed in banner type alongside. To the right states his educational experiences: "Student at South Carolina College 1895–1899" and "Teacher in Cedar Springs Institute 1899–1908." To the left are two more biographical statements: "Born January 9, 1875" and "Made Blind by the Accidental Discharge of his Gun while out Hunting January 13, 1888."[95]

This public declaration of his disability is arguably an extension of Swearingen's desire to prove his masculinity. Timothy Beneke explains that physical manifestations of suffering—such as tattoos, muscles, and scars—become symbols of masculinity: "Such symbols convey a willingness and capacity to suffer for a masculine identity, an achieved and

JOHN E. SWEARINGEN
Candidate for State Superintendent of Education

I have entered the race for State Superintendent of Education because I wish the honor and privilege of working for the development of our public schools. Politics is not my profession, but I have always cherished the ambition to serve my native State. My interest in public affairs has been second only to my interest in education, and for years I have tried to be an earnest student of both.

The office is one of dignity and importance. It is educational rather than political, and affords to any man an inviting field of work and opportunity. It demands constructive leadership of a high order, for it imposes responsibility to the future as well as to the present. The truest interests of the State center in its schools and colleges. Education is the birth-right of the child and the duty of the commonwealth. Our age is intellectual no less than commercial, for thought dominates the activities of man and renders intelligence the motive power of the world. The nation, the class, or the individual, that does not feel and recognize its power can never be anything more than a hewer of wood and a drawer of water.

But education to be effective must be practical. It should train boys and girls to make the most of the opportunities that lie about them, should show them the dignity of labor, and should fit them to be masters rather

Born January 9, 1875. Made Blind by the Accidental Discharge of his Gun while out Hunting January 13, 1888.

Student at South Carolina College 1895-1899. Springs Institute 1899-1908. Teacher in Cedar

than creatures of their surroundings. Agriculture is, and must remain, the chief resource of the State; hence any education that trains away from the farm cannot produce the best results. The exodus of country folk from the farm to the town is largely due to educational conditions. The most prosperous communities in South Carolina today are those where farmers have stayed on their lands and built better schools for their children instead of moving off to find educational advantages. The agitation for rural school improvement is full of promise, for it seeks to bring to the country districts the same skill and professional supervision which have already been secured in the cities and larger towns.

At present there is often a lack of thoroughness in our teaching. Shallowness and inaccuracy are allowed to become fixed habits the correction of which costs no small proportion of our productive energy. The State Superintendent, with the cooperation of the State Board of Education, should use every effort to remedy this condition by providing a suitable course of study and by seeing that teachers are qualified to handle it. The standard of efficiency is higher now than ever before, thanks to Winthrop, but it can be still further improved.

My experience stretches from the country log school house to the State university. Nine years of teaching has taught me some of the difficulties that confront boys and girls, and have deepened my sympathy with older students who are striving for an education. The inspiration I received from my teachers I have tried to impart to my pupils, with what success these can best testify. My record, character, and fitness are open to investigation. If elected, I shall give to the work my time, my energies, and my best thought.

Figure 1.5 John E. Swearingen, candidate for state superintendent of education

visible toughness." As such, Swearingen's blindness can be perceived as an ongoing symbol of suffering and, as such, a solid expression of his masculinity. Considering that many Civil War veterans hosted a variety of disabilities from the war, such a belief in the link between suffering and masculine worth is not a large leap.[96]

Even as he was fulfilling socially accepted definitions of masculinity, Swearingen was also subtly beginning to create a new definition of masculinity. Swearingen demonstrated a paternalistic tone while concomitantly equating education with masculinity: "Public office is under any circumstance a public trust to be administered for the public good, and he who holds the office of State Superintendent of Education is permitted to work for childhood and youth hungry for high ideals of manhood, citizenship, and religion." With that, Swearingen digressed from traditionally accepted definitions of masculinity, arguing that to be masculine was to master one's environment: "Modern agriculture calls for brain more loudly than for brawn, and the aim of our educational system should be to make masters and not merely possessors of the soil."[97]

Swearingen began his platform by explaining the reasons why he sought office. "I have entered the race for state Superintendent of Education because I wish the honor and privilege of working for the development of our public schools." His terms are no less grandiose when describing the office itself. "The office is one of dignity and importance. It demands constructive leadership of a high order, for it imposes responsibility to the future as well as the present." Becoming philosophical, Swearingen explains his view of the necessity of education in South Carolina: "Our age is intellectual no less than commercial... The nation, the class, or the individual, that does not feel and recognize its power can never be anything more than a hewer of wood and a drawer of water."[98]

Swearingen's desire for vocational and agricultural education was apparent. Using the terms and ideas that would characterize his term in office, he wrote that "education to be effective must be practical. It should train boys and girls to make the most of the opportunities that lie about them, show them the dignity of labor, and should fit them to be masters rather than creatures of their surroundings."[99] To Swearingen, farming was the key to success: "Agriculture is, and must remain, the chief resource of the State; hence, any education that trains away from the farm cannot produce the best results." Using this same logic to call for improved rural schools, Swearingen argued that the most prosperous regions of South Carolina at the time were "those where farmers have stayed on their lands and built better schools for their children instead of moving off to find educational advantages." Thus, improving rural schools was a priority because "it seeks to bring to the country districts the same skill and professional supervision which have already been secured in the cities and larger towns."[100]

The impatience and frustration with teachers about which Swearingen wrote during the beginning years of his teaching career became another plank in his platform. "At present there is often a lack of thoroughness in our teaching. Shallowness and inaccuracy are allowed to become fixed habits," noted Swearingen. The cure for this, he argued, was in better teacher training at the college level. In effect, he sought to extend his paternalism from the State Board of Education into universities by "providing a suitable course of study" for future teachers and "seeking what teachers are qualified to handle it."[101]

During the campaign the old societal notions of ability, physical and intellectual, once again reared their ugly heads: Swearingen's opponents began attacking him because of his blindness, playing on the voter's ingrained notions that the blind were intellectually inferior. However, Swearingen's friends and family would not allow such accusations to slide. Dr. George Bunch, the cousin whom Swearingen so helped in their first couple of years at the South Carolina College, was quick to publicly leap to the defense in a letter to the editor. Thanking him, Swearingen wrote, "Ma says she almost shouted when she read your reply to Hoyt, and Your [sic] action helped me allover [sic] the state by supplying specific refutation to the only argument my opponents had against me."[102] Likewise J. J. McSwain sent a powerfully worded missive to editors of newspapers across the state, providing a wealth of testimony to Swearingen's abilities:

> That the absence of sight may be shown to be no disqualification of Prof. Swearingen to discharge all the duties of the office of State Superintendent of Education, a few testimonials may be used.
> Said Dr. F.C. Woodward in June 1898: "Though deprived of the power of material vision, I gladly bear witness that no man in my acquaintance sees in reality, more clearly."
> Says Hon. J. Wm. Thurmond, of Edgefield, when asked if absence of eye-sight would disqualify Prof. Swearingen from properly discharging the office: "If any man, eyes or no eyes, can fill the office, John Swearingen can."
> Says Dr. E.S. Joynes: "The sure [?] absence of the sense of sight [results that] Prof. Swearingen possesses the intellectual grasp, the energy and patriotism necessary to the full accomplishment of any task he undertakes."
> Says J.J. McSwain, Esq., of Greenville, S.C.: "My old college friend John Swearingen can do anything he undertakes. His blindness is absolutely no obstacle to any official duty. His moral and mental attainments, his sympathetic insight into educational conditions, his comprehensive understanding of civic and social problems, his practical common sense view of

life, all qualify him preeminently for the office of State Superintendent of Education."[103]

As the campaign rolled on, it became more and more obvious that Swearingen would win outright. Upbeat messages from supporters around the state rolled in as early as August, when S. H. Graham wrote, "I am very much pleased to say in this that all the information I have up to this writing is of the most encouraging nature and I am obliged to think that we are going to roll up the biggest majority for the Blind Man, that was ever obtained in Marion County for any State Official that ever made a race of it."[104]

So it was that Swearingen again confounded societal opinion regarding the position of the blind. Society dictated that the blind could receive only a limited education; Swearingen excelled through his tenure in Cedar Springs. Society dictated that the blind could not succeed at higher education; Swearingen excelled in his academic career at the South Carolina College. Society dictated that the blind would not make successful political campaigns. However, some 30,000 South Carolinians were reminded by Swearingen, his family, and friends, and all those faculty and students who knew him at the South Carolina College, that often society is wrong. Swearingen led a very successful whistle-stop round of county seats in South Carolina, and on August 25, 1908, Swearingen and Mellichamp emerged victorious from the primaries. To further confound societal opinion of the capabilities of the blind, on that rainy Election Day, September 8, 1908, Swearingen won. Three months later, he assumed the duties of the office. While the work of the first campaign was over, the real work was only beginning.

2

Fighting the Good Fight, 1907–1915

> With a firm reliance in the patriotism, chivalry, courage, pride, and sense of justice of the Southern people, with a profound conviction of the necessity of universal education for the preservation and perpetuation of democracy, with an assurance born of the evidence of all past experience and all past history that the only means of universal education are the public schools.
>
> —J. Y. Joyner, Address to the People of the South, 1904

At the time of Swearingen's victory, the schools of South Carolina—particularly the secondary schools—were still primarily nineteenth-century institutions. During his tenure in office, particularly when working with governors who viewed education as an issue of importance, Swearingen worked diligently to move the schools into the twentieth century. While establishing routines in his office that both comforted his staff and established efficiency, he took control. Soon he established himself as a force to be reckoned with politically and legislatively, working to enact much needed reforms almost as soon as he entered office.

The Call for Secondary Education in the South

By no means was Swearingen alone in perceiving the schools of South Carolina—and across the entire south—as being in need of significant reform. In April 1904 a meeting of the Association of the Superintendents of Public Instruction of the Southern States was held in Birmingham, Alabama. At this meeting, an address was given by J. Y. Joyner of North Carolina, later unanimously adopted by the representatives of all states present. Intended to be an open call, it was titled "Address to the People of the South" and effectively laid the groundwork for the furthering of public education across the south. It was written in three sections, subtitled so there would be no doubt as to the message of the address: "Inadequacy of our Public School System," "Remedies," and "Equality of Opportunity for the Children of the South."[1]

In the writing process, state superintendents from Tennessee, Mississippi, Texas, Louisiana, Georgia, Alabama, Arkansas, Virginia, and Florida, as well as South Carolina's O. B. Martin, assisted Joyner. The address opens with almost blunt clarity: "The public schools of the South, the only hope for the education of nine-tenths of the people's children, are still sadly inadequate to their stupendous task, unequal to the educational demands of this century of education, and inferior in most respects to the public schools of other sections of our common country." Joyner then cited a variety of comparative statistics, pointing out that, in all respects, the southeast was sadly lagging in education.[2]

In pointing out the weaknesses of the Southern schools, however, the committee was also quick to deflect any blame for these weaknesses. In fact, the address went so far as to assuage the consciences of the southern superintendents: "Far be from us any intention of ridicule, blame, or discouragement in reciting these facts in regard to the educational conditions." Clearly, the committee had moved to the second phase of the New South rhetoric when they wrote: "To those familiar with the obstacles that had to be overcome—social and political revolutions, destruction and reconstruction, poverty, robbery, misrule—the wonder is that these conditions are as good as they are... we have only admiration, gratitude, commendation."[3]

The address went on to cite seven remedies to the underdeveloped schools across the South. The first was a call to improve the physical plants of schools. The second remedy was to raise teacher salaries in order to ensure qualified personnel, and to extend the school term so teachers would be full-time employees. The third remedy was for competent supervision of the schools: more training and higher salaries for administrators. The fourth remedy was longer school terms, calling for terms of between 150 and 190 days a year. The fifth remedy was for better classification and gradation by consolidation, structures of at least two rooms with two full-time teachers. The sixth remedy was a call for public high schools: "A public school system without public high schools is sadly incomplete, like some magnificent structure with only the lower rooms complete." The final remedy offered in the address was for more money through more taxation, local taxes supplementing state taxes to support public schools.[4]

After outlining the remedies, the address took on an almost religious tone in its conclusion. It asked the question of whether the South would offer its support of schools for children, posing the question as "the everlasting yea or the everlasting nay." Calling support of public schools a "sacred duty," the committee ended the address with a powerful conclusion: "By the tradition of the past, the facts of the present, the hopes of the future, by the love that you bear your children, by the duty that you owe your country, yourselves and your neighbors, we appeal to you, the people of the South, to rally to the support of your public schools and make them adequate to their high mission and their stupendous task."[5] The rhetoric of this address would shape the vision of Swearingen, as well as superintendents across the South, for years to come.

The year 1906 saw this call for high schools repeated and extended in Superintendent Martin's annual report to the state legislature. Devoting many pages to the call, Martin himself opened the arguments by writing that "the most important educational legislation that can claim the attention of the General Assembly must be a plan for encouraging and establishing high schools."[6] Martin used a variety of arguments in his writings, reminding the legislature that high schools were good for all schools as they set the tone for each district and provide a qualified teaching force. A good system of high schools would improve the colleges and universities as well, wrote Martin, allowing universities to eliminate their preparatory departments.

The call for public high schools took on clarion effect with the section of the annual report simply titled "To the People of South Carolina." In this section, a committee calling itself the Campaign Executive Committee, consisting of D. C. Heyward, D. B. Johnson, and Superintendent Martin, explained that not one but two different high school bills had been sent before the legislature. They wrote that "the prosperity and advancement of South Carolina depend upon the high school, because the school system of the state is inadequate without it."[7] They went on to write that every county in South Carolina should have a public high school open and free to all children of that county. Furthering the high school/college funding debate, the committee wrote that "it is better to have a first-class high school than a low class college."[8]

The next year, 1907, one of the final years of Swearingen's career in Cedar Springs, was a benchmark year in the development of the public high schools. During this time, two major events took place, the first being the South Carolina State Legislature finally passed "A Bill for the Establishment and Maintenance of Public High Schools Within the State," otherwise known as the High School Act. This act, with all the amendments that were later attached, was the most influential piece of legislation affecting secondary schools in South Carolina. Its 11 sections established size, term, regulations, and funding for a statewide system of secondary education in South Carolina.

Section I of the bill stated that any township or aggregate of townships could establish a high school. Section II stated that a town needed at least 25 eligible students for entrance into high school before putting the matter to vote. Section III stated that the high schools would fall under the control of the State Board of Education that would regulate qualifications of high school instructors, courses of study, tuition fees, procuring board and lodging of nonresident students, and certificates of graduation. Section IV said that each county district must keep the state appraised of the condition of high schools within it. Section V stated that local boards of trustees could levy school taxes between one mill and ten mills on the dollar specifically for the support of the public high schools. Section VI stated that local boards of trustees could select students to receive scholarships to attend their high schools, paid for out of local funds. Section VII stated that local boards could sell property or obtain bonds in order to secure funding for the construction of a high school. Section VIII established a yearly appropriation from the state legislature specifically for the support of public high schools. Section IX stated that the State Board of Education would be responsible for dispersing the appropriation to high schools, as long as the local board provided at least 50 percent of its own operating budget. Section X called for a repeal of all previous acts inconsistent with the current act, and Section XI provided the date of effect.

The second major event of 1907 affecting public high schools was the suggestion that the State Board of Education adopt a uniform high school course of study. Suggested by William Hand and forwarded by Superintendent O. B. Martin in his 1907 report, the suggestions to unify a course of study at the secondary level were highly detailed. It determined that courses should be weighted in units, each unit consisting of five weekly periods, meeting for not less than 40 minutes each day, over a total of no less than 36 weeks. Schools in turn should be organized and accredited by the number of units offered, as 8-unit schools (2-year), 12-unit schools (3-year), or 15-unit schools (4-year) (Tables 2.1 and 2.2). However, the same citizens of South Carolina who opposed state control over the schools balked at what was seen as the state's attempted takeover of the schools.

In spite of the nominal conflicts aroused, the effects of these actions were felt almost immediately. In the 1908 report to the state legislature, Martin stated that "the high school situation this year has improved very materially in comparison with last year…the high schools were

Table 2.1 Course units recommended for accreditation[9]

Course type	8-Unit school	12-Unit school	15-Unit school
English	2	3	3
Mathematics	2	3	3
History	1	1	1
Science	1	1	1
Elective	2	4	7

Table 2.2 Course descriptions recommended for accreditation[10]

English	Mathematics	Latin	History	Science	Electives
Rhetoric & composition	Algebra to quadratics	Form & prose composition	Greek & Roman history	Agriculture	Greek
American literature	Algebra, quadratics, & beyond	Four books of Caesar	Medieval & modern history	1 unit each of physiography & physiology	Modern languages
English literature	Plane geometry	Six orations of Cicero	English history	Physics	Bookkeeping
		Four books of Virgil	Modern history/civics	Chemistry	
				Botany	

improved at least 25 per cent during the past year."[11] However, State Inspector William Hand was quick to amend the gains. For example, Hand inspected one hundred public high schools, but only four of them were housed separately from the lower grades. High school teachers were still ill trained, and there was a real need for specific high school equipment, such as maps and laboratory apparatus, in all schools.[12]

One of the biggest issues facing the schools, then and now, is how rural schools could meet new standards. Martin, perhaps demonstrating his shortsightedness, stated that there was no need for high schools in rural areas. "We have found that it is impossible to establish many such schools because there are so few children ready to enter the high school grades," wrote Martin. "In hundreds of communities it would be impossible to establish high schools, even if we could give them five times as much aid."[13] Instead of supporting the rural high school, Martin called upon the legislature to provide more funds for rural elementary schools to produce students ready for high school work.

Many county superintendents echoed Martin's thoughts about rural education. Even in a somewhat more urban setting like Charleston,

E. P. Waring, county superintendent of education, wrote that "owing to the comparatively small white population in this county, distributed over a large area, we have not yet been able to take advantage of the high school opportunities, and therefore are forced to continue the high school grades in our grades schools."[14] However, not every district took Martin's view of high schools in rural areas. Many districts built high schools and allowed them to guide the lower grades. In Darlington County, for example, Henry Burn, county superintendent of education, wrote of the role of the high school in Hartsville: "We note that...the high school at Hartsville cost more money (and it is well spent) than the thirty-seven white rural schools of the entire county." However, Burn was also quick to notice that the high school created a need in the area: "We begin to realize the weakness of our rural schools, and the great work that is required to give us ideal rural schools."[15]

Resistance came from many quarters. Wrote Hand, "The people are not supporting their High Schools. They are putting neither their money nor their children into them."[16] Money was the chief problem in most districts. Superintendents from the Pee Dee (Marlboro County), Midlands (Orangeburg County), and Coastal Regions (Horry County) echoed the refrain: "The cry is: better houses, better equipment, longer terms, and trained teachers," but were unwilling to support a new tax to achieve these ends.[17] Even the universities were not supporting public high schools. Instead of working with the public high schools, the universities became competitive institutions: they offered preparatory courses for entering students, a condition Hand railed against powerfully in his statement, writing: "The evil genius which dominates our colleges is greed for numbers. Boards of trustees, faculties and the people are all under the magic spell."[18]

Race complicated the issue of high school support even more; considering the privileged, masculine view that dominated school boards and the politics of the time, establishing high schools for African Americans was not even a consideration in many districts. In Barnwell County, for example, the county superintendent reflected deficit thinking when he wrote: "One of the greatest drawbacks towards educational progress in some of our districts is the large Negro population." Explaining the process of constructing schools, he provided an example. "Three districts along the Savannah River, large in area, and composed mostly of plantations with Negro tenants, have an enrollment of 780 negroes, and only 150 whites." Rather than provide schools for the majority, instead the district decided on a different plan: "Three school-houses for whites are now being erected in these districts, and more are needed."[19]

Handling the Office

Against this backdrop of recent gains but huge challenges, upon assuming office, Swearingen hit the ground running. Before his first day officially on the job, Swearingen was a featured speaker at the December 31, 1908, South Carolina Teacher's Association conference. The prescient title of his address was "Needed Educational Legislation." Interestingly enough, the closing address at that conference, on New Year's Day, was delivered by one Senator Benjamin Tillman. Once he assumed the office, Swearingen knew he had to establish a routine that would allow him to work efficiently and keep his sighted staff at ease. For starters, Swearingen applied his gifted memory to learn the route from his home on Blanding Street to his office so he could make the trip unaccompanied. As explained by his son John:

> In his early days as state superintendent of education, his office was in one of those tall buildings. We called them skyscrapers, but I guess they were, what, fifteen, eighteen stories. And he used to walk from the house to his office by himself. He knew around, and in those days there weren't that many cars on the street. And he was able to manage those things for himself. He did it without any problem at all.[20]

His office was, in fact, located near the top of the National Loan and Exchange Building, described as being "Away up near the top of a skyscraper building...whose windows overlook the country for miles around."[21] Organization and efficiency governed Swearingen's efforts while in office. His staff quickly grew used to his daily routine: enter, have mail dictated to him, type responses, make calls, and handle other bits of official business. Assuming that the argument put forth by Beneke is correct—that success at work is a visible demonstration of masculinity—it only makes sense that Swearingen was out to prove his worth not just as a disabled man, but also as a masculine man.[22]

Swearingen did not just attend to straightforward office duties, however; as an elected official, there was much more to the job. Swearingen would hardly ever refuse an invitation to a barbecue, picnic, family gathering, political campaign meeting, graduation ceremony, or school dedication. Swearingen was extremely hands-on in the duties of his office, a trait that was respected by many, seen as autocratic by many more. This was probably an extension of the paternalistic attitude that drove him to office.

Whether it was loyalty to the state, a real sense of duty in his position, a means to prove his masculinity, or more attempts at confounding social opinion, Swearingen would travel the state frequently, conducting business. One typical duty that took Swearingen out of the office regularly was the inspection of new school buildings. At the outset, builders and superintendents alike would doubt Swearingen's abilities in this capacity; however, he took great pleasure in performing highly detailed inspections that frequently caught construction errors missed by his sighted colleagues. Working with Clemson University's architectural department, Swearingen began a program of planned construction of the schools throughout the state. Thanks to the standardization of the plans, he was familiar with dimensions, lighting, and other characteristics of the buildings.

An inspection by Swearingen was amazingly thorough. Wife Mary recalls a county superintendent telling her once that Swearingen could "find out more about a building with one trip than [he could] by watching them build it." He was methodical in his work.

> With his cane he checked the height of the ceiling and quickly stepped off the width of the room. With his sensitive perception to light, he could face the windows and remark, "I see you have your windows where you get good light." Some spectators were ready to swear he had a magic sense of some sort. He tested floor strength by his shiver-the-timber method. He would find a strategic point and suddenly bounce up and down energetically. If from two or three vantage points he could hear no rattles, he was happy. If, however, a carpenter had not braced his sills well enough, Mr. Swearingen was quick to suggest with some asperity that "these sills should be strengthened and steadied..." He would ask about the desks, the blackboards, and the heating facilities of the school building.[23]

His travels around the state were either by train or, more to Swearingen's preference, by open car. Frequently, Swearingen would have the county superintendents tour him around their district. One such trip took him to Anderson County, with Superintendent J. B. Felton behind the wheel. At every stop, Swearingen would ask, "Where are we now Felton?" Eventually, with the poor conditions of the roads of the time, the car skidded on a patch of slick red clay and slid into a ditch. Both men were thrown forward, Swearingen breaking two ribs in the process. "At the moment of the accident though," recalls his wife, "he only groaned a bit and asked stoically 'Well, where are we now, Felton?'"[24]

Swearingen did not limit himself to trips in the state; he would attend educational conferences all over the country. His son remembers Swearingen using the railroad extensively—boarding and departing trains, and navigating stations—by himself. Ironically, while Swearingen was completely at ease in these settings, his son was afraid of the danger of the old steam locomotives.

His staff grew extremely loyal to Swearingen, and were extremely capable of running the office in his absence. Clearly, Swearingen was able to not only compensate for his blindness while in office but also perform all of the duties in a much more direct fashion than many of his predecessors. This quality characterized not only the routine tasks of the office, but also the entire view Swearingen took of his professional responsibility. Not only was it good enough to maintain the public schools while he was in office, he also wanted to affect significant change. To do so, he would alternately cooperate and battle with political and philanthropic forces at the state and national levels.

Each year, by constitutional decree, the state superintendent of education in South Carolina had to generate an annual report. These reports were given to the state legislators and governor; in addition, they were made available to the public. These reports provided the authors—the state superintendents—a means to raise awareness of issues critical to the schools and a bully pulpit from which they could sound their ideas for educational reform. Swearingen was very quick to begin using these reports as both; they now provide a good account of his aims, ideas, and opinions.

Swearingen spent much of his first report, issued in 1909, conducting a blunt, honest assessment of the state of the schools upon his taking office. He began by lambasting the state legislature for the inequities that resulted from the existing high school law. Swearingen used his background in economics to present a dollars-and-cents breakup of how the existing law hurt more districts than it helped. "Is it wise to cripple the schools," he wrote, "because her people are awake to the advantages of education?"[25] Most noticeably, however, Swearingen called for a clearing up of the "educational atmosphere" surrounding the public high schools. He levied his criticism on teachers and curriculum in this matter. Swearingen lamented the fact that there was no differentiation between elementary and secondary teaching credentials and no set high school curriculum. He wrote that all schools would benefit from "a definite enrolment, a definite teaching force, a fixed minimum equipment, a well ordered course of study, an orderly program and seven years' instruction in its common school department."[26]

One high note of 1909 was the passage of the Act to Increase the Average Length of the School Term and to Improve Efficiency of the Public Schools in This State. The act, which provided the state superintendent with the power to govern it, was an attempt to lengthen the school term of rural schools across the state. Schools offering terms of less than 100 days could apply for state aid, up to $100, in order to increase their length of term to over 100 days. This funding was specifically designed to lengthen the term of rural schools. While the amount wasn't much, and even less for the colored schools, it was a great step in the legislature taking an active role in school funding.

In 1910 Swearingen managed to get Legislative Act 585, a "Commission to Examine and Revise the School Law of the State and to Recommend Changes in Same." The commission was a positive step forward in making the legislature, and the people of the state, aware of the real needs of education reform. By accepting the fact that the needs were great enough to form a commission on the subject, the legislature appeared to be acknowledging the deficiencies in public education. While this group called for several improvements in the public schools of South Carolina, Swearingen would have to fight with the office of the governor and the legislature to get any of the commission's recommendations enacted.

Notably, Swearingen's first report included an entirely separate chapter on the condition of African American schools around the state. This would begin a trend that would follow Swearingen throughout his term in office; he realized that you could not educate just one population of the state without educating all of it. While addressing the state of white and African American schools in separate sections, Swearingen presented identical sets of statistics from both, with the exception of an analysis of revenues brought into African American schools.

The question of why emerges at this point: why would Swearingen take the wholly unpopular stand of coming out in favor of making white and black schools more equitable? There are three potential reasons, all established in the examination of his personal life presented earlier. First, Swearingen felt discrimination on a personal level as he constantly was underestimated because of his disability. This would probably create sympathy for populations who faced the same societal discrimination. Second, Swearingen felt a great love for his state. In his desire to make lasting contributions to the state as a whole, it is unlikely that he would isolate one population over another to devote his service. Indeed, it was becoming common knowledge at the time that true upliftment could not occur in the South as long as any segment of the population remained educationally behind. Third, Swearingen spent much of his life proving his masculinity. On one level, he probably adopted an extension of this by adopting a paternalistic attitude toward African Americans. Probably, this paternalism was also an extension of his familial attitudes toward the African Americans who tended the family's extensive lands.

By 1910, when discussing the condition of the high schools in the state, however, Swearingen was not as effusive. While beginning by stating that the high schools "had a prosperous year," Swearingen quickly cited some of the problems facing secondary schools—and schools in general. A lack of thorough elementary education in the state led to poor high school students. Worse, the colleges were producing teachers little prepared for their positions, subjecting the students to "all sorts of educational quackery." Swearingen repeated the call for a formalized course of study for the high schools. "For four years the State has exerted every energy to establish an adequate high school system," stated Swearingen. He quickly added that "this cannot be done without a uniform course of study to be used throughout the State."[27]

Swearingen also saw a follow-up to the legislation approved in the previous session. In 1910, An Act to Appropriate Sixty Thousand Dollars to the Public Schools of South Carolina was approved. Meeting many of the same criteria as the previous year's act, this one increased the amount of aid the legislature reserved for schools to $100 annually. The legislature explained the purpose of the act was to increase "the average length of the free school term in this State." The act specified that only schools open for terms of 100 days or longer would qualify for any aid.[28]

High school inspector William Hand's 1910 report began with a summary of the increases made by the high schools since the passing of the High School Act. He described, in tabular form, just how much increase there was in secondary education (Table 2.3).

Hand used these statistics to explain that the people of the state were finally becoming convinced that secondary education was necessary to the state. Praising the increase in number of schools, Hand cited that the development of public high schools clarified the link between elementary and college, as well as elementary and secondary, education. He was not

Table 2.3 Growth of secondary education in South Carolina, 1906–1910

Statistic	1906–1907 School year	1909–1910 School year	Percentage growth
No. of high schools	95	162	59
No. of high school teachers	160 full time 75 part time	355 full time 84 part time	54 total
High school enrollment	4,812	8,030	60
Public high school teacher salary	Unknown ($146,028 in 1907)	$246,002	59
Cost of school buildings	$129,500	$309,200	42

Table 2.4 National comparisons of high schools

State	White population	High school teachers	High school pupils	Public high schools	Square miles
South Carolina	557,807	439	8,030	156	30,570
Maine	692,226	600	12,076	151	33,040
Connecticut	892,424	834	14,837	65	4,990
Rhode Island	419,050	339	7,971	23	1,250
Colorado	529,046	555	12,089	90	103,925
Washington	496,304	798	15,736	167	69,180
Oregon	394,582	393	7,788	110	96,030
Nebraska	1,056,526	1,063	20,284	376	77,510
Minnesota	1,737,036	1,256	25,374	199	83,365
California	1,402,727	1,736	33,916	185	158,360

Table 2.5 Further analysis of national comparisons of high schools

State	Teacher-pupil ratio	Area served by high school, in square miles	White population per square mile	White population served by each high school
South Carolina	18	196	18	3,576
Maine	20	219	21	4,584
Connecticut	20	77	179	13,730
Rhode Island	18	54	336	18,220
Colorado	24	1,153	5	5,878
Washington	20	414	7	2,972
Oregon	20	873	4	3,587
Nebraska	19	206	14	2,810
Minnesota	20	419	21	8,729
California	20	856	9	7,582

quick to lie on laurels, though; Hand did mention that the work, while impressive, was still in its beginning stages. Hand went on to a national comparison of South Carolina's public high schools. The purpose of presenting the statistics was to show that yes, the public high school had made gains in South Carolina; however, there was still some distance to go (Table 2.4).

Hand presented these statistics with an alarmist's note; when looking at the raw data presented by Hand, South Carolina seemed to lag behind other states. An examination of these raw data revealed the minimization of the differences. In issues such as teacher-pupil ratios and schools-miles ratios, the differences between schools with similar geography were minimal at best. The best states to consider using these criteria were Maine and Nebraska, with statistics comparable to South Carolina. When factoring in white population per square mile, the disparity between the states became even less apparent (Table 2.5).

Beginning the Battle: Improving African American Schools

Though Swearingen was racist personally, he crafted a somewhat different professional persona. Swearingen was off to a quick start in his efforts to improve African American schools in South Carolina. When Swearingen took office, the state had greatly increased per-pupil spending over the last ten years for white students—a 52 percent gain—from $4.98 in 1899 to $10.34 in 1909. However, African American students were not beneficiaries of this largesse. Their per-pupil spending only rose 17 percent, from $1.42 to $1.70. Funding disparities were in every district in the state; however, they were slighter in the up-country than in the low country. There, the funding disparities actually exceeded the average spending; in the up-country, where overall spending was lower, the trend was reversed (Table 2.6).

The 1909 Act to Increase the Average Length of the School Term and to Improve Efficiency of the Public Schools in This State was relatively and contextually almost color-blind: in its first year of operation, the act funded seven colored schools across the state. However, the amounts offered to colored schools reflected the general trend of colored versus white school funding (colored students received much less). For example, Anderson School in Darlington County, a white school listing 64 students, received $100, whereas the African American school in Dorchester County, also listing 64 students, received only $40.[29]

Swearingen attacked the disparity between white and African American schools, starting with his 1909 report, writing, "Public education is

Table 2.6 Selected per capita expenditure according to enrollment (in dollars), 1908–1909

	White	Negro	Average, both	Difference
Up-country district				
Anderson	7.63	1.92	5.53	5.71
Greenville	5.56	2.00	4.81	3.36
Spartanburg	8.42	2.43	6.08	5.99
Union	6.83	3.37	4.93	3.46
Low country district				
Beaufort	31.86	3.09	6.62	28.77
Charleston	35.70	2.55	13.56	33.15
Colleton	8.73	1.77	5.30	6.96
Georgetown	14.76	3.15	7.53	11.61

admittedly the only means of securing public intelligence." This philosophy guided him as he explained the educational impasse facing the state regarding the color barrier in education: "The problem in South Carolina is found in the adjustment of the free public school to the conditions of our social, industrial, and economic life, for public education here means a dual instead of a single school system."[30]

Swearingen cited a variety of funding disparities in his report, county by county, African American versus white. However, more telling statistics are cited by Anderson, who examines high school enrollments by age and race. In his work, Anderson presents a listing of enrollment statistics, white versus African American, across the South. A detailed examination of the information reveals that South Carolina was lagging far behind the rest of the South in providing equal opportunity for African Americans in public secondary education. This condition cannot be explained away by historical forces, such as resistance to Reconstruction, as the same conditions applied to the majority of the southern states (Table 2.7).

Table 2.7 High school enrollment in the Southern states

State	Blacks enrolled in public high schools	Whites enrolled in public high schools	Blacks enrolled in private high schools	Whites enrolled in private high schools	High school enrollment, black students, 15-19 years (%)	High school enrollment, white students, 15-19 years (%)
Alabama	1,680	14,025	1,290	2,012	2.9	12.3
Arkansas	366	6,227	606	1,304	1.9	6.1
Delaware	65	1,661	86	227	4.7	11.6
Florida	187	3,099	433	375	2.0	7.7
Georgia	648	19,833	1,528	3,063	1.7	15.2
Kentucky	1,342	6,874	563	24,537	6.7	14.7
Louisiana	98	4,778	1,101	864	1.6	5.7
Maryland	496	7,641	318	1,786	3.5	9.0
Mississippi	387	7,349	1,427	1,111	1.6	10.1
Missouri	1,183	31,705	363	3,237	10.5	10.9
North Carolina	880	13,470	2,224	4,347	3.9	11.0
South Carolina	198	7,964	919	488	1.1	11.5
Tennessee	538	9,094	1,296	5,728	3.4	8.1
Texas	1,363	29,096	1,488	3,600	3.7	9.5
Virginia	688	10,879	2,405	3,165	4.1	9.9
West Virginia	87	3,949	300	779	5.9	4.0
Total	10,206	177,644	16,347	56,623	2.8	10.1

Table 2.8 African American high schools in South Carolina, 1911

School	Weeks in school year	Years in course	Full-time teachers	Part-time teachers	Pupils
Anderson	40	2	2	2	U
Beaufort	36	2	0	2	13
Barinerd (Chester)	34	2	0	4	22
Bennettsville	28	2	1	0	12
Columbia	36	3	2	1	119
Darlington	36	3	2	0	U
Florence	36	3	1	2	41
Friendship (Rock Hill)	32	4	5	0	95
Georgetown	36	3	2	0	U
Greenville	36	2	1	0	67
Lancaster	32	4	5	0	66
Marion	32	2	0	1	5
Orangeburg	27	1	0	1	7
Sumter	36	1	1	0	36
Sterling (Greenville)	32	4	3	1	41
Union	32	2	1	1	27
Benedict (Columbia)	32	4	3	4	199
Claflin	30	4	4	4	197
State normal	28	4	5	0	170

Note: U = unreported.

In terms of reportage, 1911 marked a significant year for African American schools. For the first time ever, High School Inspector Hand's report included a detailed list of high schools serving African American students. While his report did not differentiate between public and private, it did detail the 19 secondary institutions active in the state. The data is not surprising; when compared to white high schools in the same towns, African American high schools offered fewer weeks in the school term, fewer years in course, and fewer full-time teachers (Table 2.8).

Personal and Professional Challenges

When Swearingen took office in 1908, he moved to the city of Columbia. He had proved his independence on the campaign trail, riding trains from county seat to county seat, delivering his message to as many people as possible. He maintained his independence upon moving, mastering the walk from his house to his office in order to do it unassisted. Single at the time, Swearingen's primary family commitment was back home to his mother and siblings—rather than in the city: he maintained steady ties and frequent communication with his family back in the upstate.

Starting in January 1909, the same month that he led a toast before a formal dinner honoring Robert E. Lee by saying that "it was in education common to all that the destiny of the free republic of America was practically settled,"[31] Swearingen began receiving letters from his brother and sister informing him that his beloved mother was very ill, probably dying. In March, his brother George wrote to explain that their mother had "vertigo of the blood." Five days later, he received correspondence explaining she had become "reconciled to die."[32] By that time, Swearingen was being encouraged by both his siblings to spend as much time with his mother at home in Edgefield as possible, as she was not going to live much longer. His sister returned home to tend to their mother on a full-time basis. His mother, the woman who helped move him down the path of education and success, who goaded him into overcoming his disability, and who was one of two people in his life to ever learn to read and write in Point Print Type, passed away in August.[33]

To Swearingen, the loss was devastating; he would describe it as the greatest blow that ever befell him. Gone was the woman who, as he wrote to family friend Dr. Mitchell, "For the last twenty-two years she has read for me, studied with me, guided me by advice and precept and been to me the strongest influence that ever touched my life."[34] These words are neither pure melodrama nor hopeless "mama's boy" ruminations; Anna Tillman was, quite literally, the woman who moved Swearingen out of the darkness into the light. She was the woman who not only taught Swearingen as a sighted youth, but also continued urging his education after his accident, one of two people to learn to write to him so he could read without assistance, and supported him in his efforts to confound what society said he was capable of. In his correspondence, Swearingen was uncharacteristically demonstrative in letting his feelings show and paying homage to the woman who made his career. To a Miss Lee Wharton of Woodruff, he continued in this vein, writing, "My Mother had been everything to me for many years, and since the loss of my sight, she has allowed me the unstinted use of her eyes."[35] To Dr. A. J. S. Thomas of Greenville it was, "For twenty-two years she has been eyes to me, and now that she is gone, I hope to discharge properly the duties she has fitted me to undertake."[36]

Swearingen needed to take time both to settle his mother's affairs and to mourn properly. His staff knew him well, though, and knew that his sense of duty would bring him back to Columbia well before he should. To this end, they drafted a letter to him in an attempt at putting his mind at ease. The letter reveals in its brevity how efficient the office was, and also the level of respect and candor they shared:

> Everything is o.k. The mail basket is empty, and there is nothing to require your attention here. I have cancelled engagements at Heath Springs, Berea, and Pelzer.
> Dove will go to Lexington, Prof. Hand to Orangeburg, Mann to Georgetown, Dr. Mitchell to Kingstree and Bamburg. Prof. Hand thinks Supt. Evans, Dr. Mitchell, and Mrs. Daniel will be enough of Bamberg, since they are all long-winded.[37]

Through August and September, Swearingen grieved with his family in Edgefield and corresponded with his office in Columbia. The loss of his mother, to Swearingen, meant that he would "never find so patient, so unselfish and so loving a friend again in life."[38] While usually accurately prophetic in matters personal and professional, in this area Swearingen was blinded by grief and had no idea who was about to come into his life. Ironically enough, in the midst of the health crisis facing his mother, Swearingen received a letter of recommendation from one T. O. Mabry, Professor at Winthrop University. In it, Mabry recommended a young woman, one Mary Hough, as a "fit science teacher."[39] Swearingen received a follow-up letter on Ms. Hough, informing him that she had been employed in Denmark, South Carolina. Little did either Mabry or Swearingen know that this correspondence would mark the beginning of the other most significant relationship in Swearingen's life: the woman who would become the love of his life and future wife less than a decade later.

It wasn't just his personal life in which Swearingen faced challenges during these early years in office. In South Carolina, as in many other states, the ultimate arbiter of educational policy is the state legislature. While the office of state superintendent can make recommendations on policy, law, and funding, ultimately it is the state legislature that determines which recommendations will be adopted and which rejected. Swearingen's relationship with this body was as convoluted and unpredictable as all the other elements in his life. On one level, Swearingen refused to "play politics," either refusing favors from various elected officials or taking them to task publicly for lack of effort. On another level, Swearingen still had an enormously politically influential uncle in Ben Tillman; it is a safe assumption that many of his efforts were rewarded in the hope that Swearingen would use his influence with his uncle. When things went well for the schools, Swearingen was effusive in his praise for the legislature. For instance, when recalling the significant educational legislation passed in the previous two sessions, Swearingen wrote that they "may well be called 'An Educational Legislature'" and urged them to continue their work: "I most heartily recommend prompt and widespread use of the advantages placed at our disposal."[40]

However much he praised the legislature, Swearingen's wife recalls Swearingen having difficulty working with the state legislature. Acknowledging that Swearingen's "busiest time of the year was when the legislature was in session," Mary remembers him working "around the clock" in a variety of areas: "The first problem came in working out legislation that would be acceptable and workable in all areas of the state. Moreover, it had to further his plans for over-all progress instead of favoritism for certain localities for political advantage." It was not all contentious, though. Mary further explains that many of the state representatives were "unselfish and patriotic with whom he [Swearingen] could work. He recognized their authority, and they believed in his sincerity."[41]

Some state legislators made education a priority when serving in office. Mary recounts some who worked effectively with Swearingen, many of whom she probably entertained during dinner parties organized by her husband. For example, she remembers a family friend representing Newberry County, one Dr. C. T. Wyche, who was "as anxious to help educate other people's children as he was determined to educate his own." In addition, she describes:

> Senator Ed McCravey of Pickens County, who went to bat for any school cause he believed would help the children of the state. I remember Senator Alan Johnstone of Newberry, a grand old man who for many years led the way toward progressive legislation in other fields as well as in education. I can see today Senator George K. Laney of Chesterfield as he pleaded literally from head to foot for school legislation he believed in. He would wave his hands, walk the floor, run his fingers through his disheveled hair, and beg his hearers to support legislation that would "make South Carolina great again." The work of these men and of my husband may not be completely remembered or recognized today, but it laid the foundation for the public schools from which our children and their children profit now.[42]

While getting along well with those with strong positive views on education, Swearingen was not afraid to "mix it up" with those who did not. One reason for the contentiousness of his relationship with many legislators, as well as with other groups, was his straightforwardness: some would consider it blunt, others would consider it insulting. Swearingen considered tact nothing more than a form of evasion and confusion, almost a form of lying. Swearingen was particularly succinct with legislators regarding schools. For example, Swearingen frequently pressed the legislature for funding in five areas: rural schools, high schools, school construction, adult education, and supervision. During the ensuing heated debates, Swearingen carried on the following conversation with one of the state's legislators:

> One watchdog of the treasury deplored the size of the request. "Mr. Swearingen," he queried, "if we cannot find funds for all five of your requests, which one would you rather have eliminated?"
> "Your honor," replied Mr. Swearingen instantly, "if you had five children, which one would you want to starve?"
> "Don't you know, Mr. Swearingen, how necessary it is that we exercise economy?"
> "I have practiced economy all my life, sir," he replied, "but I never believed it was economy to buy one sock instead of a pair."[43]

Swearingen, Ansel, and the Progressive Movement

While the state legislature was resistant to many of Swearingen's reforms, in particular during the reign of the years of the following governor, Cole Blease, it could not resist reform forever. A spirit of progressivism was sweeping through the nation as a whole; try as it might, the South could not resist forever. Many of the better minds in public service adopted a philosophically progressive platform in the ensuing years, bringing in some real reform across the South generally, and across South Carolina specifically. It was, in part, the highly politicized atmosphere surrounding schools that made Swearingen's tenure typical of the reform movement of the Progressive Era, both nationally and locally. Institutions across the nation, not just limited to the schools, were experiencing a period of reform unlike any that had come before, and South Carolina was no exception to this rule. As noted by Walter Edgar, "From 1908 to 1918, with the notable exception of Cole Blease (1911–1915), South Carolina's voters elected men who, if they were not progressive, at least did not try to derail reform."[44] While Coleman Blease was elected governor in 1910, running on a platform that included promised pardons for white men convicted of lynching and a rejection of compulsory attendance laws, he lost his senatorial bid in 1914. Voters' opinions in national politics followed the trend as well. While South Carolina voted for William Jennings Bryan in the 1908 presidential election, South Carolina cast its nine electoral votes for Woodrow Wilson in the 1912 election.

Progressivism was becoming wrapped up with masculinity as well. National reformers put a masculine face on reform, countering underlying assumptions about reformers' manliness. One of the most visible men of the era, Theodore Roosevelt, explained that there are two types of success: that derived from talent and that derived from labor. The first was to be achieved only by a certain elite few; however, the second could be achieved by almost anyone. Roosevelt claimed that his successes were a direct result of "hard labor...careful planning" and a third virtue he called "moral": rational judgment, emotional discipline, and self-control.[45] Many reform movements of the period soon took on masculine characteristics. One interesting example came from a pamphlet by J. F. Houchins, titled "Progressive Politics, or Why No. 3," sent to Tillman from the Holley NY Standard. Arguing for women's suffrage—a cause Tillman vehemently opposed—it argued against masculine politics while using masculine imagery to prove its point:

> On these grounds I should be excused for advocating the inalienable right of ALL citizens to participate in a government that ALL are taxed to support, without regard to sex prejudice. And finally, when I see arising under the "manly" system of government a Tammany Tiger, an Old Guard or Black Horse Calvary, a Jackpot Lorimer sitting in the Senate of the United States, the White Slave Traffic fostered and abetted by the Saloon Traffic, gnawing at the very vitals of our proud cities, it is obvious that my early conceptions of right and wrong were and are correct, that my position is therefore on the right side...The battle line is formed and the Great Progressive movement in our national government is going to win.[46]

Evidence of South Carolinians taking steps toward philosophical progressivism abounds. For example, women began to take a proactive role in getting their voices heard during this period in spite of the schools. A sample textbook of the time, written by Nixon Waterman, reflected the traditional notion of what a woman's role was. The text, titled "The Girl Wanted," advertised itself as a series of "friendly talks to young women, telling them how they can mould their temperaments and shape their characters to sweetest and noblest influence."[47] Combatting this notion, in 1910, the South Carolina Federation of Colored Women's Clubs was organized to give African American women a social and political voice.[48] Women were not alone in reform efforts in South Carolina. In an attempt to remove some of the corruption and graft in the legal system, in 1910, the State Board of Law Examiners was created.

Swearingen fit in well with the reform ethic sweeping the state. He did not want politics to affect his office; as such, when asked for political favors by anyone, from constituent to governor, Swearingen would simply refer these political petitioners to the proper county authority or the State Board of Education, deftly sidestepping the issue. In addition, Swearingen upheld the educational laws of the state and would not allow any political machinations.

In this respect, Swearingen reflected the attitudes of the voters. As noted by Edgar, "Education was an area of great concern" to the voters of South Carolina in the first decades of the twentieth century. By 1910, for example, South Carolina had only 13 "proper" high schools of the 166 secondary institutions and was the second most illiterate state according to census figures. As such, South Carolinians pushed for better-qualified teachers and newer school facilities.[49]

Swearingen would enjoy this support during the majority of his years in office. He kept up a strong public persona, doing whistle-stop runs during campaign years and school inspections in off years. For most of his tenure, the state legislature worked with him in implementing significant educational legislation. This cooperative attitude carried through to the office of the governor as well; Swearingen developed relationships with varying degrees of positivity with three of the four governors who held office during his term. The office of governor is critical in South Carolina for a number of reasons. While it is the state legislature that ultimately enacts or refuses educational legislation, the power of the governor's office often makes a significant difference in these campaigns.

When Swearingen took office in 1909, Martin Ansel was in the governor's office, and would hold this position through 1911. Born in Charleston in 1850 to German immigrants, Ansel was a product of the common (public) school system. He began his study of law in 1868 and was admitted to the South Carolina Bar in 1870. After spending six years in private practice in North Carolina, Ansel returned to his native state, holding private practice in Greenville. He served in the State House of Representatives from 1882 to 1887 and as solicitor of the Eighth Judicial District from 1888 to 1902, at which point he made an unsuccessful gubernatorial bid for the Democratic Party. He was more successful in the 1906 election, running unopposed in a token contest. However, by the following election, Ansel was unopposed again because of his popularity in office, doubling his vote count. During his two terms in office, Ansel oversaw several reform efforts at the state level. He eliminated Tillman's state liquor dispensary program, a first step toward statewide prohibition. Ansel additionally oversaw the founding of the Confederate Veteran's Home in Columbia, the State Department of Insurance, and the Office of Public Health.

Ansel, "a good progressive and supporter of local option"[50] and a product of the common school system, realized that education was one of the tools through which South Carolina could improve itself. As such, he took a very proactive role as ex officio chair of the State Board of Education and in his working relationship with Swearingen. In March 1909, for example, the state's library contract was due to expire. At Swearingen's urging, Ansel took time to inspect and review copies of books that were coming up for adoption. In July 1910, Swearingen wrote to Ansel about a textbook company representative that was paying for teachers' expenses in Florence County—but only the teachers who were using her book. Swearingen was clearly troubled by the news, writing that he could "find no authority in the law for interfering with her action, although it is clearly in opposition to its spirit." Rather than treat the matter lightly, or simply encourage Swearingen to handle it in-house, Ansel chose to take up the issue, encouraging Swearingen to "file the letter and bring the matter up at our next meeting to see if any action should be taken upon it."[51]

As further evidence of their strong relationship regarding education, Ansel and Swearingen coordinated efforts to attend the Conference on Country Schools and Country Life. The purpose of the conference was "to ascertain the main deficiencies of country life," and to decide what roles the schools, among other institutions, should play in order "to create a broad satisfying permanent rural life." Ansel took three actions regarding this conference. First, he sent the statements published by the Commission to the majority of the newspapers across the state for publication. Next, he called a meeting of all county superintendents of education to discuss the findings of the Commission. Finally, he requested that Swearingen be present at the conference and report his findings duly.[52] Ansel maintained frequent correspondence with Swearingen, liking to be kept "in the loop" in school matters ranging from administrative, such as knowing who the county superintendents were at all times; to curricular, asking for the most popular songs performed in the schools; to geographic, asking the location of a particular schoolhouse.

Ansel and Swearingen grew to share a personal and professional respect for each other. They often spoke on the telephone, and by 1910 Swearingen was comfortable enough with the governor to write to him, asking for "personal and official" favors. One such example was when two districts didn't send in their annual reports for Swearingen to complete his state report. Swearingen wrote to Ansel, asking the governor to intervene and get the district superintendents to act. Ansel responded by sending immediate letters to the superintendents in question, and wrote to Swearingen requesting to know as soon as the reports were submitted so he wouldn't take further action.[53]

Battling Northern Philanthropy

While Swearingen was an advocate of vocational education, he was not a supporter of one of the nation's most significant philanthropic agencies that backed this work. One of the primary sources of private funding for African American schools in South Carolina was the General Education Board (GEB), a group funded primarily by the Rockefeller family that operated out of New York City. By the time the board finished its work in the 1950s, it had devoted literally millions of dollars toward funding schools throughout the nation. During its heyday it oversaw research into various movements impacting the public schools, such as the Gary system, and the free, widespread dissemination of this research; the overhauling of the nation's medical school system; and providing matching funds for the building and development of private and denominational universities and colleges (seeking purposefully to avoid aiding state institutions as these were the recipients of tax dollars, which most private institutions were not).

Of particular interest to the GEB, however, was funding schools that served historically marginalized populations. In its Southern Program, the GEB funded African American K-12 schools and institutions of higher education, provided for state agents to supervise rural schools and African American schools, and worked with universities to develop secondary schools throughout the South. In South Carolina, for example, from July 1917 to December 1918, the GEB funded the construction of 10 new school buildings, the expenses of 11 Rosenwald School teachers to get further training at Tuskeegee, and 18 teachers to attend institutes at the Hampton Institute, as well as made several contributions to building funds across the state.

However, much of the historiography on the GEB argues that the board cannot be recognized as an entirely positive force in Southern education, particularly for that of African American students. As described by Charles Biebel, this organization sought to assist education in the South by "infiltrating Southern universities and government agencies with its own paid evangelists" in order "to promote a reorganization of 'general education' through a coordinated national effort."[54] Biebel was correct in his assertion that the GEB wanted a coordinated national effort; the men on the board viewed the spread of public education with the same business sense as they looked at building railroads or expanding oil holdings. When the GEB met, they looked at factors such as population density, railroad traffic, and concentration of wealth when deciding whether or not to fund a particular school. Location and local support weighed just as heavily as worth of the curriculum of a school; the GEB wanted to maximize "bang for the buck," so to speak, and funded schools where they would have the most impact.

As part of this national plan, the GEB favored schools operating on a vocational/industrial track, similar to the model that Swearingen envisioned. The personnel of the GEB in and of itself demonstrates this opinion; key board members and contributors, such as Robert C. Ogden and George Foster Peabody, also served as board members and/or contributors to Tuskeegee University, and stated publicly that the Hampton-Tuskeegee model was "the solution to the southern race problem."[55] To the GEB, the South included the wide swath of the nation that was driven primarily by an agriculture-based economy; it funded schools and state agents in what are commonly thought of as being southern states—Alabama, Arkansas, Florida, Georgia, Kentucky, Louisiana, Mississippi, North Carolina, South Carolina, Tennessee, Virginia, and West Virginia—the District of Columbia; more western states, including Missouri, New Mexico, Oklahoma, and Texas; and even rural education programs in Minnesota and Maine.[56]

South Carolina was fertile ground for the GEB to plant its Hampton-Tuskeegee seeds. As early as 1904, an auditor for the GEB reported after her examination of Voorhees School, a private African American school operating in Denmark, SC, that the school was offering both an agricultural and an academic track; therefore she "plainly expressed my opinion that she and other teachers undertake too much."[57] In this context "too much" means, of course, academics and agriculture. The GEB continued their insistence on Voorhees School following the industrial model even into 1917. Writing to Voorhees principal, Jesse Thomas, GEB supervisor Ruford Stinson discouraged all but vocational training in the school: "I think that you will find that home projects of girls, indoors, and boys, outdoors, will be among your most effective demonstrations of the methods advocated by your school for farm and community betterment."[58]

Other examples of this funding pattern abound in South Carolina. The Mayesville School, for example, was cautioned by the GEB not to listen to a "fake Negro philanthropist, one Boley," who asked the school trustees to develop an academic curriculum rather than an industrial one.[59] Within three years, the GEB was funding three academic positions in Mayesville—an assistant in academic work, an elementary teacher, and a music teacher—and nine vocational/commercial teachers—a normal program, carpentry, domestic science, blacksmithing, music, nature study, woodwork, cooking, and sewing. Schools such as the Bettis Academy in Trenton, Heath Springs Model School in Rock Hill, St. Helena Island

Rural School, and the Florence High School for Negroes all followed similar funding patterns well into the twentieth century.[60]

This pattern was not unique to South Carolina. Biebel, a critic of the GEB, asks "whether the Board's contribution to the survival and success of particular organizations...and to the demise of others was in the long run in the best interests of the country." Bibel also describes the board using the same tactics "disparagingly ascribed to the entrepreneurs whose fortunes had created and sustained these large foundations," in order to get their educational program approved across the South. After describing the board members as wealthy, white, and Protestant, Biebel presents a harsh critique of the GEB:

> It is hard to escape the conviction that the officers and trustees, representing a foundation which by its nature was private, elitist, and paternalistic, could not transcend their collective vested interest in sustaining a social and economic order largely created by their class—all in the name of democracy and the public interest.[61]

Biebel's critique of the GEB is both accurate and inaccurate. It is accurate in the sense that the board's principal contributors were cutthroat businessmen, elitist and paternalistic, and applied this sense to their contributions. However, it is inaccurate in the sense that the Rockefellers, as well as other primary movers on the board, did not take a direct interest in the funding of the GEB, instead naming to its membership leaders in education and trusting their judgment to distribute the funds in the most effective manner. In the eyes of philanthropists such as Rockefeller, this was not just "in the name of democracy and the public interest," but also genuinely intended to make the nation as a whole better. However, the case can be made that the GEB was acting out of paternalistic instincts that can be viewed as problematic. As explained by David Leverenz:

> Paternalism inheres in any social structure that features inequality. The term includes attitudes of benevolence as well as charitable or philanthropic acts. Beyond helping people down on their luck, paternalists often aim at social improvement, sometimes even reform. In its more admirable aspects, paternalistic behavior says to oneself and others, I'm helping less fortunate people to uplift themselves. Less admirably, paternalism is an enforceable attitude that says, I know what you need better than you do, and, Remember I am your superior.[62]

Regardless of the motivations of its founders or the purpose of its field agents, Swearingen opposed GEB intervention in South Carolina's schools for a variety of reasons. This proves to be another complication in the understanding of Swearingen's life. On one hand, he was an outspoken proponent of vocational education in all its forms, including the Hampton-Tuskeegee model. On the other hand, his notion that a well-rounded education was necessary to producing good citizens surely would have allowed him to believe that both industrial and academic educations had their place. Swearingen was unique in his state-level resistance: in his article on GEB funding, James Anderson describes Southern resistance to the GEB's efforts as a "series of isolated incidents" in which GEB-funded positions were seen as "unwanted agents of Northern philanthropy." However, the only specific example of this resistance Anderson presents is that of Swearingen.[63]

Swearingen had patriotic and academic reasons to oppose the GEB; however, his background more than likely shaped his obstinacy as well. Swearingen, it must be remembered, was a product of the Reconstruction South while living in the New South. Like many of his contemporaries, he was mistrustful of outside agents—in particular those from the North—who attempted to move into the South, spread money, and exert influence. He probably viewed the GEB akin to the carpetbaggers that came in during Reconstruction—and most definitely didn't want to become a scalawag himself. On another level, Swearingen was probably working from a paternalistic instinct to improve African American education; as reminded by Joel Williamson, there existed a "pervasive ethos of paternalism among the white elite"[64] of the South, of which Swearingen was most definitely a member. If Swearingen was acting in a paternalistic fashion toward African American schools, he might have viewed the work of the GEB as a violation of his efforts, much like a father would resist parenting advice from a stranger.

Whatever the motivations, Swearingen frequently expressed resentment of his role in GEB funding in South Carolina directly to the board. Directors of the board itself, as well as its representatives, were subjected to Swearingen's frustrated invectives. Early twentieth-century correspondence had a level of politeness, cordiality, and formality not seen since. Pleasantries were always exchanged, polite enquiries made, and, if something was controversial, it was approached with all the caution of a hiker in unfamiliar woods encountering a strange animal. Except for Swearingen.

For example, he was asked to present an accounting of all GEB funds spent in South Carolina, in addition to his annual reports. In a letter of response to Wallace Buttrick, a director with the board, Swearingen wrote, in part, "You have the absolute right to do as you choose with your own funds. I decline, however, to play the part of the fish dangling at the end of your line."[65] Swearingen continued his rant to another director, Abraham Flexner, writing, "I have received three letters from your office that I do not relish and it is high time for a clear understanding between all parties. The use of your contributions means nothing to me individually and I cannot afford to be harassed and bedeviled by meddlesome dictation and afterthoughts."[66] In another missive to Flexner, Swearingen declared, "If you do not wish to support the work, simply keep the money... I am tired of being deviled with variations and uncertainties that will not allow me to plan definitely for the activities."[67]

Swearingen demonstrated his distrustful, prickly nature even further when, in 1918, the GEB tried to bring together all the state agents to take a course together at Harvard, paid for in full by the GEB. In every state except South Carolina, the biggest questions asked by state superintendents regarded how many employees could be sent at the GEB's expense. Swearingen, however, threatened to refuse to allow his employees release time to attend the event. Writing to GEB Secretary Abraham Flexner, Swearingen averred that while he was "grateful for your cooperation and the cooperation of the General Education Board," funding positions in his office, he "cannot consent to have in this office a man who is not under the direction and supervision of the State Superintendent of Education and responsible to the State Superintendent of Education."[68]

Flexner's reply was uncharacteristically blunt in his handling of Swearingen. Opening with a note of reassurance, Flexner began by reminding Swearingen, "As Dr. Buttrick explained to you, when first we made provision for the support of state agents, we do not wish in any way to interfere with the direction and supervision of their work which is always and entirely in the control of the state authorities." However, Flexner's temper flashed in the next line, as he commented that Swearingen surely "would not wish to imply that the General Education Board has in any way departed from its settled policy, when at the request of state agents it consented to provide the funds necessary to arrange for the summer work at Harvard."[69]

Swearingen, somewhat cowed but still completely unwilling to relinquish alpha status, replied, "No state superintendent can afford to have in his office any sort of employee or assistant who is disloyal or insubordinate." However, he was quick to add that he was "profoundly grateful for the two men given to South Carolina through the cooperation of the General Education Board," as well as being "grateful for the University professor of secondary education, whose salary you pay." Even in gratitude, Swearingen still felt compelled to prove his masculine dominance in the repartee, adding that "At the same time, I hope you will impress upon these three men the importance of serving the pupils, teachers, taxpayers, and schools of South Carolina, and the necessity of rendering this service through the recognized and lawful channels established by South Carolina." To the GEB, this demand in the name of state's rights was as close to capitulation as they would ever receive from Swearingen. In a handwritten note on Swearingen's letter, Wallace Buttrick commented to Flexner, "Dear F., He is clearly coming around to a reasonable position—I would not answer this—we will see him in the Fall. WB"[70]

Progressivism and the Education of Marginalized Populations

As noted by educational historian William Reese, progressivism as a political movement tends to "defy easy explanation or description." The age, roughly from the 1890s through World War I, is "characterized by diverse, shifting coalitions of reform parties, voluntary associations, and activist citizens." The definition of progressivism is further confounded when contemporary audiences take regionalisms into account; what could be argued as being generally progressive by Southern standards, for example, might have been already commonplace by Northern standards. Reese further explains that historians doubt "the existence of any single progressive movement, and the search for a typical progressive reformer remains quixotic."[71]

Statewide reform came in many examples during Swearingen's tenure. In 1914, Jane Bruce Guignard led the suffragettes of South Carolina from the capital, attempting to secure women the right to vote in South Carolina. Another example of reform, in the field of academia, came as South Carolina began to reform the literary and academic notoriety of its scholars and authors by founding the University Press (later called the University of South Carolina Press) in 1914.[72] The mill population was getting into the progressive spirit as well. In 1914, mill workers in Greenville organized under the Industrial Workers of the World and led a wildcat strike around issues such as higher pay and limited hours in their workday.

Under Swearingen's tenure, the group that benefitted the most from his progressive notions was that of African Americans. No one can really know the amount of soul searching and effort it took for Swearingen to be able to put aside his personally held racism, as well as that of his family and general society, to make such gains in this area. Swearingen's efforts toward helping these marginalized groups in South Carolina were aptly summarized by the man himself. Writing to his uncle Tillman, in support of an education bill before the US Congress, Swearingen described educational progress as having social and political ramifications:

> Enclosed herewith I am sending you my copy of H.R. No. 57 relating to the removal of illiteracy. On the democratic club rolls of 1915 some 22% of the white voters signed their name with a mark. If something can be done to help these men by given [sic] them renewed ambition and a rudimentary education, it would prove a great blessing. Among the white women, the percent of illiterates is said to be still higher. Our negroes are almost wholly illiterate. If something can be done to improve them, it ought to prove serviceable to the State.[73]

Swearingen fully understood that the welfare of the state as a whole could never be elevated as long as any group remained in ignorance. As time went by, Swearingen increasingly broke free from being held hostage to familial and societal racisms, probably attributable to both his masculine paternal sense over marginalized populations and his sense of the wrongness of injustice owing to his own personal treatment at the hands of his blindness. However, while in general his sentiments became more philosophically progressive, by the middle of his career Swearingen was not much more color blind than most. Writing to Governor Blease about African Americans serving as trustees in school districts, Swearingen demonstrated his inherent racism:

> I have heard of isolated districts in which the County Board of Education have deemed it advisable to commission negro trustees. I have always advised against such negro appointments, but having no power over the State Board of Education or over the several County Boards of Education, I have not deemed it advisable to do more than enter my written protest and express my dissent in writing. I am opposed to negro trustees for the publi [sic] schools just as I am opposed to negro jurors on the panels, or negro electors on the registration books. No woman can be commissioned as a public school trustee... I should welcome a thorough investigation of this situation by the State Board of Education. I should be glad to see the investigation extended to any school district of the State where a negro is now serving, or attempting to serve, on a board of school district trustees.[74]

Blease's response was predictably gracious; it was one of the few times the two men saw eye to eye on anything. Blease heartily admitted he was "very much obliged to you" and felt the two men could take the matter up together and "do some removing ourselves or have some other folks removed."[75]

In spite of this racism endemic in the man, Swearingen continued his campaign to try and improve the education of African Americans in South Carolina by perpetuating his gentle rebukes of the state legislature in his 1912 report. Of the 2,441 schools serving African American students, only 43 had four or more teachers (less than 2 percent); the vast majority, 2,272 (93 percent), were one-teacher schools. By comparison, of the 2,635 white schools in the state, 1,910 (72 percent) were one-teacher schools and 197 (7 percent) had three or more teachers.[76] However, rather than simply lamenting the state of African American schools, Swearingen lay blame. "The district trustees know little or nothing about the actual operation of such Negro schools," he wrote. Swearingen further explained that these district trustees sometimes "have difficulty in locating the building in which the school is conducted. They rarely see the teacher except when their signatures are wanted." One end result of this situation was corrupt reporting of student enrollment in order to obtain more state funds:

> The members of the district board do not visit the Negro school, nor are they expected to do so. Nobody questions the padded rolls, and everybody seems willing...to accept the sworn report of the beneficiary teacher, and to apportion the school taxes accordingly. The result is a great stimulus to school enrollment with but little heed to school attendance.[77]

This disconnect between the reality of the schools and the reportage to the state department and state legislature was neither unique to South Carolina, nor unique to education. In fact, as noted by historian William Link, "practitioners of southern social policy in education and public health shared a common bond of powerlessness." The state system of control in education caused isolation from the day-to-day realities in the classrooms. "Aside from the collection of mostly inaccurate statistics, the writing of annual reports, and periodic tours to the hinterlands," explains Link, "state education superintendents and state health officers remained isolated from developments in the heartland, and they exercised little effective control over local communities."[78]

Swearingen's efforts to raise awareness continued in his 1913 report; for the first time, counties reported the summaries and statistics of both their white and their African American schools, which were then presented by Swearingen in his report. For almost the first time, county-by-county disparities of attendance were detailed in the report: African American attendance was poor at best. There were fewer and fewer places for white superintendents to hide the shocking state of the African American schools in their respective districts. For example, in Georgetown County, 89 percent of African American school age children were enrolled in the schools; however, in Marion County, only 53 percent were enrolled. In cities such as Newberry, located in the central part of the state, African Americans had less than half the average attendance rate of white students. "The problem of non-attendance is clearly indicated," wrote Swearingen. "Is it wise for taxpayers, school men, and lawmakers to let this condition go unheeded?"[79]

Attendance was not the only disparity Swearingen addressed in his annual reports; he also cited funding disparities between white and African American schools, in particular in cities with populations over 2,500. In towns and counties that had low attendance rates, spending was deplorable. In cities such as Marion, located near the eastern coast in the Pee Dee region, there was a 93 percent difference in per-pupil spending. Even in cities such as Union or Bennettsville, where African Americans had much better average attendance, the expenditures were completely unequal. In fact, the only exception to the rule that cities funded white schools more completely than African American was Laurens, in the upstate (Table 2.9).

One lingering effect of these multitudinous factors was a separation between public and private in African American schools. Between these funding disparities and the fact that up to 1913 South Carolina (as well as

Table 2.9 Facts for sample cities with populations above 2,500

Name of city	Enrollment, 1912–1913		Pupils regularly enrolled (%)		Per capita expenditure based on average attendance	
	White	Af. Am.	White	Af. Am.	White	Af. Am.
Charleston	3,525	2441	75	74	$30.48	$28.56
Columbia	2,816	486	76	75	34.17	13.48
Spartanburg	2,339	1,675	70	68	26.36	7.83
Greenville	2,020	1,334	75	75	17.90	6.44
Rock Hill	1,262	817	75	57	27.58	2.58
Florence	942	690	88	61	27.48	12.37
Orangeburg	772	777	73	50	20.19	4.83
Union	1,698	673	59	71	15.91	4.11
Newberry	807	420	84	40	18.49	5.50
Georgetown	460	789	93	80	20.31	5.68
Laurens	569	332	78	44	25.75	54.53
Abbeville	574	598	88	73	16.29	2.82
Aiken	367	821	84	48	20.32	5.80
Marion	522	234	86	64	141.81	10.02
Sumter	889	1,059	83	88	32.42	4.72
Darlington	622	635	72	65	36.62	28.39
Bennettsville	495	373	79	80	30.83	1.75

Mississippi, Louisiana, and North Carolina) had no public four-year high schools for African American students, the majority attended private secondary institutions. Anderson states that during this period, "southern black public secondary education was available primarily through private institutions... scarcely a fourth of the black pupils enrolled in secondary grades in the border states were in public schools, [while] slightly more than three-fourths of the pupils" in the Southern states were in private institutions.[80]

Swearingen was not monolithic in his views on African American teachers. While insisting on holding high standards for certification, Swearingen was open to teachers who had been certified by what are today referred to as Historically Black Colleges, but at the time were simply called "colored schools." One teacher, trained at Spelman College in Georgia and certified in that state, had applied for South Carolina certification and then governor Coleman Blease was opposed (a trend that would distinguish the relationship between the two men, as detailed in chapter 3). Swearingen wrote to the racist governor, clarifying that he wasn't going to lower certification standards for teachers in South Carolina regardless of color. However, Swearingen was quick to note that "Other graduates of this college are scattered throughout the State." While reassuring the governor that he did "not approve of giving them greater credit in South Carolina than they receive in Georgia," Swearingen once again wanted to follow the law and do what was right: "If this institution is accredited by the State Board [of Georgia] and this applicant is considered deserving of a State certificate, I shall take pleasure in issuing the necessary license."[81]

It wasn't just African Americans who Swearingen chose to advocate for: women in education was a real problem from the outset of Swearingen's term—and one that he, and his agent William Hand, chose to address immediately. However, sex roles in the schools made a step forward in 1913. In a step that demonstrated how Swearingen's desire for genuine improvements often overrode other factors in his life, such as his definition of masculine roles, Swearingen described an "experiment" in which women were given the power to supervise schools to assist the superintendents. At the time, women were not seen as being capable of stepping into administrative roles; that Swearingen would support such a program was testament to his progressive view on many issues of identity. The results of the experiment were "eminently successful." Swearingen explained that in districts that hired women supervisors of schools, there was "better cooperation, well-trained teachers, improved methods, increased enrollment, more regular attendance, and the awakening of a county school spirit." While only 16 districts had instituted the policy, Swearingen noted that all districts in the state could benefit from it.[82]

Swearingen's 1913 call for the increased presence of women in supervisory roles may have been entirely philanthropic; however, there may have been a pecuniary motive toward this call. Teaching had been considered a woman's role since the nineteenth century. As noted by William J. Reese, as early as 1860, "The hope of finding a job as a teacher attracted many girls to high school in the first place, and other desirable positions and prestigious professions were largely closed to them."[83] As such, the teaching corps was becoming increasingly feminized in South Carolina specifically as well as across the nation. However, as explained by Tyack, just because there were more women in the profession did not guarantee equal pay. In the early decades of the twentieth century, women received much less pay for doing the same educational tasks as men. For example, a survey of 467 city systems conducted by the National Education Association (NEA) reported average salaries for different educational occupations. Male high school teachers earned $1,303, while female high school teachers only earned $903 (a difference of 31 percent). The difference was more marked in administration: male principals earned an average of $1,542, while female principals earned $970 (a difference of 37 percent).[84]

While Swearingen argued for increasing the role of women in schools, both as teachers and as administrators, he encountered resistance within his own office. State High School Inspector William Hand argued that such a discussion was "rash, impolitic, and dangerous" to have. Hand hoped to remove the "sentimentality...blarney and patronizing gallantry" that normally accompanied such a discussion, arguing not to remove women from the ranks of teachers or to prove that male teachers were in any way superior to female teachers, but argued that there existed a need for both sexes in the ranks of high school teachers, and, as such, the decrease of male high school teachers accompanied by a 50 percent increase of female high school teachers was a matter of some concern to him.[85] Hand's discussion of sex in teaching also echoed national debate. Again, as noted by Tyack, "leading educators began to have doubts about the benefits of the feminization of the profession." However, feminists were quick to sound their outrage. It wasn't enough that women were forced to obey male supervisors, paid less than men, and barred from advancement because of their gender, now critics were saying that too many women were harmful to boys.[86]

In spite of the occasional resistance, Swearingen made tremendous inroads into improving the schools of South Carolina, particularly as it impacted marginalized populations. This was largely owing to his positive relationship with the governor and members of the state legislature. However, this positivity was not always the case; in fact, it was the highly contentious relationship with one governor that would not only distract Swearingen from his mission for many years, but also ultimately lead to his political undoing.

3

Political Triptych: Swearingen, Blease, and Tillman, 1911–1915

There exists no better explanation of the role politics played in South Carolina during this time or how politics impacted Swearingen's efforts while in office than the triptych of John Swearingen, Benjamin Tillman, and Coleman Blease. To say the relationships between the men were convoluted is an understatement; there existed layer upon layer of discussions and confrontations, advice and misunderstandings, and alpha-male struggles that became increasingly heated between the "top dogs" of South Carolina politics at the time. Tillman and Swearingen enjoyed a tremendous amount of personal and professional respect. Tillman intervened early in Swearingen's life and provided the political tools necessary for success; Swearingen served as Tillman's ears back home, frequently writing his uncle events from the state legislature. Blease and Tillman were alike in many ways: both billed themselves as populist, and both were overt racists; however, Blease didn't think Tillmanism went far enough and resented the interference of the elder statesman, while Tillman resented Blease's upstart fashions and set himself in opposition to him. Swearingen, by extension and by action, would develop an antagonistic relationship with Blease that would hound and ultimately end Swearingen's political career. Knowledge of the respective roles that Blease and Tillman played in the populist tradition of South Carolina is necessary to fully understand the wrath and ire, *sturm und drang*, that was Swearingen's 1922 campaign.

Governor Coleman "Coley" Blease

A disciple of Tillmanism and populism, Coleman L. "Coley" Blease was born near Newberry in 1868 and educated at Newberry College, the South

Carolina College (though expelled for plagiarism), and Georgetown University, where he graduated from the law department in 1889. Blease rode Tillman's coattails to both legislative houses in the state, the House of Representatives from 1890 to 1900 and then State Senate from 1900 to 1910. He served as governor from 1910 to 1914, and finally as US senator for one term, 1924–1930.

To understand Blease and his following, referred to as "Bleaseism" (followers are referred to as "Bleaseites," just as followers of Tillman are "Tillmanites"), the reader must understand the people who supported him most strongly: the working-class whites of the textile mills. The mill workers of the state were an increasingly important voting bloc fed up with politicians telling them what to do and how to do it. Mill workers needed their children in the mills, not in schools; reformers campaigning for compulsory attendance laws did not meet a receptive audience. As such, when Coleman "Cole" Blease began campaigning on the single-plank platform of less government intervention, his blue-collar message fell on sympathetic ears. William Bradford also notes that Blease had the support of "two or three fraternal orders with which he was connected," although he never specifies which specific orders those were, leaving latter-day readers to speculate.[1]

Some 50 years after the fact the founder of Spartanburg Methodist College, Reverend David English Camak, described the working-class voters, writing, "No richer field for shyster tricks and demagogic activities could possibly be imagined." He lumped politicians such as Blease with "agents for enlarged pictures in huge gilded frames, patent medicine quacks, religious fanatics and imposters," and wrote that those thieving groups, along with political demagogues, "lost no time in beginning their nefarious practices among them—bowling, befuddling and deluding the people, and growing rich on their own sophistication." Camak actually attended a Blease political rally that he described in his book *Human Gold from Southern Hills*, subtitled "A story of the word that swept down from the hills of the stuff about the turn of the century and a man who caught a vision of their great need... Not a novel but a romance of facts." Camak described attending one of Blease's 1912 campaign stops:

> One day a political meeting was held in our town. On the way to the 'speaking' someone pinned a white ribbon on my coat. White was the color of the Jonesites, followers of the chief justice of the state Supreme Court, Ira E. Jones, who had resigned his position for the purpose of unseating Governor Cole L. Blease, whose administration—and especially his open advocacy of lynching—had got the state an unsavory reputation throughout the nation. The Blease followers wore red badges.

On this occasion I not only meant to get a good view of the arch juggler of human passions, but the people also—the people to whose intellectual, social, and spiritual well-being I was giving my life. So I found a comfortable seat on the low-hung limb of a tree overlooking the excited throng. Soon a young man wearing a red ribbon climbed up to a seat beside me, then another, and so on until there were seven—all red-ribbon wearing fellows.

I ordered a watermelon. The Reds helped pay for it. We enjoyed the red meat and threw the white rind away in disgust. But I held onto my white ribbon despite their good-natured insistence that the color was no good and I had better go with the winning crowd. I was careful to conceal my identity as a minister that I might do better study my true companions. Consequently I was subjected to such a shower-bath of profanity and obscenity that in sheer desperation I begged for a little clean atmosphere. The topics of conversation were liquor, prisons, pardons, and automatic pistols.

"Wonder whut this automatic 'ud do," said one, "if I turn't her loose on thet crowd." He patted his coat pocket proudly. "Hit'd git yer in the pen," replied another, "but 'Coley' 'ud git yer out." They all laughed.

While the numerous lesser lights of the campaign were speaking, I saw six of my seven tree companions eat barbecue dinner on the original tickets procured by the two who went first to the table. They bought tickets, slipped under the ropes without surrendering them and brought them away for their comrades to use. They made no effort to keep their thievery from me.

In the meantime thousands of impatient, petulant people listened reluctantly to the several speakers and yelled anon for "Coley" who was last on the program by preference. Finally he came with dash and tawdry show, borne on the shoulders of his henchmen. And when the tornado of shrieks, yells, and whistles have finally subsided he sprang to the fray. With glib tongue spouting billings-gate he launched a broadside of invective against his opponents, prodding his coarse deluded admirers to one shrieking yell after another. With consummate art he played upon the passions of the mob, without offering one constructive measure. Then came the hand primary. "All you dear people who are going to vote for me, hold up your hands." He had it! There they were there, and there was no doubt about it. And they were holding up their hands; many of them both hands. What if the loudest and most prominent of them were imported from other counties or states, and some were the grateful hands of criminals he had pardoned? The crowd knew no difference. To most of these simple-minded folk it was a clear demonstration that he held the winning hands, and they loved it...The crowd surged forward and swept him off his feet. He was born back to his car on the shoulders of the "dear boys."

By now my seven Red companions had joined the happy throng and on to glory gone. I slipped down from my seat on the lam and boarded a streetcar. The human society, for those well-being I lived and worked, seemed slipping into the sea, and I was sick with the slush of it. The trolley was crowded. So far as I could see, I was the only man on it who wore a white ribbon. If there were other Joneses supporters aboard, they were acting very discreetly. As I swung off at my corner, a red-faced man with a red badge said, "I hope ye've got 'er nough."'

"Yes," I replied. "I have enough," but my irony was wasted. I was sick with despair. What could I do to show the people that they were being toyed with? Was there really any use trying to educate a few when the great mass behaved like this?[2]

Blease, sensing the attitudes of South Carolina voters, left the state house and made his first, successful, run for governor in 1910. Amongst the planks in Blease's platform was opposition of using white taxes to support African American schools and the separation of convicts along racial lines in South Carolina prisons. Blease pitched his rhetoric almost directly to the blue-collar workers of the state, and his call rang in sympathetic ears on many issues. Many of the political and social progressives of the period viewed the mill workers as "'unfortunates' and 'children' in need of 'uplift.'" These progressives, in the eyes of many of the mill workers, placed too much blame on the workers and too little on the mill owners. All too often, and at least in part because of the rhetoric and efforts of the reformers, "Working class whites, struggling to maintain some control over their lives, resented reformers as 'do-gooders.' The mill workers' resentment gave Blease the political leverage that he needed to win public office."[3]

To the mill workers, he promised them the right to raise their children as they saw fit—without inoculations and in the mills, if they wanted. To the rest of the white population, he promised to pardon any white man convicted of lynching—a promise he made good during his term. He appealed to the working-class white citizens with his "laissez-faire attitude toward prostitution, drinking, and gambling," and won 57 percent of the mill vote, helping him to carry the state and become governor.[4] During his tenure as governor, Blease opposed "anything he viewed as a threat to family unity and individual dignity," fighting tooth and nail "any law or regulation concerning safety, wages, public health, or education." His battles placed him in direct conflict with the press, the state supreme court, and the state legislature. The full ramification of Blease's tenure cannot be measured as, when he left office, he purposefully destroyed all paperwork.[5]

Blease was a near-perfect example of someone working to maintain alpha-male status. He would physically threaten opponents, promising sound thrashings to anyone who questioned or opposed him. His messages to the state legislature frequently had to be censored owing to the abusive and profane language they contained. On one level, Blease was the logical culmination of the masculine and populist politics that had ruled the state since before the Civil War, when South Carolina representative Preston Brooks physically caned Senator Charles Sumner of Massachusetts.[6] This uber-masculinity appealed to South Carolina's voters and, for decades, Blease was particularly adept at tapping into it: races with Blease as candidate had the highest voter turnout in the twentieth century. As summarized by Walter Edgar: "'Coley' might upset 'respectable folks,' but he surely had a lot of friends. Bleaseism was a last hurrah of a dying world, a world in which all whites were equal and blacks were the mudsills of society."[7]

Blease: The Public Face of Racism

In some regard it was the echoes of an unreconstructed South that led to Blease's popularity: he was a proudly public face on racism, which directly led to his popularity amongst white workers. Yet this is only a negligible part of the overall picture. The attitudes of white workers, mainly textile workers in the up-country region, combined concerns about race, class, and gender. Blease was skilled at tapping into these interwoven concerns, recognizing that to the workers, independence was woven with citizenship, economic autonomy, white supremacy, and masculinity.[8]

Interestingly enough, the governor's racism did have limits: it all depended on his audience. In order to win a race, Blease would campaign to African American audiences. During such campaigns visits, his "tone was one of moderation, displaying his ability to win any crowd by telling it what it wanted to hear." One example of this occurred at a campaign stop at the historically African American Allen University. During this visit, "the auditorium rocked with cheers of approval, Blease shouted: 'You are coming in to higher things. They can't hold you back, despite what I or any other man may say.'" African American audiences were sadly very receptive. All too often, they falsely attributed Blease's violent racism as campaign tactics. One African American "Episcopal bishop dismissed the harsh things said by Blease on the stump as intended 'only to tickle the ears of the voters and thereby gain their support.'"[9]

Blease's racism is best exemplified in his stance on lynching. An integral component of his campaign platform was his proclivity to pardon any white person convicted of such a crime. "From the stump, and newspaper interviews, and for messages to the legislature he preached his doctrine of accelerated justice." In fact, Blease "would take no official action to prevent others from carrying out their duties as Southern men. 'I will never order out a militia company, so help me God,... And tell my home boys and girls to shoot down a white boy, their neighbor and their friend, to protect a black brute who has laid his hands upon a white woman.'" It took a little while for the full import of this message to sink in amongst South Carolinians: "He attributed the absence of lynchings during his first six months in office to the Negroes knowledge that the militia would not be called to save him from the mobs."[10] Admittedly, lynchings were not simply a Southern thing; they and race riots occurred throughout the nation. To wit, there were more than 30 examples of "anti-Black collective violence" between 1885 and 1910 in just Ohio, Indiana, and Illinois. Granted, this number seems low compared to the fact that, for example, there were 27 examples of such violence in Virginia alone. However, when these numbers are considered per capita population, they equal or outweigh those of the South.[11]

In the Palmetto State, where overt political support from the State House existed, it would not be long before lynching became front-page news. The banner headline of the October 11, 1911, edition of the *Anderson Daily Mail* was all too common. "NEGRO RAPIST WAS LYNCHED AFTER CONFESSING HIS CRIME: Prisoner Was Taken from Officers After an Exciting Chase Through Three Counties." The article describes that "there were at least 5000 people in the crowd who witnessed the execution," and that the mob was led by a local judge, the Honorable J. W. Ashley. Unfortunately for the 17-year-old lynching victim, he was wrongly killed. Near the end of the article the newspaper admits that "there are many people in Anderson, a number of them among those who went to Honea Path to witness the lynching, who believe that Willis Jackson, the Negro lynched, was the wrong man. Officer V. B. Martin, who was with the Negro boy from the time he was taken from the jail until he was caught beyond Greenville, is one of those who share this belief."[12]

In addition to the terrible loss of life from these lynchings, there was another side effect: white citizens of South Carolina felt (albeit morally wrong) they were entitled to treat African Americans in any way they saw fit. The day after the Anderson lynching, for example, an African American man who had the audacity to ask a white man to make room in the road, "was given a severe whipping at the lumber mill at tony path this morning." Trying to get to the mail to pick up a load of lumber, over 200 white men had the road around the site of the lynching completely blocked. The African American man said that "he had as much right to the road as anybody." Under Blease, sentiments such as these were cause for pain and humiliation: of the two men who administered the whipping, only one was placed under bond but released soon after.[13]

The governor's racism, like all of society at the time, extended well beyond simple black/white terms—if you weren't white, you didn't count. While it would be several years before the US Supreme Court would issue its *Gong Lum v. Rice* ruling that in 1927 essentially divided the country into two camps, white and other, Blease was well on his way to pre-affirming this decision. In 1913, a Chinese student attempted to enter the USC and Blease denied them entrance. One fan of the governor's actions wrote in support, "My feelings and sentiments are identical to yours in the matter of not allowing any student who is not a full blooded white man or woman to enter the University. I hope to see you carry your point in this matter. We don't want our Colleges to lose their place of distinction."[14] In response, the governor was "glad you endorse my position in the matter in regard to which you write. I believe in speaking plainly about such matters."[15]

As if being a violent, virulent racist wasn't bad enough, Blease was also extremely sexist. Typical of many men during the period, Blease believed women were property and, once married, conceded all rights to their husbands, regardless of circumstances. One opportunity Blease took to demonstrate this belief came in December 1914. A distraught mother wrote to the governor, asking for special dispensation to obtain a divorce on behalf of her daughter—whose husband comes home "drunk and cursing and threatening her life and told her if she left it would become another Sam Hyde case" (Sam Hyde, convicted of murder in Anderson in 1911, was then murdered by Ernest Mulwee, who was sentenced to the electric chair).[16] The mother asked for an annulment as divorce was illegal at the time in South Carolina. Blease's response was typically sexist: "There is no chance in this world to get loose from marriage ties in this State. You can have the fellow placed under a peace bond, to keep him away from your place. If his wife does not want to live with him, she can leave him, but under no circumstances or conditions are divorces granted in this case."[17]

Putting the Bully into Bully Pulpit

As governor, Blease viewed the entire state as his: every resource was at his disposal, and all its politicians at his beck and call. Whether this was because of his uber-masculine approach leading to a perverse sense of paternalism or relatively more simple egotism is debatable; for whichever reason, Blease put the "bully" in "bully pulpit." He would threaten and cajole people publicly and privately, and the universities of the state were no exception to his whims. Even an institution that, theoretically, should have been supported by Blease wholeheartedly such as the Citadel was not above bearing the brunt of his egotistical desires. In 1911, the Citadel Corps of Cadets was invited to march in a parade for the Atlanta, Georgia Peace Conference. While the Citadel had been invited, Blease was not, and he took deep offense. Bearing the brunt of Blease's scripted ire was O. J. Bond, then superintendent of the institution: "I object. The officials of that conference...purposely refused to invite the Governor or other officials of this State to participate, and I think it would be the height of discourtesy on your part to allow even one of your cadets to attend; and, if you do so, I will bring the matter to the attention of the Board, and, if possible, secure your resignation, which meeting I will call by wire if you intend to carry out your intention of sending cadets to that event."[18]

Bond, however, was nonplussed by Blease's threats. Responding, he explained that Blease was completely wrong, only governors from four northern states that were involved in the original project were invited, that there was no truth in the statement that Blease was being discriminated against, and that, in fact, "the State was honored by having the Corps of Citadel Cadets among the specially invited guests." To Blease's threat, he simply responded, "As to the very unpleasant threat contained in your letter, I have only to say that my resignation will very promptly be placed in the hands of the Board of Visitors upon any intimation from them that my services are no longer useful to the institution over which they elected me president."[19]

Like all bullies past and present, once he was stood up to, Blease backed down: "I...see that the information given me was incorrect, and that it was the Board of Visitors who acted in the matter and not you. Therefore, if I have done you any injustice, I beg your pardon." Cowing is not the same as accepting blame, however, and Blease was quick to exert the paranoia that characterized many of his interactions, blaming the Citadel board of trustees: "I am not surprised at their action, in view of the political feeling some of them have against me individually." Even with this admission, Blease was defiant at the end of his missive: "I am proud that the Executive Committee could not find money enough to assist the Georgia Officers in charge of that matter in carrying out their snub to South Carolina and to her State Officials. It is a pitty [sic] that it was only for want of money that caused them to resent this snub; still, this is one time I am glad the Citadel was poor."[20]

No state official was immune to Blease's rants, which almost always came with little reason and less warning. To E. J. Watson, secretary of agriculture and Blease appointee, he raved, "In my opinion, you were appointed Commissioner of Agriculture for South Carolina and not for the United States, and I would advise you as a friend to remain in the state and quit running about as you are now doing," and threatened, "If you do not discontinue this continual running around over the country, I will be compelled to put someone in your place who will not neglect the duties thereof. If you make another trip out of the State without my permission, an official order, declaring your office vacant will be made and your successor appointed."[21]

Watson's confused reply began, "I have received yours of even date with utter astonishment for I have been absolutely unconscious that I have been doing anything in contravention of the administrative policy." He continued in his own defense, "God knows I have honestly, sincerely, and without the remotest thought of self-interest done all in my power to advance the material interests of our State and her people in just the same manner... I have endeavored to work in perfect harmony with your policies." In terms of explanation and as a means of salving the governor's ego, he continued, "When I have gone out of the State this year it has been with no idea of self-advancement, but always after something I felt would do the State the greatest amount of good, and it has been but seldom that I have gone. I believe that I have lived up to my promise to you to accomplish the hardest year's work of my life." Seeking to jog the governor's memory, he concluded, "I talked with you, as you will recall, of the objects of the recent trip to Chicago, and urged you to be there, and I had not the remotest idea that you were any way opposed to my going. A word from you would have kept me here."[22]

It wasn't just individuals that Blease attempted to bully; often he would take on entire groups, such as in January 1914 when he tried to have the entire state hospital board resign or be removed. Threatening to once again go before the state assembly, Blease wrote a letter copied to the entire board. It began, "I have a very important matter, in reference to your personal and public life which I desire to read to you, and, at the same time, to read to you a message which I have prepared to send to the General Assembly in regard thereto. Your Associates on the Hospital Commission have been requested to be here at the same time. I beg you to be sure to attend." By way of explanation, Blease simply wrote, "Your personal character, as well as your public actions, have been seriously questioned so much that I feel it is absolutely necessary for me to call it to the attention of the General Assembly, and I want you to first know of it directly from me."[23]

However, if you were a friend of "Coley," you were probably able to get away with almost anything. For example, the man responsible to auditing alcohol sales and consumption in the state was Blease's old friend

Harvey Mitchum who, when on break in Charleston, got so drunk he was arrested and imprisoned. The irony of the situation—the state alcohol auditor being arrested for public drunkenness—was completely lost on Blease. However, rather than ranting and raving or sending threats, he was gentle to his friend. In a very brief letter, Blease wrote, "It has been reported to me that you were in Charleston recently on a drunk, and that you were arrested and carried to the guard house. I would like to hear your side of the matter."[24] Of course, no punishment was forthcoming, and no demands for resignation were made over the public embarrassment.

Loyalty went both ways; Bleaseites were willing to go to any length to defend "Coley's" honor, even throwing a wounded Confederate veteran from the hospital or going to jail. In 1913, Major H. W. Richardson, director of the Confederate Infirmary, did both. It seems one of the inmates, called "Soap Jones," did not have a very high opinion of the governor and began talking about him with two other residents. Director Richardson "showed him where his animosity to you [Blease] would be no excuse for the insult to the high office of Governor. In a very short time after, this man again started a report connecting your name with a negro woman living back of the Mansion and who he said a policeman told him that he had frequently seen you at night in this woman's house and that she kept a bull dog for you." For telling such stories, "I [the director] charged Jones with disorderly conduct, iniquitious influence over the other inmates," and removed him from the hospital. Jones hired lawyers, filed suit, and got reinstated; however, the director would not allow him in. Richardson unsuccessfully contacted the attorney general to get it overturned, then contacted Jones to state that "his bed and room space was [sic] occupied by another more worthy and needy Veteran, and that it was needless for him to return." For refusing Jones reentry, Richardson was "arrested for contempt of Court" and the other two inmates accused of spreading gossip were allowed to stay.[25] It wasn't just within the Palmetto State that Bleaseites lived; during his tenure, Blease corresponded with people supportive to him and his work well beyond the state borders. For just two examples, US Senator Jonathan Bourne (R-Oregon) wrote asking for copies of Blease's speeches, and the Prudential Insurance Company of Newark, New Jersey, asked for printings of Blease's speeches to put in their library.

However many his supporters and fans, by the end of his terms in the governor's mansion, Blease had turned his venom on anyone and everyone within reach. Responses to constituents that used to either be ignored or have a brief note of dismissal now earned the governor's full wrath—he was taking his anger at his election loss out on everyone. To one, who had incorrectly requested notary status, he quipped, "If there is any such office in the State as 'Notary Republic' I have never heard of it. There may be a special act in your county requiring you to be one of those things, whatever they are, in order to be a commissioner, but I have never heard of any such law."[26] To a distant relative, writing to request a pardon, he was equally short-tempered: "I have never heard of any law by which I could pardon anybody before he is tried. You had better get a lawyer and have him look after the matter for you, for I cannot be running around looking after such matters, especially at this time, when I am very busy getting matters in shape for the coming Legislature, and to turn over the office of Governor to my successor."[27] By "turn over the office," Blease—who was irate at his electoral loss to a progressive politician—meant destroying all government documents and resigning his office early. This forced the lieutenant governor, Charles Smith, to serve for five days in January 1915.

Tillman vs. Blease

Tillman and Blease both had roots in the populist movement even if they weren't necessarily members of the People's Party. Blease and Tillman were, at first, natural allies. In 1910, Tillman was so happy with Blease's election he immediately sent a telegram of congratulations that read "Let the heathen rage."[28] As late as 1911, Blease was comfortable enough with Tillman to write asking for a letter of reference to get his nephew a job as safety appliance inspector at the Inter-State Commerce Commission. In terms of qualifications, Blease wrote, "He was born and reared in Newberry; is fully competent to perform the duties; is entirely honest; does not taste, touch, or handle whiskey, beer, or wine in any manner, shape, or form; is married and has three children." Blease even concluded on a friendly, personal note, "I hope that you are quite well, getting along nicely, and will be pleased to see you at anytime that you are in the City."[29] During Blease's early days in politics he professed to be a Tillmanite, bringing him the support of Tillman's branch of the Democratic Party.

Almost from the get-go there were distinct differences between the two. Tillman's populism was a reflection of the old southern notions of gentlemen farmers and agrarian lifestyles; Tillmanites were men of the earth. Blease represented the working-class men of South Carolina; Bleaseites were men of the mills. As early as 1911, Blease was making this distinction clear to any and all. The *Journal of the Progressive Farmer*, a paper with a history of supporting populist politicians, wrote to Blease asking his opinion on cotton futures. Rather than shouting across the hall or sending an aide to find out, Blease sent a rather abrupt (though politically schmoozing) telegram in response: "Your wire. Am not a farmer; therefore, not in position to advise farmers what to do. Regret very much the low price of cotton. If I was able to loan farmers money to handle the distress cotton, in order that they might hold for higher prices, I would do so with great pleasure, charging them no interest."[30]

Heading into the 1912 election, Blease and Tillman were still on cordial terms. However, the press began circulating rumors that Blease was speaking out against Tillman. Blease quickly wrote the senator either in an effort to cover himself and/or an effort to clear the air. "You are so use [sic] to being lied on by the newspapers yourself and I have seen so much of it on me, that I feel that it is absolutely useless for me to write you in regard to the many malicious lies that are now being circulated," he began. Quickly explaining the motives of the press, Blease continued, "I am satisfied that this is being done for the purpose of trying to cause you and I to fall out, and am still further satisfied that the old gang of sore-heads and liars cannot bring about that desired result by the publishing of such lies as they are now resorting to." However, Blease wasn't entirely conciliatory in his letter; a bit of his ego did come forth. "Of course, I would be glad to have your vote and influence in my race for Governor; but, to be frank, I do not believe that it is absolutely necessary to my success." The reasons for his lack of worry about Tillman's endorsement were twofold: "I have not yet reached the point where I believe that any man can dictate to the people of South Carolina as to who they should or should not have in office" and "from information received from all parts of the State, I am satisfied that I will be re-elected, regardless of who may oppose me."[31]

Tillman's response was conciliatory and direct. After explaining what he believed the source of the misinformation to be, he declared his neutrality to Blease: "One thing you may rely upon: If I decide to have anything to do with the governor's race, you will be the first man I tell. As at present advised and as I feel now I shall be absolutely hands off as I have said more than once." However, there were the beginnings of the cracks that would split the two populists, at least in terms of politics. Tillman explained, "Some of my strongest and most intimate friends noted what they thought was an effort to link your political fortunes and mine together, and have urged me to disavow any alliance. But I have not thought it right and as there is nothing of the kind in existence or likely to be I have felt that the attitude I have assumed was the right one and wisest one." Overall, though, Tillman was quite positive about Blease's campaign, complimenting Blease with, "If you continue to make speeches like that I heard you make at Orangeburg and hustle around among the people, it will be difficult for any man to beat you." After a few sentences of sound political advice regarding the state legislature, Tillman's advice turned to a more personal nature. Almost sounding like a scolding parent talking to an unrepentant child, Tillman chided Blease:It has always been the custom in this State to give a governor two terms and I imagine it will continue to be so unless the governor should do something disgraceful to shock the people's pride. I do not know whether you are drinking now or not. You recollect that in a former letter I advised you to cut it out absolutely and I take this occasion to renew my advice. I hope you will not take offense if I presume to further advise that you keep your mouth shut as much as you can for everything you say or are likely to say will be distorted and twisted out of all recognition of truth. You are traveling the same road I traveled once, only I think I was less spectacular than you have been, and always followed my maxim to find out what my enemies wanted me to do and not do it. You seem to have done what they wanted you to do and events will determine whether your way is better than mine.[32]

Correspondence does not bear out his claim of neutrality. Writing to a local politician in Anderson, Tillman wrote, "I do not care to mix in the fight between Jones and Blease, but it is very clear to my mind that Jones will make a far better governor than Blease has made. Tillmanism will not be perpetuated by Jones' election, but Tillmanism will become more respectable that it is now since it has become adulterated with Bleaseism."[33] Tillman wrote twice to newspaperman Leon Green around the same time. On the first occasion, after Green's request for an interview regarding Blease, Tillman responded, "I do not know your motive for asking me to answer your questions...I do not care to have anything to say about him just at this time lest what I say would be misunderstood." Demanding things go off the record by writing, "I do not mind telling you privately what you already know," Tillman explained that he "did prepare an article for publication indorsing [sic] Blease in the second primary as against Featherstone, but suppressed it at the persuasion of warm personal friends that it would do me no good and might make Blease mad. While the time may come when I would be willing to have the interview published, I do not believe that it is appropriate that it should come out now. I must therefore decline to answer any of your questions and hope you will understand why."[34]

Whether it was over Blease's reported slights of Tillman, the governor's extremist stances on issues, the inability of two uber-masculine alpha figures to coexist, or Tillman's cautionary words, Tillman and Blease parted company in very public fashion; in 1912 a war of words began in earnest. Opposing Blease in the 1912 gubernatorial race was former chief justice Ira B. Jones. Jones was successful in the courtroom, but his abilities "on the stump" were very limited. While Tillman worked to remain publicly neutral during the election, privately he wrote to friends a series of letters marked "private" and "not for publication," cautioning against Blease. Tillman wrote to supporter W. Lee Johnson, explaining in part his change in support. "I wrote him a letter after the primary election two years ago in which I gave him some advice, which he has not seen fit to follow," the senator explained. "If he had, he would have been elected Tuesday beyond a doubt. As it is now, I hope he will be defeated for he has made anything but a good governor and his election next Tuesday would be little short of calamity."[35] One of his friends, Bose Crewes, ignored those words and released the letter to the press, who immediately seized upon it and made it national news. In an open letter to several media outlets sent after the election, Tillman explained the reasons for his decision at length, blaming Blease's poor decision making:

> I realize that things are in a very bad shape in the state and Blease seem[s] to be sweeping everything before and felt that it would be a calamity if he were elected governor again. But I was not willing to take any part in it after having said what I did about neutrality without something of the kind giving me an excuse...a letter came from Mr. Sims at Orangeburg to which I responded. I had no dream that anything would result from my reply such as happened and was thunderstruck a couple of days later to receive a telegram demanding to know if Blease who was not "eminently qualified" too. This was followed by scores of letters of the same tenor, and some of them in a peremptory manner demanded that I say as much for Blease...I wrote to several men and pointed out wherein Blease differed from Tillman...The clamor in the state about my intermeddling grew greater and greater and there was a more persistent demand on the part of Jones' friends for me to come out and give my reasons for preferring Jones to Blease...For about 10 days I was at war with myself...I received information from South Carolina that my letter was being used to bolster up Blease and injured Jones. Three days before I gave out the interview I received a letter from Governor Blease protesting against what I had done and enclosed a copy of a letter I had written to a Mr. Sullivan at Townville, Anderson County, which I had marked "private and confidential". I realized that I was being whipsawed and was very uncomfortable in the false position I was occupying. My judgment was with Jones; my sentiments with Blease because my wife supported him. Finally I decided to get rid of the whole mess and be relieved in mind so that I could sleep and I dictated the statement.
>
> Until I gave up the statement I felt very uncomfortable and was being ground between the upper and nether millstones of contending feeling. I had no reason to love Judge Jones and I did not give him out the interview because of any love or friendship for him. I did not have any reason to antagonize Blease except for a feeling of a public duty to the state. His rash

actions and wild utterances have demonstrated him to be wholly unfit to be governor.[36]

Tillman began to speak out against the perceived excesses of the Blease campaign (Figure 3.1). Anti-Bleasites, such as Swearingen's friend J. J. McSwain, were incredibly proud of the senator's new stance. Reminding Tillman that "I knew you in your house in 1896 (then a student visiting John Swearingen in Edgefield)," McSwain included high praise: "Pardon me just a word on reading your open letter to Gov. Blease printed in

Figure 3.1 Tillman on Blease, *Anderson Daily Mail*

today's papers. It is the final fact that stamps you a patriot. Naturally I am delighted that so many of my 'anti' friends now see you as I have for 16 years." Beginning a political career of his own, McSwain was quick to jump on Tillman's coattails: "In a few minutes address in Opera House here, Aug 23, I contrasted Blease with yourself, exposing his false masquerade as Ben Tillman II. I have often said that History (50 years hence) will accord to you greater place as a constructive statesman than even Calhoun."[37]

In his response, Tillman was gratified, if a bit melancholy about his own legacy. "I am not ready to discuss my place in history with anybody yet, but think perhaps your diagnosis of my work in South Carolina may be assigned a place somewhat like that you spoke of in the opera house...But, my dear sir, don't you know that nobody writes South Carolina history. South Carolinians make history, but none of them ever write it," he added in a somewhat humorous vein. However, knowing that coming out against Blease would hurt him in the long run, he added, "No one can take from me the honor and glory, if glory there be, of having founded Clemson and Winthrop, but every once in a while I see signs of someone being willing to chip off a brick from those monuments. After I am dead and gone I have no doubt the claim will be strenuously contested. My good deeds will be obscured and buried under the dust."[38]

Tillman knew specifically he was losing the mill vote by his actions, but still felt compelled to speak out the way he did. "The mill people who have always been my friends think now I have deserted them and gone over to their enemies and oppressors," he wrote. However, he made clear that "nothing is further from the truth. They are so prejudiced and aroused at this time that they would consider themselves dishonored if they do not stick to Blease. I expect to lose 30,000 or 40,000 votes on account of my attitude and these will all be from among the best friends I ever had." Tillman was resigned to the effects of his decision, honestly believing he was in the right: "I have done my duty and they say angels can do no more...my conscience is clear, and that is the only thing to be considered now as I am too old to think about political results."[39]

This loss of the mill workers may have had implications on Swearingen's campaigning. Though Swearingen never tried to ride his uncle's coattails, the two men were linked in South Carolina politics of the time. Someone as politically savvy as Swearingen would understand that his own campaigns would be swallowed up in the split in populism and Tillman's losing the mill workers. Very likely this would explain why Swearingen grew more aggressively progressive after this period: he had already lost the mill worker constituency, and therefore didn't need to curtail his efforts to appease them.

Tillman was not content to let his political battle with Blease lie with the voters of South Carolina. Understanding the national ramifications as then governor Blease was making noise about a possible senatorial bid, Tillman took his case to no less than President Wilson. Asking Wilson to change his mind on candidates for the attorney general and US Marshall in a letter stamped "personal," Tillman wrote that he "had two objects in life in a political way, to wit: to make your administration a success, and to keep Governor Blease from coming to the Senate. I believe religiously that if you make this appointment of Mr. Weston it will make Blease's election a certainty." After a fairly detailed (though time would tell slightly incorrect) analysis of the political landscape of South Carolina, Tillman pleaded with Wilson to "appoint Mr. Thurmond District Attorney and he and every one of his friends will do everything possible to beat Blease... if Blease is allowed—and it cannot be prevented by anyone but yourself—to go up and down the State shouting to the Tillmanites that Tillman has been trampled underfoot by Woodrow Wilson and thrown aside, while the Haskellites and Anti-Tillmanites have been given all the patronage, can't you see Mr. President, that nothing but a miracle could keep Blease from being elected?" He concluded with the cautionary explanation that "Tillmanism, as I understand it is genuine Democracy; and Bleasism is mobocracy and demagoguery."[40]

It wasn't just a political battle, or vengeance over a perceived betrayal, that fueled the battle between the two men. To Tillman, his struggles with Blease were no less than a battle between good and evil, and he frequently used biblical references in his correspondence. To Rev. G. W. Bussey of Fountain Inn, Tillman wrote, "He shall not make the people of South Carolina 'sweat blood' if I can help it. I know God is too good not to aid me."[41] Similarly, to J. G. Anderson of Rock Hill, he wrote, "Contrary to the expectations, which were almost universal, Blease has been re-nominated and will be governor two more years in spite of the world, the flesh and the devil. His followers believe he is the salvation of liberty; his enemies believe he is the devil incarnate. There is middle ground I hope."[42] To Anna Lewis at his beloved Clemson College, Tillman clarified even more: "The forces of good and evil in the State can array themselves under the two banners, Tillman's or Blease's as they see fit. I have no doubt of the final outcome. Morality, Cleanliness of life and patriotism are bound to win."[43] The battle became, when writing to Ferdinand Muckley of Easton, Pennsylvania, a struggle between "the elements of honesty, decency, and character are on one side, while the cutthroats, black guards, gamblers and crooks are on the other."[44]

Tillman's health had taken a serious blow at this point, though, and he couldn't travel the state to reassure supporters and let the common people hear his powerful, inflammatory oratory. The efforts he could make, largely correspondence and newspapers, were for naught, as amongst the voters of South Carolina, "a new generation had arisen that knew not Benjamin." In fact, Blease sent a highly egotistic but altogether accurate telegram to his campaign staff, saying in full, "Tillman letter will not hurt me. We will win."[45] The common, working-class person of South Carolina had taken to rallying around Blease, believing wholesale all of his rants as demonstrated in one letter received from a supporter (all errors in the original text): "Don't be discourage in your race for the senate. If the majority of the Delegates was anti Blease Its you are stronger in Williamsburg County to day than you was two years ago. When you come to Kingstree to speak don't sling any mud but give it to Smith. Straight. Make a clean race as you did on your last go round no one believes the News Papers. I hope you will win."[46]

To little surprise, Blease won reelection in 1912. To his former friend and mentor, Blease sent a telegram of insult, reminding Tillman of his former support now viewed as betrayal: "Trenton SC Sept 1910—'Let the heathen rage' they still rage Cole L Blease."[47] Tillman was despondent over the issue. Writing to a family friend, Tillman relied once again on Christian imagery: "Up to this hour everything indicates that Blease will be our governor for two more years in spite of the world, the flesh and the devil, and specially of the devil."[48] Referring to Blease as a "pinch-back Tillmanite" and saying the governor would make "a magnificent Nero," Tillman shared his harsh assessment with friend W. H. Glenn:

> I did all I could, but delayed it too late perhaps as Blease has been re-elected in spite of it and we will have to endure two more years of this would-be tyrant...The result of this primary makes me doubt the wisdom of ever having emancipated these "wool-hat one gallus" men from the domination of oligarchy. If Bleaseism is to become a substitute for Tillmanism, I know it was a mistake. As Bleaseism has come 22 years after Tillmanism was born it shows that the people are not capable of governing themselves unless they are taught. Jefferson's maxim was "teach the people and trust the people" and the only reason why such men as Blease has [sic] come to the front so rapidly is because the teacher was too weak to continue to point out the difference between the two ideas contending for mastery.[49]

Not to take any insult or perceived threat to his publicly masculine image lying down, soon after winning the election Blease went on the attack. His arena of verbal combat was the floor of the South Carolina State House, detailing a series of what Blease considered outrages committed against himself by Tillman. Stating Tillman had a "weak" and "enfeebled" mind, Blease accused Tillman of "reprehensible conduct,"[50] and of conspiring with the newspapers to try and undo his campaign. To this end, Blease submitted an act to the legislature, asking that newspapers be severely curtailed and removed from any and all political writing. Living up to his promise to be Tillman's "eyes and ears" in the state house, Swearingen sent an immediate and detailed warning to his beloved uncle:

> On entering the Hall of the House of Representatives at 12:40 p.m. today I found that the reading of this message was in progress. Immediately upon the conclusion of the reading, Mr. Rembert moved that the message be received as information and published in the Journal...Mr. Stevenson moved that the message be received as information and that you should be given the opportunity to reply...The message and the reply are then to be printed consecutively in the Journal in accordance with the action of the House.
> Both factions in the legislature are apparently anxious to escape from the necessity of an open clash, but the goading of the Governor may cause a rupture at any moment. A division-vote has not yet come in the House, but it is imminent at every stage of the proceedings.[51]

In his reply, Tillman returned the attack with a vengeance. Writing about his plans to his nephew, Tillman explained:

> I am very much obliged to you for your kindness in sending the message to me in the way you did as it enables me to come back at him in the most effective way which is by communication to the General Assembly itself and will thus get into the permanent record the antidote going with the poison and charge. I imagine that there will be some lively doings in Columbia soon, for Blease is so constituted that unless he is fighting, he thinks himself obscured entirely. He will, therefore, keep the Legislature in hot water as often and as long as he can.[52]

Tillman asked an open letter to Blease be read to the legislative body. It began by explaining that Blease's motive was "to keep the minds of the people stirred up and not allow the waters to clear sufficiently to see what sort of man he really is" and whose primary skill was in "bamboozling the people." Tillman accused Blease of conspiracy and theft, as well as blatantly lying to the state legislature.[53] Claiming that Blease had been riding his political coattails up to that point, Tillman demanded a stop. Asking to "explain briefly the difference between Tillmanism and Bleaseism," Tillman (loftily and inaccurately) wrote:

> Tillmanism means genuine democracy, the rule of the people—of all the white people, rich and poor alike, with special privilege and favors to none,

with equality of opportunity and equality of burden to all...Bleaseism, on the contrary, means personal ambition and greed for office—the office to be used nor for the welfare of all people and the State, but office for "Blease and his friends. None others need apply."[54]

Blease allowed his sense of betrayal to govern many of his actions during his second term. If the governor already viewed the state as his personal playground in 1914, he began trying to, like a spoiled child who didn't get their way, take his toys and go home. Nobody and no office was safe from his invective, and anything associated with Tillman was particularly in trouble. Tillman's beloved Clemson was one of the first things Blease began trying to undermine. Writing to D. B. Johnson, president of Winthrop, Blease was blunt in his assessment: "I would be glad to see your college have all the money as I think Clemson has enough already."[55]

Blease used the legal system as well as his fists and voice to vent his anger and extract revenge on those he considered to have done him wrong. In September 1913 he filed suit with the US Attorney's office against W. O. Saunders, publisher of a small weekly paper called *The Down Homer*, on charges of obscenity for mailing copies of two articles, one titled "Cole L. Blease Ought to Be Shot" and the other "Cole Blease Up In the Air." In an interesting strategy, attorneys for the defense wanted Blease to take the stand; ostensibly their belief was that if a jury was to hear the governor's rants firsthand, they would surely acquit. Accordingly, they subpoenaed Blease. The governor, probably sensing he was in over his head, refused to travel to testify, writing that he would not "be dragged around over the country by a character of his kind and compelled to pay my own railroad fare and hotel bills."[56] The case settled when Saunders pled guilty and agreed to stop publication of his journal.

Not content merely to be the thorn in the sides of Tillman and Swearingen, by 1914 Blease launched paranoid attacks on Tillman's son, Henry. In a bit of convoluted "he said, she said" that would be instantly identifiable to any schoolchild but has no place in adult discourse, Blease explained he was trying to clear up the misconception that "I have been informed that one W.P. Beard stated to you that Mr. C.C. Wyche, of Spartanburg, had told me certain things in reference to the office of your father, Senator Tillman, as coming from Mr. C.C. Wyche's brother." Blease offered his usual refutation: "I wish to state to you that it is a lie out of the whole cloth, and I can not [sic] imagine why Beard would manufacture such rotten cloth." And, in a final burst of characteristic egotism, Blease concluded, "I write this letter merely to set Mr. Wyche straight. So far as I am concerned, personally, of course it doesn't make any difference what people say or think."[57]

Blease and Tillman would be at each other throughout the remainder of their careers. One example of a battle between the two men came in 1913 when Blease was attempting, through his usual questionable means, to close the Hospital of the Insane. That it was owned and managed by relatives of Tillman and Swearingen very likely had much to do with this decision. Blease went on the attack first, sending letters to influential South Carolinians around the state leveling various forms of accusation against the management of the hospital. Tillman's response was swift and direct. Writing to a sampling of senators from around the state (those representing Prosperity, Bascomville, Florence, Charleston, Moncks Corner, Barnwell, Edgefield, and Newberry), his message was simple. "I learned while in South Carolina on my recent trip home for the Christmas holidays that there will probably be an effort made to oust Dr. Babcock from the Hospital for the Insane. Governor Blease's underlings and satellites want to manipulate the sale of that property and the building of the new institution out at State Park...An effort will be made to smirch Dr. Babcock and his lady assistant, Dr. Saunders, as these men must have some excuse, you know, and are not at all scrupulous."[58]

Blease vs. Swearingen

During Blease's tenure, at no time would the job be easy for Swearingen; not only were he and Blease ideological and political opposites, Blease took out the wrath he felt against Tillman on the nephew. Blease, a racist populist, and Swearingen, a tolerant progressive in beliefs, were almost ordained to clash from the start. Swearingen overcame his personal beliefs to publicly oppose discrimination and racism, and believed there was a place for the government in helping others.

Worse, Blease felt Swearingen was inherently inferior because of his blindness, and constantly underestimated—and undermined—Swearingen's efforts at every turn while in office and after. Because of his attitudes and his disability, white wage workers never saw him as a "real man" like Cole Blease. The governor had long dismissed those with disabilities as being a kind of second-class citizen worthy of pity. When a friend of Blease entered the Telfair Sanitarium in North Carolina, known for treating alcohol and drug addictions as well as nervous conditions, the governor wrote as if he were addressing a small child: "I hear you are getting along nicely and doing fine and will soon be home with us again; so just go ahead now, be a good boy and when you start back, come by Columbia and spend two or three days with me."[59] However, for someone being treated for nerves, two or three days with the governor was likely one of the worst treatments imaginable.

Worse, Swearingen was from a wealthy family, placing him firmly in the class of "aristocrats" so detested by a working class that viewed individuals of a privileged background as a threat to their own rights. Men like Swearingen threatened working-class masculinity. Blease oversimplified masculinity and capitalized on such (mis)perceptions, wrapping himself in Southern manhood and claiming that reform efforts were thinly veiled attempts at emasculating South Carolinians. Conversely, Swearingen's complex view of his own masculinity incorporated reform and service as extensions of manhood. The two views would collide frequently.

At every turn, Blease proved to be the exact opposite from his predecessor, Ansel, in his relations with Swearingen. While Ansel and Swearingen attended educational conferences together, such as the Conference on Country Schools, Country Life, Blease refused to attend any at all. When Swearingen would send information or requests for him to attend conferences, Blease would send a reply that he was too busy to attend. Blease did enjoy trying to toy with everyone else, though, exerting his power as best as he could. Often, in spite of the fact he had no intention of attending, he would write to university presidents to ask they rearrange the trustee meetings to accommodate his schedule. Throughout Blease's term, Swearingen would send him minutes from the various educational committees in efforts to keep the governor "in the loop," though Blease consistently refused to participate.

Blease and Swearingen were also polar opposites in the realm of intellectualism. Throughout his life Swearingen used his gifted mind and memory as assets. Blease was an outspoken anti-intellectual who encouraged a blatant distrust of intellectuals as part of the aristocracy. By the end of the nineteenth century, anti-intellectualism was intimately associated with Southern masculinity, empowering Blease to react to liberal reformers as infringing on gender norms. When it came to proving masculinity, Blease and Swearingen would be in direct competition for alpha status.

The year 1911 brought more professional turmoil for Swearingen as he and Blease came into opposition on a wide variety of issues. Blease refused to commission county board members for personal, rather than professional, reasons. For example, when C. W. Wolfe of Williamsburg County was nominated to the county board, Blease wrote to Swearingen and explained that "he is personally offensive to me and I decline to commission him."[60] Blease tried to extend his patronage system into the field of education, attempting to appoint friends to positions in the State Board of Education. Swearingen was compelled to remind Blease that such patronage did not follow the laws of appointments. Worse, Blease and his friendly appointees had exhausted the expense accounts of the State Department of Education—conditions that Swearingen had tried to counteract twice that year. When the funding was finally spent and members of the Board began to complain to Blease, the governor in turn railed against Swearingen, whose reply was characteristically direct:

> I have twice reported these conditions and requested the Board to take action to correct them. My report was passed over in silence on both occasions. The appropriation for the State Board of Education has now been exhausted. The conditions mentioned in the letter of Prof. Daniel and Prof. Rembert have existed for months. The men who brought them about cannot expect me to assume to take up the matter a third time at this late date.[61]

Soon after winning reelection in 1912, Blease took his ire against both Swearingen and the South Carolina College before the South Carolina Assembly. In January 1913, Blease appeared before the collected assembly and accused Swearingen and the College of diverting $90,000 of Peabody funds that were supposed to be directed to Winthrop toward "the education of free negroes." First, speaking of Carolina president Mitchell, Blease bellowed, "Certainly the president of the South Carolina College has no place in the educational department of South Carolina." Blease next tapped into his old standbys—masculinity and racism—to launch his attacks. "If he would rather take that money to educate negroes than to give it to the white girls of South Carolina, he certainly has no place in my administration." Launching into his typical fight mode, Blease continued with the ridiculous analogy, "If the two colleges are to fight each other—if Winthrop is to fight the University, let Winthrop fight the University like a man."[62] This assertion is made all the more ridiculous when one remembers that, at the time, Winthrop was an all-women's college.

Blease partisans in the state house demanded an investigation, and a joint committee of six was formed. Hearing testimony from February 5 through 14, the joint committee called as witnesses Blease, Presidents Mitchell and Johnson (of Winthrop), an agent of the Peabody Board, ex-governor Ansel (who now sat on the Peabody Board), Swearingen, and representatives from both boards of trustees. The joint committee's report, issued on March 1, found that Blease's attack was based on misunderstood hearsay—which by all accounts, had Blease actually attended any of the meetings of the various education boards on which he was an ex officio member, he likely would have understood the truth. Worse, owing to the investigation and subsequent delays in distributing that year's Peabody funds, the state actually lost "between $200,000 and

$400,000, which Winthrop and her friends feel sure the College would have received if it had not been for this attack."[63]

Blease was, of course, not satisfied with the results of the joint committee's report. Accordingly, he rejected almost every item in the university's budget request for that year while approving Winthrop's funding wholesale. Fortunately, Blease was overridden, and the university received its largest appropriation. Not finished, Blease actually began attending university trustee meetings—of course, solely to introduce resolutions calling for President Mitchell's resignation. While the trustees voted it down 8–1, Blease took his campaign public. He informed the press that he was determined to force Mitchell out, and trustees who were in elected positions (Swearingen and two others at the time) "would hear from the people in no uncertain terms when they stand up for reelection." Blease added that if Mitchell showed him any discourtesy, "I most assuredly will slap his face."[64]

Many groups and individuals encouraged Mitchell to stay. The Columbia Chamber of Commerce and the student body both made "strenuous efforts" to change his mind and keep him in Columbia. Prominent judges and politicians from all over the state wrote letters of support. Voices from outside the state chimed in as well; the chancellor of Vanderbilt University voiced his outrage at Blease's actions, writing, "I do not know if I ever saw anything so little or so contemptible." Tillman wrote,"I hope and believe that you are too much of a man to retire under fire—especially from such a source. I am certain that Governor Blease, in his crusade against you, does not voice the sentiment or wishes of any considerable number of people."[65] Fortunately for Mitchell, unfortunately for the university, Mitchell accepted the presidency of the Medical College of Virginia and resigned, effective June 1913.

As Swearingen became more and more aware of the corruption and patronage that marked Blease's term, it was evident to Swearingen that some battles were worth fighting with the governor's office, and some were not—and Swearingen became adept at picking his battles. An example of a battle worth fighting to Swearingen involved a student's choice of district in which to enroll. When Blease was working with a citizen to get the citizen's children into a better school district, Swearingen was quick to react. "You have confused township lines and school district lines," Swearingen wrote to the citizen, carbon copying the governor. "I have written to you fully because of your apparent unwillingness or inability to understand the situation," Swearingen wrote to the citizen, possibly intending the message for the governor as well. His concluding remarks, though, were clearly for Blease's eyes: "I cannot, however, violate the law, although I should be glad to serve you if I had the right or the means to do so."⁶⁶

A battle not worth fighting to Swearingen was that of the certification of a teacher from Georgia. Blease had told the teacher that South Carolina would certify her without first checking with Swearingen and even though she "had not filed the customary papers required for all applicants." Swearingen admitted that he did not "approve of giving greater credit in South Carolina" than in Georgia. But Swearingen was quick to defer to the governor in this matter: "as Chairman of the State Board of Education you have more authority in these cases than I do."⁶⁷

The year 1913 also saw a gender and racially charged controversy between Governor Blease and Swearingen. In December of that year, Blease wrote to Swearingen that he had discovered that Rosa Cooley, a white woman, was named school trustee of an African American school on St. Helena Island. Blease was so incensed that he wrote to Swearingen "I do not understand it. There must be some mistake about it...I would certainly love to have her immediately removed."⁶⁸ In matters such as this, Swearingen truly demonstrated his caginess. While existing laws forced segregation and barred women from holding trustee positions, Swearingen was able to find a loophole and therefore keep the governor from firing Cooley. Since Swearingen had never received an annual report from the school in question, he told the governor to assume that it was a private institution. As such, current school law did "not give the State Superintendent any jurisdiction over private schools and colleges of any kind...The State Board of Education makes no appointments of school district trustees, and employs no teachers." In short, Swearingen was able to counter Blease's wrath and ensure that Cooley and the Port Royal Agricultural School both had happy holidays.⁶⁹

Blease would continue his openly racist practices in regard to the state's schools, even taking matters before the state legislature. In 1914, Blease urged the state legislature to pass a bill "forbidding white teachers in colored schools," a proposal that ran counter to much that had been taking place in South Carolina's schools. Blease's proposal was something "that Charleston did not want," as white teachers serving African American schools were common in the low country. Fortunately, when the state legislature met, they "killed his two cent rate bill" and the teachers were allowed to remain in their schools.⁷⁰

It was against the backdrop of the 1914 campaign and Tillman's attacks that the most bitter exchange of words between Blease and Swearingen took place. Writing to Blease, Swearingen asked the governor to explain his view on rural graded schools. He wrote, "At the 1913 session of the

Legislature, you opposed State aid to two-teacher and three-teacher schools in the country. I understand that your position...is still unchanged. If you care to express your views on this policy, and your attitude toward rural graded schools, I shall be glad to learn your position."[71]

Blease's response was furious, full of invective, and typical of his attitudes in regard to politics in South Carolina. "I want to state to you, sir, that that statement is absolutely and unqualifiedly false," Blease's defense began. Rather than address what his policy toward state support of schools actually was, though, Blease instead attacked in heated rhetoric. "I do not care to speak of your infirmity—but unless you have been imposed upon by reasons of your infirmity, I cannot understand this statement." Then, in spite of Swearingen's efforts to keep politics out of the office, Blease begins a political attack. "I can understand why your uncle, Senator Tillman, has endeavored to injure me politically, and I presume his influence over you, being afflicted as you are, caused you to write the willful [sic] and malicious falsehood." In his anger, Blease even moved toward direct threats against friends and coworkers of Swearingen's. "I understand that your Mr. Tate is now a trustee of a private Negro school," wrote Blease. Tate was considered for a newly formed position in the State Department of Education to be funded by the GEB. Blease wrote that he was "opposed to him, in any manner, shape, or form, handling any school matters in this State,"[72] though nothing ever came out of the threat.

With the advent of World War I and the ensuing growth of the mill industry, the mill workers became an ever-growing segment of the South Carolina electorate, and Blease campaigned heavily with them in mind. South Carolina was unlike many other Southern states in this regard; as noted by historian Bryant Simon in his work *A Fabric of Defeat*, the voting disenfranchisement of African Americans did not carry over to poor white males. "Because millworkers represented a quarter of the electorate, politicians sought their support," and "laborers' ideas echoed through wider discussions about the meaning of public power in the state."[73]

One example of this echoing was the debate over a compulsory education bill in South Carolina. Reformers such as Blease's opponent for reelection, Ira Jones, were touting compulsory education laws under which all children under the ages of 14 (or 16) would be required to attend school. Blease countered these arguments, saying that compulsory education was just another means by which the government was trying to control the mill people's private lives. As noted by Simon, "Cotton mill people, he continued, 'should be left alone...and allowed to manage their own affairs...Compulsory education means disrupting the home, for it dethrones the authority of the parents and would place paid agents in control of the children which would destroy family government.'"[74] As such, Simon notes that between 1906 and 1916, textile workers went to the polls and voted for Blease as a solid bloc with ritualistic repetition.[75] In this torrent of vitriolic debates, a questionable election in which the "criminals, lunatics, paupers, and illiterates" voted heavily, Blease won reelection as governor.[76]

In 1914 Blease decided to attempt to move from Columbia to Washington, DC, running for senate. A move to the national stage may have seemed natural to Blease; however, his reputation preceded him. Worse, Blease dealt with national officials with the same bullying, belittling tone used against those in his home state. In 1914, for example, then secretary of the navy Franklin D. Roosevelt requested that states with naval militias participate in extra training and engage in practice drills. Blease, as usual, refused to take orders from anyone and, acting as commander in chief of the state's forces, refused the state naval militia permission to participate. Trying to remedy the situation, Roosevelt wrote to Blease asking what happened and requesting the militia "make a cruise or participate in such instruction as the Navy Department may prescribe, as long as the present Commanding Officer hold his commission in the Naval Militia. The Department respectfully requests information as to what steps, if any, are being taken, or will be taken, to remedy the condition complained of."[77] Blease sent his usual curt reply: "Your letter of October 15 was received this morning. So long as the present commanding officer holds his commission in the Naval Militia of this State I shall take no steps whatever to remedy conditions you complain of."[78]

Blease opposed the incumbent E. D. Smith but was opposed in his bid by Lang D. Jennings and W. P. Pollock. As ever, Blease was attacked from all sides. These attacks included the "lucrative practice in obtaining pardons" formed by lawyers in Columbia and his extremely derogatory treatment of female employees. Upon being called out in this fashion, Blease "denounced as liars" all challengers and "challenged his critics to fistic combat, which was barely prevented on the spot."[79] Worried about the mill worker vote, many progressive politicians took political steps to counter, if not eliminate, their bloc influence. "Under the guise of political reform," explains Edgar:

There was a concerted effort to reduce the political influence of the mill workers. In Columbia (1910) and Spartanburg (1913), the city commission form of government replaced the old aldermanic system with its wards. All commissioners would be elected at large, thus diluting the influence of votes from the mill wards...The at-large method of election that was so common in South Carolina towns and counties until recently can be traced to the efforts of the progressives. They were determined that mill operatives, whom they viewed as threats to stability and progress, would have as little voice as possible in the government of their communities.[80]

Sensing the tides rising against him, Blease did what was to be expected: began to levy paranoid accusations across the boards. On the eve of the election, Blease sent telegrams to voting precincts in South Carolina calling for extra caution. "Reported that money has been sent to your county to be used in primary election tomorrow. Appoint special deputies." Of course, Blease couldn't admit to losing an election outright—it had to be the work of his rivals. As such, he ordered local supporters to "watch polling precincts and campaign headquarters and arrest all parties who you can find using money or whiskey for influencing voters, and all parties who you find attempting to intimidate voters. A strict observance of this is requested and demanded of you."[81]

By November 1914, Tillman began to sense a political undercurrent shifting in South Carolina. To this end, he wrote to his nephew for help. "You are at the headquarters of politics in South Carolina," reminded Tillman, "and I would be glad for you to dictate a letter giving your ideas about politics in the state, the Blease-Smith race and the effect of my recent letters."[82] Swearingen's response was swift and direct: "In the senatorial race I am of the opinion that the Governor has the best chance today. If Senator Smith can be forced to assume a defensive attitude, he will certainly lose out. Already efforts are being made to transfer the center of interest from South Carolina to Washington. Both candidates have records, and each man should look after the facts in his opponent's history."[83]

Taking his nephew's words to heart and worried that Blease may soon join him on Capitol Hill, Tillman again came out against Blease; this time, however, his efforts proved to be more successful. In a speech delivered on August 14, 1914, Tillman blamed Blease's popularity on social injustice in South Carolina. Tillman even managed to reverse an argument of the populist Blease on the candidate: Tillman argued that Blease was supported by "resurgent Bourbonism." Tillman concluded that it was a shame that even after twenty-four years of primaries, South Carolina voters were still "an easy prey... to the wiles and tricks of demagogues."[84] The clash between Tillman and Blease would even garner the attention of *The New York Times*:

> To outsiders it would seem cruel that senator TILLMAN of South Carolina should take pleasure in the defeat of his old friend COLE BLEASE. When BLEASE was first elected governor, TILLMAN in his joy telegraphed to his successful friend, "Congratulations. Let the heathen rage." Two years later, when BLEASE was reelected in spite of TILLMAN, who had seen a new light, the governor telegraphed to him "They still rage." Now that BLEASE

has been overwhelmingly defeated in his effort to get the Senatorship, it is TILLMAN's turn again. This is his message: 'Hon. Cole Blease, Columbia, S.C.: "The heathen still rage." But the people rejoice. See Deuteronomy, third, two to fifteen. Good bye. (Signed) B.R. TILLMAN.' The theory in South Carolina, except among BLEASE'S loyal followers, and there is still a host of them, is that TILLMAN has profited from the bad example of his former friend, and now views politics with a purged vision. His biblical reference is worthy of his contemporary, WILLIAM of Hohenzollern. OG, it seems, was delivered into the hands of the enemy by the Lord.[85]

Standardizing the Schools

The 1914 election was a turning point in South Carolina politics. Not only was Blease not reelected (and wouldn't be again until 1924), every candidate who had aligned himself with Blease was defeated. Richard Manning, another progressive, prepared to move into the governor's office. Blease resigned five days before his term ended rather than have to meet his successor.[86] As a last act, Blease refused to allow South Carolina troops to march in Woodrow Wilson's inaugural parade in Washington, DC. The public reason Blease stated was, to little surprise, racist. The marching order of the parade would have had South Carolina troops marching behind a regiment of African American soldiers, and to Blease this was an unforgiveable affront.

In his pettiness at losing office, Blease attempted to create as much turmoil as possible—including disbanding all militia units in the state. Tillman suspected this was in order for Blease to be able to stir up armed revolts at his loss with no militia to quell them, and sent word to local authorities via a telegram to newspapers across the state. Trying to reach as many South Carolinians as possible, Tillman's telegram was sent to the *Spartanburg Journal*, the *Piedmont* (of Greenville), the *Daily Mail* (of Anderson), the *Post* (of Charleston), the *Times* (of Florence), the *Herald* (of Augusta, GA), and the *Columbia Record*. "Members of the South Carolina delegation have received various telegrams from different officers in the militia about Governor Blease's remarkable order disbanding the South Carolina Militia," the telegram began. He then used his national office to trump the governor's authority, something rarely done before or since: "Consultation with the Secretary of War leads me to advise that the militia do nothing, but be prepared to quell riots if any occur, as citizens under the orders of the sheriff. Everybody sit quiet in the boat until Governor Blease's term expires, when Governor Manning will take charge of the situation."[87]

Blease made unsuccessful runs for governor in 1916, 1922, 1934, and 1938, as well as equally unsuccessful attempts for US Senate in 1914 and

1918. Even with those losses, he remained active in politics for some time to come, lending support to various candidates throughout the state and continuing his political vendettas. In 1924, Blease was elected to the US Senate, the last time he would hold public office. However, in spite of his personality, his time in DC was uneventful, probably because so many had been attuned to his behavior in advance. With Blease out of office, Swearingen was able to refocus his reform efforts in the schools of South Carolina. When not having to enter a political fracas with every recommendation, Swearingen was able to use the remaining eight years of his time in office moving the state forward and making up decades of lost progress.

The years that Swearingen held office were marked by significant reforms throughout society of the United States, not least of which involved the schools. Various educators improved greatly or overhauled completely curriculum, pedagogy, and administration during this period. It was incumbent upon school leaders, such as Swearingen, to sort through the reform efforts and guide their schools in those deemed most effective during this turbulent period. One journalist described the conditions when Swearingen took office, casting him as a hero. "Dynamic he was, is, and has needed to be. The task of providing adequate educational opportunity for the children of his state is a man-size job," begins the unknown author. Describing the state's overall condition, the journalist describes South Carolina as being "rich in tradition, but mighty poor in ready cash." Moving on to education, "when Swearingen entered office the percentage of literacy was appalling. In some of the western counties it reached nearly 30%, while the average for the state was over 10%... The money set aside by law from the tax revenue barely sufficed to maintain the old standard." Describing the legislature's attitudes toward education, the author stated they were "either ignorant of the imperative need of a radical advance in the school system of the state, or else indifferent to it."[88]

Even in the face of Blease's racism and anti-intellectualism, Swearingen "began his fight against poverty, ignorance, and indifference. Thoroughly familiar with the splendid work being done in many other states, he fearlessly attacked conditions in his own." From the outset, Swearingen's efforts were far-reaching. "There was scarcely a branch of the existing system that did not need heroic treatment, and to accomplish anything he must have money. It was an uphill struggle; but Swearingen's blood was up," and the new superintendent was off and running.[89]

One area of reform was implementing high school standards and accreditation. After years of arguing through statistics and educational benefits, High School Inspector William Hand used a different approach:

"The State undertakes to protect its citizens against unwholesome food and against swindling insurance schemes," he argued, "why should not the State take the same position in regard to educational institutions?" Keeping in mind the reform ethic sweeping the nation, if not the state, he argued for education in the same terms as reformers of the food industry: "Until the State inspects and classifies the education given or sold to its citizens with as much care as it inspects the meat or milk given or sold its citizens, it is not doing its duty... Whenever an institution offers its wares to the public the State should label the wares."[90]

In 1912, this goal was finally achieved. Courtesy of the Association of Southern Colleges and Preparatory Schools (ASCPS), there was now a "clear-cut definition of the minimum requirements for a standard high school." Following the ASCPS (known in the future as Southern Association of Colleges and High Schools) guidelines, Hand categorized the schools using a set of minimum requirements. However excited he was in publishing this categorized list, though, he neglected to include

Table 3.1 ASCPS guidelines for high school classification[91]

	Class A	Class B	Class C	Class D	Class E
Curriculum	Four-year curriculum, no less than 14 units	Three-year curriculum, no less than 12 units	Three-year curriculum, no less than 10 units	Four- or three-year curriculum, fewer than 10 units	Unspecified
Teachers	Three or more full-time teachers, all with college diplomas	Two full-time teachers, third part-time teacher	Two full-time teachers	Two or more full-time teachers	Less than two full-time, but at least one full-time teacher
Recitation periods	Not less than 40 minutes in length	Not less than 40 minutes	Not less than 40 minutes	Not less than 30 minutes	Unspecified
Length of term	36 weeks	36 weeks	36 weeks	32 weeks	Not less than 32 weeks
Facilities	Buildings, laboratory, library, and all other needed equipment for courses offered	Equipment necessary for courses offered	Unspecified	Unspecified	Unspecified

one significant piece of data: African American schools. This might have been done because of their exclusion as public high schools; most African American secondary institutions were private. It is unknown whether ASCPS allowed or even considered African American schools in their accreditation. Just as likely, however, is that Hand realized that inclusion of African American schools would skew the state results even more heavily toward Class D and E schools, shining an extraordinarily unfavorable light on the state's educational system (Table 3.1).

Accreditation agencies such as the ASCPS were a relatively new phenomenon in the public schools. The first such commission, the North Central Association, defined standards for four-year high schools in 1895. This association formed the national guidelines in 1901. The Association of Colleges and Preparatory Schools of the Southern States was formed in 1895; however, owing to the slow development of public schools across the south, this association didn't begin accrediting schools until 1911, and didn't examine public high schools until 1912. Therefore, the first year that the association began accrediting high schools, Hand brought them into South Carolina.[92]

Swearingen's examination of the public high schools was reflective of trends taking place nationally during this period. As explained by Edward Krug, reformers had looked to the lower levels in previous times—but now:

> The main object of attention was the public high school. In the minds of many critics it was still a citadel of reaction, less so perhaps than the college or the private secondary school, but at the same time more vulnerable to attack. The academic tradition had survived the oratory of G. Stanley Hall, the onslaughts of vocationalism, the first wave of social efficiency, and the besieging of the college. It was battered, but still intact.[93]

Echoing this close examination of the high schools, Swearingen began to attempt to enforce his will and issue calls for changes, beginning mildly, and then developing in intensity. Indeed, Swearingen began to work diligently, again mirroring national trends, to standardize the secondary school system of the state. To this end, while Swearingen wrote that the schools had demonstrated "significant progress" and that the work done by the schools was "perhaps better than ever before," he also detailed the flaws of the High School Act.[94] First, since very few towns could meet the student requirements of the act, Swearingen called for an amendment to change this minimum requirement. Second, since towns over 2,500 people in population were excluded, many of them did not offer public high schools; Swearingen called for an amendment to change the population limit. Third, since some counties needed to support more than one public high school because of population differences, white settlement pattern differences, and land size differences, Swearingen called for an amendment to change the maximum amount of state aid to any one county.[95] In addition, he called for a plan to develop teacher training in the public high schools, specifically establishing teacher-training courses in ten four-year high schools in ten counties. This would allow more students in the state to become certified, making for a wider, more highly qualified, better-quality pool of teachers to staff even the most rural schools.[96]

In 1911, Swearingen continued his efforts at the standardization of the high schools by adopting, for the first time, a comprehensive list of textbooks for use in the high schools. Swearingen listed the texts adopted by the State Board of Education for four years of high school study. Getting four years of high school texts on the approved-to-purchase list was a significant first step toward adopting a statewide high school curriculum. These texts reflected the trend of high schools toward a humanistic, classical curriculum. Noticeably absent from the adopted texts are any texts on the teaching of agriculture, or home economics. In spite of calling for instruction in these fields, specifically agriculture, Swearingen was unable to get the texts approved for any but a third year course in business methods.[97]

William Hand's report of the conditions of South Carolina's high schools was more optimistic in tone that that of Swearingen's. He cited the continued growth in number of high schools (1), number of high school teachers (33), and enrollment (510). In addition, Hand showed a decline in the number of private secondary institutions in the state; of the 69 towns with populations over 1,000, only 5 still had private secondary institutions—Charleston, Columbia, Spartanburg, Rock Hill, and Bamberg. The public high schools were rapidly becoming the dominant form of secondary education in South Carolina.[98]

Furthering the push for standardization, 1911 marked the first year students received state high school diplomas at graduation, during which 16 high schools had students eligible for state diplomas.[99] Meeting this standard unit for graduation, Hand finally published an approved guide to standard high school units. A standard unit was defined as 5 weekly recitations of 40 minutes or more for a minimum of 36 weeks (a minimum of 120 hours of 60 minutes each). In spite of both Hand's and Swearingen's calls for increased agricultural education, the outlined course of study still followed the humanist classical curriculum. The only commercial or vocational course of study was in drawing.[100] One possible explanation of this humanistic approach is a movement that was sweeping the nation— one of the first back-to-basics reform movements. As Tyack reminds us, many districts nationally were responding to parental requests and returning their schools' curricula to a classical approach: "What citizens wanted, and what the teachers gave them, was 'honest school work,' upholding the 'standards of manners, of morals, and of real work,' not 'fads' and 'pedagogical experiments' or 'showy effects.'"[101]

Another progressive education element implemented by Swearingen was the development of professional educators in the roles of county superintendents to improve education. When discussing education and literacy in the state, university leaders did "not give the State a literate citizenship... This task has fallen to the County Superintendent." Swearingen continued in biblical terms: "To make brick without straw has always been a burden." To provide the "straw" to make the bricks, the superintendents needed to be better paid than their teachers and guaranteed four-year terms.[102] In making this call for the professionalization of superintendents, Swearingen again followed what was becoming a national trend. Later seen as a branch of the administrative progressives, schools were compared to businesses. The idea was to move toward a stable, well-paid superintendent who in essence ran the district as a professional educator in a way similar to the role that a corporate executive plays in a company. As noted by Tyack, across the nation, "the movement to institute the corporate model of school politics spread rapidly. In many ways the key element in the new model was the power of the superintendent to influence major decisions of the school board."[103]

Standards for the issuance of teaching certificates were formalized under the Swearingen administration as well. Throughout Swearingen's tenure, becoming certified as a teacher in South Carolina became an increasingly formalized process. By 1911, an examination system had been put in place, announced by newspapers such as the *Anderson Daily Mail*:

> The regular fall examination of teachers will be held at the court house here tomorrow, beginning at 8,30 o'clock in the morning. The examination is for the purpose of awarding teachers' certificates of the first, second and third grade, and it is expected that there will be a large number of teachers from the city and county [to] take the examinations. The examination will be in progress for the greater part of the day, and also expect to take it or ask to be on hand promptly. It will be conducted by the County Board of Education.[104]

It was frustrating to Swearingen that his best efforts often went for naught as county superintendents often didn't avail themselves of all the new opportunities coming out of the legislature. Worse were the ones who wrote to Swearingen, asking for special dispensation on matters that could be handled in legitimate means, such as levying a local tax. When A. H. Cox, superintendent of Anderson County, wrote to Swearingen asking for extra funds to be allocated their way, Swearingen's response was clipped, direct, and reflective of all his policies:

> It is impossible for any school district in Anderson County to secure adequate educational facilities simply by depending on its regular school funds. If you and your neighbors desire a good school, you must vote a local tax in order to secure State aid...I have written to you fully, because of your apparent unwillingness or inability to understand the situation. I am anxious to help your children, and every other man's children, to an education. I can not, however, violate the law, although I should be glad to serve you if I had the rights or means to do so.[105]

Many of the statements and demands made by Swearingen would prove to be true when ignored by others involved in education. While works such as *The Shopping Mall High School* indicted schools for watered-down, too expansive curricula, Swearingen cautioned against this as early as 1913: "Any institution that undertakes to be universal in its province or its function is doomed to break down of its own weight," he warned. He continued in words that are as meaningful in the twenty-first century as they were in 1913:

> We attempt to correct all our shortcomings and to cure all our evils, social, political, and industrial, through the public schools...The school is fast becoming the factotum in our civilization. One set of people demands that academic degrees be given for swimming and aviation. Another set hopes to reform society by giving high school credit to boys for running errands at home and for pulling weeds out of the front yard...There is a world of difference between a school's linking itself sympathetically to every good community undertaking and its attempting to incorporate into its work everything in which the community might be vitally interested. Whenever a small school undertakes to do a little of everything, to spread itself out over every community enterprise, it becomes very thin.[106]

Owing to his focus and direct dealings with the state legislature, the years in which Blease held office were not a total waste in terms of education. While Swearingen's relationship with Blease as governor was contentious, at least it was short-lived. The 1914 election of the politically progressive Richard Manning gave Swearingen the support of the governor's office necessary to continue his efforts in improving the schools. While the Blease years were rocky, the Manning years would prove smooth sailing.

4

Swept Up in Progressivism, 1915–1919

Much to the benefit of Swearingen's efforts, and to the benefit of the schools of South Carolina, Blease's term came to an abrupt end with the election of Richard Manning. While on good terms with predecessor Martin Ansel and on horrific terms with Blease, it was Swearingen's relationship with Richard Manning that would prove most fruitful to the people of South Carolina. The voters of South Carolina would get caught up in the general wave of social and political progressivism that swept the nation, and Manning and Swearingen were all too happy to ride that wave in making improvements to the state. This is not to say that there were no challenges that occurred while the two men served. Indeed, these years saw the boll weevil, World War I, and teacher shortages impact the nation. However, there were tremendous strides both personally and professionally for Swearingen. Personally, Swearingen married and started a family, happily settling into domestic life in Columbia. Professionally, Swearingen would see the Compulsory Education Act through, as well as many other legislative successes, making vast improvements in the state's schools.

Good Times Return: Richard Manning

These improvements were largely because of Swearingen's positive relationship with Governor Manning. Born in 1859 in Sumter County in the Midlands, Richard Irvine Manning III was educated in Kenmore Preparatory School in Virginia before attending the University of Virginia. First elected to the South Carolina State House of Representatives in 1892, he served in there until 1906, when he mounted his first unsuccessful bid for governor. He was more successful in 1914, becoming the third generation in his family to be elected governor; both his grandfather and father had held the position. Although he came from one of the most wealthy and influential families in South Carolina, Manning believed that it was the role of government to provide for the welfare of all its citizens and that it was a duty of the privileged to help those less fortunate. One of Manning's top priorities in order to assist the general populace was improving the public schools.

Manning was unlike his predecessor in a variety of ways: first, he viewed education as being of extreme importance to the state; second, he had a positive working relationship with Swearingen. During Manning's four years in office, Swearingen would make hitherto unreachable goals in educational legislation. They had their work cut out for them; in 1915, Swearingen and Manning partnered to ask the state legislature to approve spending what would amount to $15 per white pupil and $2 per black pupil in South Carolina. By comparison that same year the city of Boston, Massachusetts, spent $40 per pupil.

Manning caught the zeitgeist of the populace and was a Progressive Era politician in every sense of the word. In Manning's years in office more than a dozen major acts of legislation were approved. Prohibition finally caught hold in South Carolina when, in 1915, the citizens voted by more than two-to-one to prohibit the sale of alcoholic beverages. In 1916, a Child Labor Law raised the minimum age for employment to 14. Schools, such as the South Carolina Industrial School for Girls, were created for the mentally ill and delinquent white females. The State Highway Department was created in 1917; as a result, drivers had to be licensed for the first time in state history, and they had to be semiliterate in order to pass the written portion of the driver's test.[1]

Swearingen developed quite a different rapport with Manning than he had with Blease. As explained by Manning's biographer Robert Burts, "Manning and Swearingen worked together and suggested appropriations for the public schools." In his inaugural address, Manning "enunciated the principle of equalizing educational opportunities when he said that 'the policy of the state is to educate all the people at the expense of all the people for the welfare of all the people.'"[2] Correspondence between the two men was cordial; both men frequently asked professional favors of the other. For example, early in Manning's term, Swearingen wrote to discuss the legislative appropriation for schools. "Knowing your interest in the public schools," he began, "I am writing you briefly concerning public school appropriations for 1915." Noting that many people, such as the state legislators, were citing economic needs to reduce spending in the public schools, Swearingen wrote, "I do not admit that the public schools are a fit place for economy in South Carolina today." To conclude his letter, Swearingen recommended that the governor not lessen the appropriation, but double it.³

While Manning was in office, he had much to cope with in addition to his attempts at spreading progressive reform. The period also saw a series of natural disasters that drastically affected the state, and consequently the state's schools. The year of the flood was 1916, sweeping down from the mountains of North Carolina. This flood affected the Pee Dee region of the state most drastically. In 1917, the boll weevil was first detected. This insect would destroy the state's agricultural system; for example, 90 percent of the cotton crop of the Sea Islands was destroyed by the boll weevil. An influenza epidemic hit the state in 1918, resulting in 7,400 deaths by the year's end.⁴

The natural catastrophes facing South Carolina were frustrating for its farmers; however, the legislative catastrophes facing Swearingen were just as frustrating. While Manning agreed to sponsor significant educational legislation, such as increased funding bills and a local option compulsory education act, many of Swearingen's best reform efforts were thwarted under the auspices of violation of local control. Raising teacher standards, compulsory attendance, defined school terms, and permanent state aid were all rejected by the state legislature under the local control umbrella.⁵

This resistance included reform efforts within the public schools as well. While the high schools were gaining in importance and function across the nation, there was still much resistance to high schools across the South. "The high school is, in its essence, nothing more than a mass-production factory," wrote John Gould Fletcher, "It was not and is not adapted to Southern life." Fletcher explained three reasons that the modern high schools were not viable in the South. First, the majority of the population was still agricultural and rural, creating difficulties finding skilled teachers and creating a disconnect between urban high schools and colleges with the country life to which most students return. Second, the large African American population created a difficulty. Fletcher is quick to point out that African Americans were more than willing and capable of completing high school work; however, without social and economic opportunities, secondary education would be worthless. Third, Fletcher argued, Southerners believed the system devalues the degrees earned; since all students are able to get a diploma, what is it really worth? And what does it really prepare people for?⁶

In spite of this resistance, Manning's term did mark some real reforms in South Carolina's schools. The 1915 school year was one of the "glory years" for Swearingen as superintendent as his recommendations on attendance were finally followed. That year, even with the previous opposition by Blease and the mill workers of the state, the legislature finally took note of Swearingen's annual reports and approved the *Local Option Compulsory Attendance Law*. Swearingen referred to this piece of legislation as "the most constructive pieces of legislation," although he was also quick to note that the bill did contain "some crudities" and had some "serious defects."[7] Swearingen also attempted to reform school funding by no longer holding parents responsible for paying additional fees for high school work, a practice deemed "detrimental" in his 1916 annual report. He cautioned that such fees would deter many parents from enrolling their children in public high schools owing to either economic reasons (the parents couldn't afford it) or choice reasons (the parents would rather spend their money on a private academy).[8]

Swearingen was confident enough in his relationship with the governor to make direct recommendations—something that had been soundly ignored during Blease's tenure. For example, in February of that year, Swearingen wrote to Manning to encourage the governor's signing into law two bills. The first was a new high school bill that had passed the house with one amendment, calling for a training program for high school teachers; the other provided funding for a program of teaching agriculture in South Carolina's schools, known as the Toole Act. Both passed.[9] In addition, Manning worked with Swearingen to continue the process of standardizing the schools. The 1917 Stafford Bill allowed the State Board of Education to compile and mandate a list of approved textbooks for the state high schools. Manning proposed a compulsory attendance bill that would displace the local option bill in existence. Finally, Manning attempted to standardize teacher certification in the state; he urged the legislature to approve a bill that would establish one state certification system with two tiers, one for high school and one for elementary school.

The Battle for Compulsory Attendance

However emphatically Swearingen wrote regarding the needs in the schools, he was even more verbose and detailed in calling for compulsory education legislation. Beginning his argument in 1914, Swearingen noted that a provision for compulsory attendance was written into the 1868 state constitution; however, the act had never been implemented. "It is needless to discuss in this report the causes of this postponement," he wrote. "That the time has come to improve this condition is also admitted. The only question today is the framing of a practical and practicable statue. The terms of the law will determine whether it shall be useful or useless."[10] In calling for this compulsory education law, Swearingen was trying to move South Carolina toward a goal that had already been achieved by most of the nation. Across the nation, schools were being perceived as the messianic agents to save the society of the United States; as such, students needed to compulsorily attend. As Tyack expounds, education officials "joined with muckraking journalists, foes of child labor, and elite reformers in political campaigns to translate their concerns into compulsory schooling and child labor laws."[11] Stereotypically, the Northern and Western states acted long before the Southern states; however, by 1914, many of South Carolina's neighboring states such as North Carolina and Tennessee had enacted statewide compulsory attendance (Table 4.1).

Swearingen provided ten points to the law. The first was the compulsory school age, between 8 and 14 years. The second was the length of the session, a 16-week term, for which exceptions could be made for agricultural and industrial needs of the community. In one of his few moments of shortsightedness, Swearingen argued that with this local control "the

Table 4.1 Chronology of enactment of compulsory education laws[12]

State	Year	State	Year	State	Year
Massachusetts	1852	Wisconsin	1879	Arizona	1899
New York	1853	Illinois	1883	Iowa	1902
District of Columbia	1864	Montana	1883	Maryland	1902
Vermont	1867	North Dakota	1883	Missouri	1905
Michigan	1871	Rhode Island	1883	Tennessee	1905
New Hampshire	1871	South Dakota	1883	Delaware	1907
Washington	1871	Minnesota	1885	North Carolina	1907
Connecticut	1872	Idaho	1887	Oklahoma	1907
New Mexico	1872	Nebraska	1887	Virginia	1908
Nevada	1873	Colorado	1889	Alabama	1915
California	1874	Oregon	1889	Florida	1915
Kansas	1874	Utah	1890	**South Carolina**	**1915**
Maine	1875	Kentucky	1893	Texas	1915
New Jersey	1875	Pennsylvania	1895	Georgia	1916
Wyoming	1876	Indiana	1897	Louisiana	1916
Ohio	1877	West Virginia	1897	Mississippi	1918

race problem would not be an issue," that African American students and white students would both meet their terms.[13]

The third, fourth, and fifth factors to be considered were the distance students would have to walk to school, exemptions to this, and penalties. Since no districts at the time offered transportation for students, no student should be required to walk more than two and a half miles to school, making districts place schoolhouses no more than five miles apart. The only exceptions to the law would be for students who were "physically, mentally, financially, or otherwise disqualified." For penalties, Swearingen described as what can best be described as a three-strikes-you're-out enforcement policy: the first violation would simply warrant a warning. The second violation would warrant a fine (amount unspecified). The third violation would warrant imprisonment (term unspecified).[14]

The sixth, seventh, and eighth strands of the bill regarded school census, textbooks, and truant officers respectively. Swearingen noted that South Carolina had no means of taking a school census. Until teachers knew how many students were eligible for school, they could not enforce attendance; thus, the teachers or the districts had to complete these census reports. The textbooks would be provided at district expense to "indigent" students, with those students who were not be charged for their textbooks. Attendance officers must be hired by districts as well, considering "teachers cannot play policemen" and enforce attendance laws.

The ninth section of Swearingen's proposed bill was that of cost. Swearingen quickly admitted that the "public school never raises revenues." As such, he wrote that any and all costs of compulsory attendance must be provided for by the state legislature. "Whatever the cost may be in money or in work, to refuse to meet it would be even more costly."[15]

The final section of Swearingen's proposal was enacting the law. As eager as he was to see the bill enacted, Swearingen was also realistic enough to realize that not every district in the state was prepared to immediately begin enforcing the law. Thus, Swearingen recommended two forms of local option for enactment: first, districts could enact a local one-mill tax levy; second, districts could file for permission to postpone enforcement of the law until their schools were prepared to meet the demand. "I regret the necessity of suggesting the exemption of a single school or a single district," he wrote, "but knowing the resources of the State, the condition of the public schools, and the spirit of our people, I can not permit my professional enthusiasm to overcome my practical judgment in this important matter. I am unwilling to set a head of gold upon feet of sand."[16]

The racial question was also part of Swearingen's discussion of compulsory attendance. When explaining the length of the school term under compulsory attendance, Swearingen cited that most white districts had a term of seven months; however, African American schools had no such legal length of term, although Swearingen himself "favored as long a term as practicable in the Negro schools." There was no excuse for this situation to Swearingen: this problem was due to "the unsatisfactory condition of our schools and to their inadequate terms than to any other causes."[17] Swearingen argued for direct action: "The time has come when the General Assembly ought to authorize and direct a campaign for the better health and better industrial conditions among our negroes," he wrote. "The foundation for such an effort lies in the schools. The first step in the program for their betterment would be a modest appropriation to be expended solely in negro schools." To this end, Swearingen requested a "special appropriation" of $20,000 directly to the state superintendent's office to be used "for the betterment of negro schools."[18]

Swearingen also called for an amendment to the High School Act, eliminating the population limits set on distributing state aid in the form of tuition reimbursements to high schools. "Centers of wealth and population will always be centers of education," he explained. "They do not need State aid to establish or maintain good schools." However, rural areas did not and could not support high schools; as such, many of these children paid tuition to journey into the county seats, or other towns, to attend high school. Many more students would have attended high school if they could have afforded it. Swearingen lamented that "hundreds of competent, ambitious, country boys and girls would enter the classrooms of these town high schools if tuition bars could be let down through state aid."[19]

That year Swearingen proved that he was willing to stand up to anybody—textbook dealer, philanthropist, politician, or scholar. As a member of the board of trustees of the USC, Swearingen took a heartfelt interest in the goings-on in Columbia. During the Blease regime, however, the board took matters into their own hands; 6 of the 11 board members began meeting in a secret "President's Committee." Aghast, Swearingen felt "compelled to register my protest against the method of doing business pursued by the Board. The Statues of the State, and accepted rules of parliamentary practice, should have some semblance of observance, even at the hands of University trustees." Swearingen wrote he was "opposed to the policy of secrecy pursued by this committee, and, further, to the extravagant salaries and unauthorized appointments fixed by such majority." In response, he decided to send "a copy of this letter to every member of the Board in order to register my protest against favoritism, ring rule, and extravagance. I regret the necessity for speaking thus plainly, but the University is a public institution belonging to the people. I have not endorsed, and I do not propose to endorse, either in private or public, several acts and several proposals of the majority under the name of the 'President's Committee'."[20]

Table 4.2 Revised notation of high school accreditation, 1915[21]

Category	First class	Second class	Third class		Fourth class
Curriculum	4-year	4-year	3-year	3-year	Less than 3 years
Units in curriculum	14	12	12	10	Less than 10
Number of teachers	3 full-time	2 full-time	3 full-time	2 full-time	1 full-time
Session length	36 weeks/ 180 days	36 weeks/ 180 days	36 weeks/ 180 days	32–36 weeks	Not less than 32 weeks
Recitation period length	40 minutes	40 minutes	40 minutes	40 minutes	40 minutes

In addition to taking a stand for the universities, the public high schools also saw a boost. Hand also reported that the Association of Colleges and Secondary Schools of the Southern States revised the system of accrediting high schools. More formal and structured than the previous one, the new system not only looked at length of term and number of days, but also took into account curricular issues. This newly revised system was detailed in his report and explained in tabular form (Table 4.2).

Progressive Attitudes toward African American Schooling

Swearingen and Manning saw eye to eye not only on the necessity of educating African-Americans in the state, but also on how they should be educated. Manning advocated for African American students to be taught "a core curriculum of reading, writing, and arithmetic" in addition to "occupational and vocational training to equip them better for trades and crafts." It was not all good news, particularly for colleges to serve the African American population. Rather than being the staunch advocate of these institutions one would expect, "Manning believed that the state should concentrate upon improving the broad base of education, the public schools, and omit large capital outlays for colleges, which he hoped could be maintained at existing standards of academic efficiency."[22] In spite of Manning's efforts, though, the state legislature in 1917 set aside $2,100 as part of the Rural School Improvement Association to be used specifically in improving the normal school at what is now known as South Carolina State College in Orangeburg.

This was due in no small measure to Swearingen's addresses to the state legislature. He and Manning spent much time making both houses aware that "the quality of Negro education was much poorer than the Negro schools' padded enrollment and attendance figures indicated." According to the figures he provided the governor in 1917, 95 percent of African American students, as opposed to 70 percent of whites, never finished the fifth grade. Swearingen believed that much of the money being spent on African American education was being wasted "through the incompetence and inefficiency of the Negro teachers and that it was useless to spend more money on the schools until the quality of the Negro teaching corps could be improved."[23]

Across the South, school districts continued to develop white schools at the expense of African American schools. Swearingen documented this problem in his 1915 report. In a section of the report devoted entirely to "Negro Schools," Swearingen reported that "the negro is here, and here to stay. He cannot remain ignorant without injury to himself, his white neighbors, and to the Commonwealth." However, Swearingen did cite several statistics demonstrating the dearth of educational opportunities available to African Americans in South Carolina. Of the 2,307 schools serving African Americans in South Carolina, 92 percent were located in the country; only 8 percent were in cities or towns. Also, 92 percent were still one-teacher schools, and only 22 percent of African American students were enrolled in regular attendance. Concluding the section, Swearingen asked, "Can we afford longer to allow this large element in our population to follow their present practices and to remain in their present condition?"[24]

Further compounding this lack of academic preparation was the particular sort of school funding that grew during this period: vocational-only education. The predominant school of thought, associated with Booker T. Washington and often referred to as the Hampton-Tuskeegee model, stressed the need for vocational training. As noted by Anderson, proponents of the Hampton model "believed that a particular combination of hard work, political socialization, and social discipline would mold appropriately conservative black teachers."[25] Just as Swearingen was an advocate for vocational education, he was a fan of the Washington-Hampton model. Swearingen began a section of the *Fiftieth Annual Report* by acknowledging that "the situation of these schools demands careful discussion." Focusing his attention on the "absolute incompetency and unfitness of Negro teachers," Swearingen lamented that the only higher education institution with a normal training program was the state's "Negro college at Orangeburg" and that "graduates of this college are quickly absorbed in the trades and industries." Swearingen stated that the best hope for African American teachers was to become trained in vocational and industrial arts, writing that "the industrial education of negroes has been thoroughly established throughout the South."[26]

Viewed through contemporary lenses, this belief of Swearingen's was a demonstration of his inherent racism. Critics today explain that such gradualism-promoting, vocational-only education was nothing short of racist. Inherent in it was the belief that African Americans were incapable of performing up to standard academically. This may be true in Swearingen's case; however, it is more likely that Swearingen, the student of political history and nephew of Ben Tillman, was a keen observer of the political process and realized that this model was the best chance of funding African American schools available to him. It also must be realized that this was the dominant view not just of Southern whites, but also of whites across the United States. Philanthropic agencies focused their spending on schools in the Hampton-Tuskegee model, and teachers from across the country were sent to both institutes for summer sessions to better learn industrial and agricultural techniques. In this regard, contemporary readers cannot forget even school people were products of Jim Crow.

Marriage and Running the Household

Just as the election of Manning saw Swearingen's professional career blossom, so too did his personal life take on significant happiness during this period: Swearingen married Mary Hough. Born in 1888 to Columbus Nixon Hough and Martha Love Chappell, Mary was 13 years Swearingen's junior. The couple first met when Mary graduated from Winthrop University in Rock Hill as a member of the class of 1909 and Swearingen presented the commencement address. In his letter of recommendation, professor of pedagogy J. W. Thomson described Mary as "a promising young teacher" who possessed the "scholarship which will enable her to do any work required in the public schools: her health is good; she is diligent, faithful, prompt, seems always ready; disposition seems safe, and kindly."[27]

Mary, along with three of her classmates, were hired in Denmark as teachers, "all equipped with high ideals and low salaries."[28] Happily, the town embraced the new teachers and encouraged them to set high standards for the students. Mary cites this experience above all others in her career when recounting them in her memoirs: "Almost fifty years have passed since my first experience in a classroom as the teacher, but I shall always remember it with satisfaction."[29] Owing to the low pay, Mary moved on to teach the next four years at the private Spartan Academy, a mountain mission school, during which time she had to teach several history courses to the students. During her time at the school, it was paid a visit by the state superintendent of education—one John Swearingen—who did not stay long but did comment to her that he knew she was teaching there and was hoping to see her again.

For the 1914–1915 term, Mary taught at Anderson High School. However, her sister Bessie frequently wrote, describing teaching jobs in Montana that paid the then exorbitant salary of $100 a month (nearly double what teachers in South Carolina were earning). Mary applied and completely resigned herself to relocating. As she recounts, "Had Mr. Swearingen not come along when he did, I might now be a real Westerner, a ranch woman, or perhaps an Annie Oakley."[30] While Swearingen surely felt some sense of loss at the move, nonetheless, he was able to separate his personal and professional lives in the matter. In correspondence to her, he agreed to write her a letter of recommendation, although he confided that he would feel a "personal and professional loss" at her moving.[31]

Swearingen was a bachelor at 41 years of age. Until he met Mary, he admitted to friends that he believed it was unwise for a blind man to marry. This statement could arise from two sources. One, Swearingen knew the social definition of a man's role in marriage; masculinity had stamped multiple other aspects of his life. As such, Swearingen probably had doubts as to his worth "as a man," particularly in a marriage. Another reason, though far less likely, could be construed as somewhat philanthropic: Swearingen had every intent of throwing himself into his career more than full time, which might not allow for a happy family life as well.

Neither Swearingen nor Mary recount their courtship, and in later interviews, their son remarked that neither parent would comment on it as was the dominant social custom of the time to keep such matters private. However, this uncharacteristic insecurity about marriage marked their early relationship; Mary and Swearingen decided to use the time apart to determine how serious their relationship was. In their case, the distance proved the old cliché, "absence makes the heart grow fonder." While in Montana, Mary corresponded frequently with Swearingen. It was also during this year that Mary learned the Point Print method of writing; Mary was the only person, other than Swearingen's mother, who ever learned the method. However, Mary was uncomfortable with the method that involved a tablet, stylus, and heavy paper; correspondence was punched through the paper, written backwards, so it would appear raised and frontward to the reader. While Mary could write using the method, she could not read (or make corrections on) what she had written. Her betrothed, however, told her it was fine—that he would happily decode anything she sent.

Mary's learning of this method led to another favorite family story, recounted by both Mary in her memoir and their son, John. When the first letter from Montana arrived at Swearingen's office, his staff met it with great pleasure, looking forward to reading it to the man who guardedly protected his private life as they did all his other correspondence. "Some members of his official staff later told me that consternation reigned in his office when the mail, postmarked in Montana, began to arrive in Point Print," Mary recalls in her memoir. "Several of the clerks had primed themselves to open the Montana mail for him. Their chagrin was matched only by Mr. Swearingen's own supercilious delight and satisfaction when the letters arrived."[32]

After one year, the weather proved too much for Mary and she prepared to move back to South Carolina. While Mary was in Montana, Swearingen proposed and Mary accepted; they would be wed upon her return to South Carolina the following year. So, at the end of the school year, Bessie filled Mary's "hope chest with linens, fancily embroidered lingerie, handmade laces, and crocheted whatnots...wedding clothes, shoes, and hats," and Mary returned to the Piedmont.[33] Swearingen met her train as it arrived in Asheville, North Carolina, and completed the trip with his beloved.

Swearingen's friends and family were delighted. In a letter written to his future sister-in-law, George commented that he was happy to hear of the couple's engagement, was grateful that she liked him as much as he liked her, and he respected her for going to Montana. He ended on the somewhat humorous note of requesting Mary find him a girl her equal.[34] Swearingen's friend, US Congressman J. J. McSwain, echoed George's sentiments, writing that the engagement was "good news I hear—fine business—I know her mighty well. Just suits to a T."[35] Even Uncle Bennie chimed in; buried in a letter written on senate letterhead between details of the Annapolis entrance exams and a request to be kept abreast of South Carolina politics, Tillman included the personal aside, "I have not seen you since reading in the papers about your contemplated marriage; and I must congratulate you, without knowing the woman—taking it for granted you have made a wise selection. All I can say to her, and I wish you would tell her, is that if she makes you half as good a wife as you will make her a husband, you will both be happy."[36]

June 29, 1916 marked the beginning of a new phase of Swearingen's life—that of the family man. He and Mary were married in the home of her sister in Greenville, South Carolina. Mary's former principal from Anderson, Mr. H. L. Riley, performed the ceremony. Congressman J. J. McSwain performed best man duties and "engineered all the groom's tasks such as getting the license and ordering flowers."[37] By all family remembrances, Swearingen and his new wife were extremely happy. After spending the year apart while Mary was in Montana, the couple was absolutely convinced they were perfect for each other. One acquaintance jokingly asked Swearingen how he had managed to get such an attractive woman to marry him. "You didn't expect me to look across the breakfast table at an ugly woman the rest of my life, did you?" was his jovial reply.[38]

Never one to allow a professional opportunity to pass him by, Swearingen and his new wife honeymooned in New York City so that he could attend sessions of the NEA conference held in Madison Square Garden that year. A story that was recounted in the family memoirs occurred on the train ride to New York; it would prove the need to reinforce Swearingen's masculinity. On the bumpy journey, the new Mrs. Swearingen asked a porter to offer Swearingen assistance in the dressing room. Within a few moments, the porter came back up the aisle laughing aloud. He quickly explained that, while the other men were hesitant to try and shave even with safety razors, Swearingen was "in yonder shavin' himself with a long straight razor, and everybody is a-gaping at him...Lordy, miss, that's a *man*!"[39]

During the return trip, the Swearingens visited Washington, DC, where they met with "Uncle Bennie." He gave the new couple a tour of the congress building, in which Swearingen was often mistaken for another senator. Mary recalled that other congressmen and their employees often stopped Swearingen, asking him about matters of legislative responsibility. Surely the temptation existed for one who enjoyed tweaking public sentiment as much as Swearingen, but he resisted because of his respect for their office and his uncle. Once the couple returned to Columbia, they took up residence at 1413 Blanding Street. Although in the early years the house contained no modern appliances—such as furnace, refrigerator, or washing machine—the family would spend the rest of their life in this home.[40]

Throughout their married life, Mary accompanied her husband on many similar business trips, serving as guide and mediator. Mary was well-suited to the task. After her father passed away, Mary's mother operated a boarding house, giving Mary the opportunity to interact with a wide variety of people. In addition, a neighbor's son was blind, giving Mary the opportunity to learn to work with people with visual impairments. Between learning social graces in the boarding house and learning to assist people with visual disabilities from her neighbor, Mary proved an able and pleasant guide.[41] With her educational background, she greatly enjoyed the trips, accompanying her husband to educational conventions, conferences, and group gatherings; together they traveled to cities such as

New York, Atlantic City, Washington, and Philadelphia. As she recalls in her memoir, "I met many interesting people, heard many speeches...and visited cities and places where I had never been before."[42] Swearingen's relationship with his wife was a special, loving one. Swearingen frequently commented that there were only two women in his life who learned to write in Point Print or Braille: his mother and his wife. Their son John recalls the relationship as being "truly amazing." He remembers that his mother was "always useful and helpful to my father in what he was trying to do." John also recalls that one of Swearingen's favorite names for his wife was "Christmas. He'd say 'You're my Christmas every day.'"[43]

This is in no way meant to claim that the Swearingens had a perfect marriage. Mary fully admits that she and her husband "had our share of conflicting ideas about many things," although they "never had arguments." This was not due to even temperament on either of their parts; instead, it was because Swearingen "stated his position, abided by it, and that was that." Both were aware of social definitions of masculine behavior in matrimony; while Swearingen conformed, Mary undermined. Like newlyweds throughout time, she learned to negotiate things on more compromising terms; she would "bide my time, catch him in a weak moment, and eventually gain my point." Mary soon became so skilled that often Swearingen "actually believed he was the one who thought up the idea originally."[44]

Being married to an elected official provided much material for the mosaic of the Swearingen marriage. Frequently, Swearingen would invite political friends and guests back to his home for a meal. While initially nervous in her role as homemaker, Mary proved to be excellent in this facility. She recounts the first time she had to serve as hostess to a gathering; she had offered to host the meal for her husband without looking at the guest list, a mistake she would not make again, as it included D. B. Johnson, president of her alma mater, Winthrop University; Dr. Walter Riggs, president of Clemson College; Dr. Henry Snyder, president of Wofford College; Sr. S. H. Edmunds, superintendent of Sumter City Schools; Dr. S. C. Currell, president of the USC; and no less than the governor, Richard Manning.[45]

Not all gatherings were as illustrious as that, nor were all neighbors supportive of the Swearingen marriage. Mary recalls that some people came to call on the newlyweds just to satisfy their morbid curiosity. A reflection of their society, these people came to the house with a set of stereotypes they were hoping to have addressed or reinforced. Comments Mary endured in these early gatherings ranged from the fairly innocuous, such as, "Why did you marry a blind man?" to the blithely ignorant, such as, "Aren't you afraid your children might be blind?" to the blatantly offensive, such as, "I knew a blind man who married the ugliest woman in the state. She looked like a mud fence although that didn't matter since he couldn't see her." While Mary admits that neither she nor her husband was very disturbed by these incidents, Swearingen did advise her to "terminate any of their future unsolicited visits and advice."[46]

While Mary proved to be an excellent hostess, she admits to being not the most perfect homemaker. Owing to his blindness, Swearingen provided a sense of organization to the household that was absolutely necessary for his own physical and mental well-being. While Mary would frequently lose the car keys, for example, her husband always kept a spare set in his desk drawer for such occasions. If Swearingen reinforced his masculinity in other areas of his life, these behaviors did not carry over into the house. He would frequently assume the "feminine" tasks such as setting the table, washing dishes, and putting them away. He even had a cabinet custom-made so that he could keep the house's dishes away by sense of touch. Mary recalls in her memoir that she "soon learned to let him care for many things and many duties about the house. Any especially valuable paper, article, or souvenir was always delegated to his care... He wound the clocks... sharpened the kitchen knives, locked up the house at night, kept all receipts."[47]

While assuming these household duties, Swearingen was not just expressing a physical need due to his disability, but was also a product of his times. During the years that Swearingen and his wife were settling into marriage, as explained by Margaret Marsh, "marriages required new roles for both men and women, even if we cannot describe them as egalitarian." Indeed, there existed a "cultural chasm" between societies of the "mid-nineteenth century, in which women took responsibility for the home and for the emotional tasks of parenthood while men took on the role of firm patriarch or detached observer, and that of the early twentieth, in which men could be referred to as 'homemakers.'" In this sense, Swearingen was a social progressive.[48]

Organization was the key to running the household. In Swearingen's case, it was not only for his mental satisfaction—of being able to fulfill the typical masculine duty of being head of the house—but also for physical well-being. As recalled by his son:

> He always had an admonition, which he... drilled into us children. Everything should have a place. Everything should be in its place. And you can understand his reasons... And, around the house, mother almost never rearranged the furniture. Because if he knew where the chairs and the tables and everything were, he could manage around the house without running into them. But if you changed them around, why then he had

to learn them all over again...But one thing that as a child we learned, you couldn't leave a door half opened. When he began to walk, of course he put his hands out in front of him. And if a door were open, then he could walk right into the edge of the door, and it would hit him in the nose or the forehead or something. Sometimes it hurt him badly. So we had to learn either to leave the door wide open or to leave the door fully closed.[49]

Beyond the immediate household, Swearingen was entrusted with his extended family's landholdings: he was, at least in part, responsible for the Tillman family's landholdings, including those in Florida as well. The Florida land became a frequent topic of correspondence between "Johnnie" and his "Uncle Bennie." In 1912, for example, a railroad had made an offer to the family to purchase some land hitherto used as a lumber farm. While explaining that such an offer was "most gratifying" and "highly desirable," Swearingen showed his savviness that came through his awareness of global events. He cautioned Tillman to wait on the sale as they would likely increase the offer because "large developments in this section were sure to follow the opening of the Panama Canal."[50]

More for the Marginalized

Just as Swearingen made efforts to improve the teaching and administrative roles of women and the entire school process for African Americans, he realized there was another population within the state that desperately needed educational help: the mill workers. To this end, in 1915 Swearingen expanded the role of his office in benefiting this population. Swearingen hired for the first time a supervisor of mill schools, whose job it was to align these schools with the public schools or provide assistance to well-running schools: Wil Lou Gray.[51]

Gray wrote that mill management "as a body have gone on record as favoring a State-wide compulsory school law." She also reported that 21 mill districts had, in fact, enacted the compulsory attendance law (Table 4.3).

Swearingen proved almost prophetic regarding another issue: transportation of students at district expense. Commenting that this trend was "growing in favor" with districts, Swearingen cited 72 districts in 29 counties that used 119 vehicles to transport 16,015 students. Swearingen opined that the transportation of students by the schools gave "satisfaction to teachers, pupils, and patrons." He also predicted with characteristic optimism that "the wider use of transportation, like so many other

Table 4.3 Mills enacting compulsory attendance regulations, 1916[52]

Name of county	Name of district	Name of mill
Abbeville	Abbeville	Abbeville
Aiken	Graniteville	Graniteville
Fairfield	Winnsboro	Fairfield
Greenwood	Jones	Ware Shoals Mfg. Co.
	Greenwood	Greenwood
	Greenwood	Grendel No. 1
	Greenwood	Grendel No. 2
	Greenwood	Panola
Laurens	Laurens	Laurens
Richland	Columbia	Richland
	Columbia	Columbia
	Columbia	Columbia Hosiery
	Columbia	Palmetto
	Columbia	Southern Aseceptic Lab.
Spartanburg	Spartanburg	Beaumont Mfg. Co.
	Spartanburg	Crescent Mfg. Co.
	Spartanburg	Spartan
	Landrum	Blue Ridge Hosiery
	Pacolet	Pacolet
	Whitney	Whitney Mft. Co.
	Drayton	Drayton

progressive tendencies within the schools, simply waits for increased school revenues."[53]

However, like so many other issues relating to the public schools during this period, even school transportation was broken along racial lines. As schools in South Carolina were providing transportation for their white students at district expense, as differentiated by Anderson, African American school students were another matter completely: "Unlike for white children, southern state and local governments refused to provide transportation for black children." One example cited by Anderson explained that local African American parents raised private funds to purchase a school bus as the local district wouldn't provide a bus. This refusal came even in light of many students having to leave their homes by 6 a.m. to get to school on time, and many students suffered from overexposure to cold weather.[54]

National Events Impact the Palmetto State

The year 1917 was amazing for education on a national level. Three separate events—one political, one global, and one curricular—all had serious impact on the public schools in the nation. Politically, the federal government was becoming increasingly involved in the public schools, in spite of the "delegated powers" clause in the constitution. To wit, from 1787 through the year Swearingen took office, there were only six pieces of federal legislation passed: in 1787, the Northwest Ordinance authorized land grants for the establishment of educational institutions; in 1802, An Act Fixing the Military Peace Establishment of the United States established the US Military Academy; in 1862, the First Morrill Act authorized public land grants to the states for the establishment and maintenance of "A&M" (agricultural and mechanical) colleges (such as Clemson College in South Carolina); in 1867, the Department of Education Act authorized the establishment of the US Department of Education; in 1876, the Appropriation Act established the US Coast Guard Academy; and in 1890, the Second Morrill Act provided monetary grants to support instruction in A&M colleges.

However, five federal acts were passed during the 14 years of Swearingen's administration alone. Therefore, in addition to implementing a wide variety of state reforms, Swearingen's tenure oversaw the implementation of these new federal acts, many of which were brought to his attention by his uncle Tillman. The most expansive for South Carolina was the Smith-Hughes Act that would fund one of Swearingen's dreams: vocational education. There are a variety of reasons that Swearingen, himself someone who believed in a classical, essentialist curriculum in the schools, would so strongly support vocational education. First, his love of state would make him welcome with open arms any educational program that would encourage economic growth. Second, being raised on a farm, Swearingen saw the need for agricultural education, honestly believing the land to be the key to South Carolina's future. Third, the skills taught in the majority of vocational programs—farming, tool and die making, and carpentry—were stereotypically masculine fields, appealing to his need to prove himself "a man" within the bounds of his society.

Swearingen, via Hand, began including impassioned but logical pleas for vocationalism in the high schools. Hand began his argument by calling for his audience to "accept what ought to be self-evident—that God does not create all boys and girls equal or alike in capacity, in opportunity, in taste, in ambition, or in ideals, and that it is folly for fond parents and obstinate schoolmasters to undertake to disregard the handiwork of the Almighty."[55] As such, Hand wrote, high schools should offer curricula that would benefit all students instead of "slavishly, if not blindly, following the traditions of four centuries ago" and requiring all students to complete a college-preparatory curriculum. The number of professions has grown; the coursework of high schools should concomitantly grow to prepare students for these new careers. The current curriculum, a "veritable medieval mummy" was inadequate for this purpose. Worse, there was a sort of academic snobbery taking place in the high schools—that students attempting to pursue a course of study in the commercial arts were treated as second class, or "plebian."[56]

In doing so, Swearingen was again following what was becoming a national trend. Within the public schools of the period, as described by Edward Krug, "there was beginning to develop an idea of election by courses more closely related to the occupational futures of finishing pupils." Indeed, while there did exist much antipathy, if not hostility, to the idea of manual/commercial courses in the high school, the progressive notion that "election by courses...in relation to presumed occupational choice" became more and more the norm for secondary institutions: the comprehensive high school emerged.[57]

There was resistance even in a rural, predominantly agricultural state such as South Carolina. Since school board members were mainly comprised of the leading citizens of the community, they wanted their children to go to college—and made the local schools prepare their children for college at any expense. The teachers in the schools had no thorough vocational preparation, thus did not and could not appreciate the significance of the curriculum, nor were able to teach these courses. The superintendents and principals were caught in the middle, the worst of both worlds.[58] However, quantitatively speaking, less than 15 percent of public high school students in South Carolina attended college. "The remaining 85% have some rights," wrote Hand, and hoped that when the voters of the state realized that 8,000 students were not being treated fairly by the public high schools, they would rise up and "demand fair play."[59]

The colleges and universities perpetuated the system as well. The universities in the state did not give their students college credit for courses in manual training, domestic science, agriculture, bookkeeping, and other commercial subjects. Thus, even though the universities claimed to help support a vocational system by offering these courses, there was no reason or motivation for college students to attend these classes. Worse, colleges didn't count these courses when admitting students.[60]

The year 1914 marked the publication of two works that would validate the statements of vocational needs made by Swearingen and Hand. E. L. Thorndike published what came to be known as his "theory of identical elements" that proved that only in limited situations would transfer of learning occur. This was significant because it scientifically disproved the old notions that an academic curriculum would train the mental abilities of a child enough to allow them to pursue any career, thus establishing a need for specific vocational education. Also in that year William

Lewis published his book *Democracy's High School*. Featuring a foreword written by President Theodore Roosevelt, this book was a clarion call for vocational educators, demanding an equal place in high school curricula for practical subjects such as business training, manual arts, domestic sciences (for girls), and, most significantly to Swearingen and South Carolina, agriculture.[61] Indeed, the federal government was preparing a bill that would both validate Swearingen's desire to forward vocational education and provide the means to make it possible; and, luckily enough, one Benjamin Tillman was on the committee overseeing it.

The Smith-Hughes Act passed in 1917, but it was the culmination of a national trend that had been occurring since the beginning of the twentieth century. Traditionally, the high schools did not include specific commercial and vocational training for its students. People in the United States began to realize that there was a need to create a trained labor force: if there were specialized programs of study for fields such as law, medicine, agriculture, and commerce at the postsecondary level, why not begin the process of preparation for these fields at the secondary level as well? Two views were becoming more and more popular in regard to vocational education. From a societal point of view, the American economy needed efficient service and trained workers, especially in light of the emerging war. From an individual point of view, citizens were feeling the need to make a more effective living; many citizens felt high school vocational programs would help them, or their children, in this matter.[62]

As detailed by Henry Perkinson, discussions at the NEA's 1903 annual convention led to the realization that "few self-respecting educators accepted any longer the theory of mental, or manual, discipline. Schoolmen now justified school subjects by their practical not their disciplinary value...Speaker after speaker at the symposium pleaded for practical, vocational education." Even opponents of vocational education "acceded to the pleas for vocationalism." All the opponents asked was "that the public schools not become 'trade schools.' They argued against trade schools on the grounds that this narrow education, or training, would not prepare youths for a variety of different job opportunites."[63]

Giving additional impetus to the federal government was the plethora of private sources funding vocational education. J. P. Morgan, for example, provided $500,000 to the New York Trade Schools. During this period the majority of "such commercial and technical schools founded by philanthropists had been absorbed into the public system," legitimizing vocational education.[64] This belief was most notably demonstrated in the work of the GEB, which spent millions on funding state agents of rural education to implement vocational education at both the K-12 and higher education levels, particularly in regard to schools for African Americans. In 1906, the National Society for the Promotion of Industrial Education was founded; it would later be backed by the American Federation of Labor. In 1910, the National Association of Manufacturers officially ended its support of private trade schools, instead throwing political and financial support behind vocational programs in the public schools. In 1912, President Woodrow Wilson called for a conference on vocational education in the public schools.[65]

Recognized as the legislative basis for vocational education, the Sixty-Fourth Congress passed Public Law No. 347, referred to as both the National Vocational Education Act and the Smith-Hughes Act. Specifically, the act provided federal funds to provide for the promotion of vocational education; to provide for cooperation with the states in the promotion of such education in agriculture and the trades and industries; to provide for cooperation with the states in the preparation of teachers of vocational subjects; and to appropriate money and regulate its expenditure.[66]

While providing funding for and training of teachers in vocational education, the act had three specific components that would create future difficulties in vocational education. First, individual states were required to create separate state boards for vocational education that were to expedite communication between the federal and state governments; however, these boards often did not provide organizational systems, establish state priorities, set state goals, or provide state accountability mechanisms, and ultimately "fostered the notion of vocational schools as separate and distinct from general secondary schools, and of vocational education as separate from 'academic' education."[67] In addition, the act dictated that any student receiving education from a teacher paid for with federal funds could not take more than 50 percent of their coursework in the academic curriculum, creating what is referred to as the "50–25–25 rule"; that vocational students' coursework would be 50 percent shop work, 25 percent related subjects, and 25 percent academic courses.[68] Furthering the separation of vocational and academic curricula, the act also called for a separation of funds: salaries of vocational education teachers would be paid from an account separate from salaries of academic teachers. While the intent of this provision was good, to prevent raiding vocational funds for other purposes, all this provision did was "separate the vocational education program from the mainstream of a school's operations."[69]

In spite of Swearingen's efforts to prepare South Carolina for the Smith-Hughes Act, some elements were still missing in 1918. Swearingen explained in his report that the state didn't recognize a separate board of vocational training until November 15, a date "too late to be utilized fully in the schools." South Carolina's secondary schools also resisted meeting the federal act's provisions; Swearingen described that making efforts to "revise the program so as to meet the new requirements of the Federal Board and the State plan was no easy matter." Primarily missing amongst the requirements was a formalized system of state funding to match the federal monies spent.

Swearingen insisted that "vocational instruction must be made an integral part of our high school system, if it is to succeed here."[70] Swearingen's belief tended to counter the beliefs of many educators, who tended to believe that general education and vocational education were incompatible; to combine them would lead to a watering-down of the curriculum. Swearingen wrote that he hoped "never to see a dual system of education separating young boys and girls into vocational groups and cultural groups."[71] He knew then that creating such a dual-path system would perpetuate social inequities that the children of blue-collar workers would be placed in vocational groups and the children of white-collar workers would be on the academic path. Swearingen ultimately believed in the "American dream," that schools should be a means of social and economic mobility for all of South Carolina's students.

Swearingen was absolutely correct that this dual-path system would be symptomatic of problems with vocational education across the United States. On a social level, the addition of vocational education reinforced economic roles for students. Rather than education encouraging social mobility, it reinforced class roles. As Counts wrote in 1922, "It is clear that we in America have not abandoned in practice the selective principle in secondary education, even though we have established a free public high school in almost every community in the country." He added, "The children of the laboring classes are destined to following the footsteps of their fathers."[72]

This situation was especially true for African Americans: Counts found that most African American students were in either manual training or home economics courses. He concluded:

> Misfortune, as well as fortune, passes from generation to generation...When not preserved through the operation of biological forces, the inequalities among individuals and classes are still perpetuated to a considerable degree in the social inheritance. While the establishment of the free public high school marked an extraordinary educational advance, it did not by any means equalize educational opportunity, for the cost of tuition is not the entire cost of education...secondary education remains largely a matter of family initiative and concern, and reflects the inequalities of family means and ambition.[73]

While vocational education allowed Swearingen to use his background and masculinity to once again benefit his state, a global event was beginning to unfold that would truly appeal to Swearingen's militaristic sense of duty. On June 28, 1914, Archduke Franz Ferdinand was assassinated by a 19-year-old Bosnian student. European politics had been dancing on the edge of disaster for almost a decade; the assassination was exactly the spark needed to ignite what would (rather ironically) become known as "The Great War" and "The War to End All Wars." Initially remaining neutral, the United States avoided entering the conflict until a series of events forced its hand. First, German U-boats were attacking shipping vessels of the United States at will. Second, the United States intercepted what would become known as the "Zimmerman telegram," a document from Germany to Mexico offering a deal of sorts. If Mexico would join Germany on the side of the Central Powers, it would in turn support Mexico to recover Texas, New Mexico, and Arizona. Until that point, the United States was wholly against entry into the war. Indeed, the Republican Party passed over the hawkish Theodore Roosevelt for Charles Evans Hughes in the 1916 presidential election. However, the incumbent Woodrow Wilson, who ironically campaigned for reelection using the slogan, "he kept us out of the war," asked the US Congress to declare war on Germany on April 2, 1917.

While at the time there was no existing federal standing army, by using the public schools the government had been preparing for the outbreak for years. As early as 1911, Secretary of War Robert Shaw Oliver was devising a plan to train all American boys in military techniques and history and build what would essentially be a standing national militia. Under the bill, each high school would form a corps of cadets that would engage in drill and target practice. Unfortunately for Oliver, Blease was in office and predictably refused to participate for a great variety of reasons. "In the first place I do not believe this Country is in danger of any serious war, now or hereafter," the somewhat shortsighted governor declared. On a more humorous note, he admitted that he did "not believe in educating every boy that he has to shoot somebody. They have enough of that in them already." On a much more serious note, the governor spouted his usual ignorant racism for his next reason: he was "unalterably opposed to arming negro school children with rifles and ammunition. Our state has had trouble enough with federal bayonets in the hands of negroes and their allies." White schools would suffer the most because "under the provisions of your bill, requiring forty or more students, fourteen years of age or over," there would not be as many white as African American corps of cadets formed. As the governor concluded, "In the white schools there are sometimes not as many as forty students, and they generally cease to go about the age of nineteen, while in the negro schools there are nearly always forty and they range in age from five to thirty."[74]

Issues of preparedness aside, the United States entered the Great War on April 6, 1917. While there was indecision about entering the war (6 senators and 50 representatives opposed it, for example), once the United States entered, many Americans honored the call to arms for a wide variety of reasons, patriotic and politic. For example, Swearingen's best friend, J. J. McSwain abandoned a run at congress and decided to enlist in May 1917. With the war thus hitting home in a deeply personal way, Swearingen understood that the war had tremendous impact in South Carolina. Writing to Tillman, he explained that there were political, as well as educational, ramifications to the war. Writing of the political nature, Swearingen explained, "The State is heartily and earnestly in the war," but cautioned that "many people, however, feel that the truth is being doled out in packages by too many officials. Everybody feels that the cost is to be shared by all and that blood is to be spilt by all, hence many folk are dissatisfied with evidences of inner control." Its educational impacts were noted, but not explained, with an unusually curt aside: "The war is making heavy inroads on the schools. The problem of school administration will certainly not become easier next year."[75]

While the war brought out Swearingen's patriotism, it is not to say that the war met with universal approval. In South Carolina, in the same week of the war preparedness parade in Columbia, there was an antiwar rally at the Lexington County Courthouse. Cole Blease got into the scuffle as well, accusing pro-war governor Manning of being "worse than Scott, Chamberlain or Moses, because they only stole money and he [Manning] is trying to steal the souls and bodies of your boys." However, eventually the notion of "those who are not with us are against us" won out, and 307,000 young men registered for the draft. By the war's end in 1918, some 62,000 South Carolinians would serve in the conflict, 54,000 of them draftees, and the state's patriotic fund drives would raise nearly $100 million.[76]

As the spirit of patriotic fervor swept across the nation, schools joined the war effort. Michael Sedlak explains, "Many communities increased the amount of time their schools devoted to physical education, military training, domestic science, and hygiene programs." Schools sponsored the Reserve Officers' Training Corps and Red Cross programs. Since there was such a large number of men physically unfit for military service, new emphasis was placed on health and physical fitness programs in the schools to provide a better soldier.[77] The war also affected the gender makeup of high schools; with young men enlisting or being drafted into armed service, more girls than boys enrolled in high schools. With the sweeping patriotism and concomitant xenophobia, foreign language class enrollments declined sharply during the war. Students elected to take French and Spanish during this period rather than German and Latin, as they had in the prewar era.[78] World War I also progressed so-called intelligence quotient (IQ) testing in the United States; the American military began using tests in order to determine both potential officer's ratings and the potential efficiency of soldiers. As noted by Tyack, "The army test experience prompted school testing experts to urge the use of IQ scores in vocational guidance and in the assignment of students to lanes leading to different careers."[79]

Swearingen, the descendent of a long line of soldiers and once West Point hopeful, vocally supported the war effort in his 1918 report, writing, "Every patriotic appeal and every loyal activity were enthusiastically supported by the schools." He went on in highly patriotic terms, writing that the efforts "proved again the real value and the real democracy of the public school." He also credited the schools with producing well-trained soldiers: "The American soldier is one of the best products of the American school system. His record in the fight is the best evidence of his training and efficiency."[80] The Junior Red Cross, Thrift Stamps, War Savings Stamps, School Garden Academies, United War Work Drive, and the four Liberty Loans were among the official efforts joined by South Carolina's schools. In addition to the national efforts, South Carolina schoolchildren worked toward food production, food conservation, and raising funds and materials for Belgian, French, and Serbian relief efforts. The schools adapted their curricula to include "civic intelligence and, above all, the clear understanding of the aims and principles of the War."[81]

World War I had a tremendously negative impact on the teaching profession. By 1918, there was a nationwide shortage of teachers that aroused federal intervention. President Wilson authorized the Bureau of Education to assist schools in their efforts at "finding teachers for colleges, normal schools and technical schools, superintendents and principals of schools and teachers and supervisors of special subjects in the secondary and elementary schools." Secretary of the Interior Lane estimated that, owing to the high rate of military induction of teachers, the nation was short of 30,000 teachers in their city and county systems. The Bureau of Education knew that it could "not undertake to recommend any teacher for any position"; its primary purpose was to "report names and addresses and records of education experience in other qualifications" to help states efficiently identify "a large number of persons not now engaged in teaching who are willing to work in the schools at least until conditions become normal."[82]

Nationally, the war had profound social consequences. European immigration, for example, all but ceased. As American men marched off to war, more jobs, mostly in the industrialized North, became available. This new job availability appealed to African Americans eager to leave the South. As noted by Richard Kluger, within the next 15 years, nearly 1.5 million African Americans (approximately 100,000 each year) were driven by "hate and flood and the weevil and the Klan, of Jim Crow and pauperism and diurnal drudgery" to move north.[83] Aside from the First Great Migration, the war had tremendous impact on African Americans in another way: over 200,000 African American men fought during World War I. These men who fought for democracy abroad returned to decidedly undemocratic conditions. As then colonel George S. Patton declared at the war's end, quoted in *The State* newspaper:

> When peace is declared these Negro men will return proud of their achievements and conscious of the fact that they offered themselves for the cause of freedom. They will seek for themselves and their children and rightly so, not social equality but political and educational opportunity. They will demand education and political justice. We have proclaimed the salvation of the oppressed nations of Europe—what shall we do for the Negro of the South?[84]

The State editorialized the matter in similar tones. Since African American men "offered themselves in the cause of freedom; many thousands will have made the supreme sacrifice, the last full measure of devotion to their country," it would be only natural for them to "expect to be full shares in the fruits of victory and partners in the glories of triumphant piece—a heritage justly claimed. They will seek for themselves and their children, and rightly so, not social equality but political and educational opportunity. They will demand education and political justice."[85]

This evolved into a rhetoric of a "new reconstruction," words that sent chills up the spines of most white Southerners who believed that the status quo should not change. To get the government involved in social issues such as this would be to create another Reconstruction government, with equally disastrous, equally violent results. Just as Reconstruction was an affront to white Southern masculinity, so too were the increased calls for an end to Jim Crow at the war's end. Riché Richardson argued that in spite of being "celebrated and honored in majestic parades" in some northern cities upon their return home, "Black soldiers typically met with a cool reception in the South." Indeed, it is sadly ironic that:

> For those who faced combat abroad, the threats to life and limb had become more visceral in their communities at home than they had ever

been in the battlefields of Europe. In no other place in the nation did the conflicts related to the convergence of race and masculinity play out with more brutality and intensity than on the black male body in the South.[86]

Richardson explains that "African-American soldiers carried a particularly onerous emotional, physical, and psychological burden both during and after the war." During the war, they were often treated as second-class citizens, fighting in segregated units led by white officers. Those African American soldiers who did earn promotion were not allowed to supervise white troops. Then, to add injury to insult, upon their return home to the South they "incurred the wrath of whites deeply resentful of Black men in uniform. In the worst cases, black soldiers were lynched while wearing their military regalia."[87]

In spite of—or perhaps because of—this tremendous backlash, Swearingen knew that the time had come for the government to improve the station of African Americans, and that the schools would be the beginning. The year 1918 marked a significant increase in the documentation of problems facing African American schools in the state superintendent's report. There are two likely explanations for Swearingen changing his rhetoric from a simple documentation of problems to that of calling for action. The first was the returning soldiers from World War I; with his love of service, Swearingen probably believed these men deserved something better. In addition, Tillman retired from the senate that year. It is safe to assume that many of Swearingen's actions and writings were tempered by his attempt to balance his strong beliefs while doing nothing to cause political detriment to his uncle. With Tillman's retirement, this balancing act became obsolete.

Proving that he was, in the words of one of the GEB inspectors, "quite a progressive person in favor of education for the Negro and he much encourages the idea,"[88] Swearingen addressed the problems of segregated schools. Using the strongest, most direct language to date, Swearingen explained that it was hypocritical for the state to not discriminate in funding between two white high schools in the same city, but to limit funding when one of those schools operated for African American students. "Personally I favor the use of identical standards for all schools," he wrote. Swearingen explained how a fair, just, colorblind system of schools would operate:

> If the instruction and organization of a colored high school, organized and directed by local school officers, and superintended and taught by men and women responsible to local authorities, conform to the high school standards of the State, I believe such a Negro school ought to be accepted as an integral part of our high school system. The cost of such a policy

would be small at first, but it would and should become considerable in a few years.[89]

The third issue to impact the schools was a curricular issue: the *Cardinal Principles* report was issued that same year, attempting to realign the curriculum of the secondary schools. There existed a strong debate as to the purpose and curriculum of secondary schools; a group of academics, superintendents, and teachers came together to plan what would become the future of high school curricula in the United States. In 1918, the US Bureau of Education published their "manifesto that codified the curriculum reform consensus,"[90] Bulletin Number 35, subtitled "A Report of the Commission on the Reorganization of Secondary Education, Appointed by the National Education Association." Seen as a landmark in education and curriculum history; this document is one of the most discussed documents in the field. In short, the *Cardinal Principles of Secondary Education* would forever change the face of secondary education in the United States.

The chair of the committee was Clarence Kingsley, Massachusetts state high school supervisor. The members at large included the US Commissioner of Education, one additional state high school supervisor, two college presidents, three professors of education, the YMCA senior educational secretary, one high school principal, and one teacher. There were 16 subcommittees; two general subcommittees were the Organization and Administration of Secondary Education and the Articulation of High School and College. These subcommittees represented distinct areas of secondary study: agriculture, art education, business education, classical languages, English, household arts, industrial arts, mathematics, modern languages, music, physical education, sciences, social studies, and vocational guidance.

The authors of the report were not arguing that their results would be the final step in the development of secondary education; in fact, they wanted just the opposite. If anything, the *Cardinal Principles* report expected secondary curriculum development to be an ongoing process. As written by Chairman Kingsley in his "Preface" to the work, "The translation of these cardinal principles into daily practice will of necessity call for continued study and experiment on the part of the administrative officers and teachers in secondary schools."[91]

Assimilation remained one of the fundamental purposes of education. In the report's second section, "The Goal of Education in a Democracy," the authors highlighted the need for education to efficiently and effectively prepare citizens for society. The report explained that "the purpose of democracy is so to organize society that each member may develop his personality primarily through activities designed for the well-being of his fellow members of society as a whole."[92] As explained by Graham, during World War I, "the schools performed the astonishingly successful transformation of taking many children whose family culture and often whose family language was foreign and converting them into adults who were American." Such assimilation was perceived as building good citizens: "The push to comprehensive schooling in the United States was driven by the need both to inform the citizenry so they could govern and to assimilate the immigrants so they could be constructive citizens."[93]

In this respect, the *Cardinal Principles* was not much different from the rhetoric of educators from the nineteenth century. As noted by Joseph Kett, while the report called for a wider variety in the curriculum to meet the needs of diverse students, a large segment of whom were all but ignored by the high schools. The report "consistently emphasized the value of secondary education in creating a uniform national culture."[94] In order to achieve these ends, the report recommended the adoption of seven objectives of education. These objectives showed a new focus, embodying the efforts of progressive educators: educating the whole child beyond the school environment. Secondary education was no longer simply preparation for further education: it was preparation for life. Indeed, only the second objective was traditionally school-specific. In calling for students to have a "Command of fundamental processes," the report cited that students need a strong academic preparation. Reading, writing, math, and "elements of oral and written expression" must be expanded beyond the elementary preparation.[95]

The remaining objectives moved the notion of education beyond the traditional walls of the school. The first objective stated that "it is necessary to arouse the public to recognize that the health needs of young people are of vital importance to society" and thus "the secondary school should therefore provide health instruction, inculcate health habits," and "organize an effective program of physical activities." The third educational objective called "for the development of those qualities that make the individual a worthy member of family, both contributing to and deriving benefit from that membership." Students of both sexes should learn music and art, as these fields "result in more beautiful homes and in greater joy therein," and should be taught to "exemplify wholesome relations between boys and girls and men and women." The report was sex-specific to the point of sexism in one area: that of the household arts, or home economics. The authors of the report argued that since all women would eventually make homemaking their "lifelong occupation," even those who enter other fields briefly, schools should prepare women to be homemakers first and foremost.[96]

The fourth educational objective was intended to "equip the individual to secure a livelihood for himself and those dependent on him." In a larger context, this objective should also prepare students "to maintain the right relationships toward his fellow workers and society, and, as far as possible, to find in that vocation his own best development." "Civic education," the fifth educational objective, stated that students should be prepared to "act well his part as a member of a neighborhood, town, or city, State and Nation," and provided with "a basis for understanding international problems." The sixth objective specified the role of students in their future free time: "Worthy use of leisure" was an objective meant to focus on the "avocational interests" such as music, art, literature, drama, and social interactions in order to "equip the individual to secure from his leisure the re-creation of body, mind, and spirit, and the enrichment and enlargement of his personality." The seventh and final objective, "Ethical Character," was designed to teach "the moral values to be obtained from the organization of the school and the subjects of study" by developing "the sense of personal responsibility and initiative" as well as "the spirit of service and the principles of true democracy." However, the report never provided clear boundaries as to whose morals would be taught; it is safe to assume that the predominant White Protestant values would be the basis.[97]

To a man who was a curricular essentialist, the recommendations of the *Cardinal Principles* report came as a shock. Indeed, while he remained socially and philosophically progressive, he remained educationally conservative and essentialist. It was in his 1921 report that Swearingen reported his protest of what he termed "the overcrowded curriculum," and lamented the great expansion of the high school curriculum: "Pupils are being burdened with much matter and many subjects that are of questionable value." Swearingen argued for a return to a classical education:

> Mastery of the fundamental processes is essential. Shallow substitutions for these processes ought not to be allowed. A little smattering about everything is not education. Further overcrowding of the curriculum ought to be stopped. In fact, the elimination of many subjects would do no harm today.[98]

The *Cardinal Principles* report makes an interesting backdrop for an explanation of the concomitant development of women's rights. In 1918 the South Carolina High School League finally gave official sanction to a girl's sport—basketball.[99] At the postsecondary level, women were first admitted to the College of Charleston on September 30. In addition, women were granted the right to practice law in South Carolina in

1918, with "Miss Jim" Perry being the first woman admitted to the bar.[100] Nationally, however, women's rights both gained and lost momentum. Woodrow Wilson, often seen as one of the more progressive presidents of the era, was notorious for being antifeminist, at both personal and professional levels.[101] In spite of Wilson's resistance, though, women's suffrage looked as if it was going to be approved; in 1918, President Wilson pushed a measure urging the senate to vote on women's suffrage as a war measure. With so many men overseas fighting, there was not a large enough electorate. Wilson urged the senate, arguing that "if America is to lead the world to democracy it will be judged by its acts." The senate was not impressed; the two South Carolina senators joined the rest of the senate in voting down women's suffrage as a war measure.[102] Nationally, resistance to women's suffrage was resistance to perceived infringement on what was a masculine venture; as described by Bederman:

> [Politics is] part of the male sphere...an exclusively male bailiwick. Indeed...partisan politics were seen as a proving ground for male identity. Political campaigns were male rituals celebrating participants' identities both as party members and as men. At the same time, electoral politics dramatized and reinforced men's connection, as men, to the very real power of government. Men objected so strenuously to woman suffrage precisely because male power and male identity were both so central to nineteenth-century electoral politics.[103]

The framers of the *Cardinal Principles* report did not anticipate the Nineteenth Amendment. After a long battle across the nation, the war provided the rhetoric and reasons necessary to give women the vote. Tennessee became the thirty-sixth state to ratify the Nineteenth Amendment, providing the three-quarters of states needed for full adoption, and the amendment was adopted in 1920. Nationally, women exercised their right in droves. However, predictably, the South was more resistant to the change. Women in South Carolina, for example, began exercising their right to vote upon the amendment's national adoption, but the legislature only ratified the amendment in 1969.

Schools became central to women's rights gains. Recognizing that schools were central to reforming society, women became very active in reforming child welfare and school policies. Indeed, as schools became increasingly perceived as "women's work" by mainstream society, it became almost a natural fit for women to step in to the educational arena even while they were often disenfranchised in other political arenas. As explained by William Reese, "Progressive women wanted to shape public policy and expand women's opportunities more broadly, and they demonstrated this most forcefully in multifaceted campaigns to improve neighborhood schools."[104]

Legislative Successes, Louder Calls

Even with the social and political chaos at state, national, and global levels, Swearingen was still able to make progress in South Carolina's schools. In 1917, the legislature approved five acts directly affecting the public schools. That year, the state legislature passed the Rector-Riddle bill, which set aside the largest appropriation for the support of the public schools in the state's history. Swearingen was able to get an amendment to the 1912 Graded School Act through the legislature. In addition, an amendment to the Smoak-Rector Act provided school districts financial incentives to consolidate their schools.[105]

Swearingen also spearheaded a movement to continue progress in one of the areas he deemed most critical to South Carolina's schools: the teaching of agriculture. Working on the advice provided by his uncle, Swearingen knew that the Smith-Hughes Act would pass at the federal level; as such, he scrambled to make South Carolina one of the states most prepared to implement its provisions upon passage. Coordinating with Clemson University, Swearingen had approved a position as professor of agricultural education, allowing Clemson to graduate agriculture teachers.[106] Swearingen was also able to get an act approved by the legislature, creating a State Board of Vocational Training, an offshoot of the State Board of Education. Predicting that the Smith-Hughes Act would necessitate matching state and/or local funds, Swearingen used the passage of this act to call for the legislature to set aside funding for agricultural/vocational education.

One of the banner legislative achievements of Swearingen's career was the Equalizing Act, creating a contingent fund for schools in 1917. This act guaranteed funding for a minimum term of seven months for any district voting an eight-mill tax to support the schools. Swearingen had long lamented the inconstancy of school terms in South Carolina, providing examples of some districts meeting for terms of 60 days while other districts met for eight months. Noting that under the old terms of state aid, many districts received funding as "an undesirable pork barrel aspect," Swearingen stated that the new act would provide money to "the truly needed and the really progressive districts of the State."[107]

Not every bill put forth by Swearingen and Manning sailed through the legislature as they intended. The fifth act of legislation was one actually criticized by Swearingen. An amendment to the state's local tax code, the bill stated that no district school tax could take effect if voted later than July 1 of any given year. Noting that "every improvement in the public schools during the last ten years is directly traceable to local taxation," Swearingen stated that there should be no handicap placed on this taxation. Considering that only 14 percent (272 out of 1,886) of school districts had no local tax, any hampering of it was deemed harmful.[108]

The year 1918 marked a significant change in Swearingen's rhetoric and attitudes. In that year, his uncle stepped down from national office. Beginning with this report, it becomes clear that, while forceful and outspoken in his beliefs, Swearingen had made an effort to tone down his rhetoric to avoid bringing about career deaths, both his own and his uncle's. However, without an immediate family member in office to worry about making unpopular, Swearingen began elevating the level of his rhetoric in regard to his more unpopular positions—specifically, the need to significantly improve African American schools.

Why did Swearingen wait until 1918 before becoming so political in his position and his stance on African American education? There are several events that, individually or collectively, might have provided the necessary confluence of events to foster this. Was it the election of Robert Cooper as governor, a man more progressive than his predecessor Richard Manning? Was it the birth of Swearingen's son, John Jr., and a father's desire to leave a better South Carolina to his heir? Was it the death of his Uncle Benjamin Tillman, allowing Swearingen to speak unpopular opinions without negatively affecting his uncle's campaigns? Was it Swearingen's resistance to the resurgence of Blease-ism sweeping South Carolina? There is no direct evidence to support any of these opinions; any or all could be true.

Marking the fiftieth anniversary of the annual report, Swearingen provided perspective, reminding his audience that the nation had been in existence for 143 years. He used this historical perspective to lament the poor state of South Carolina's schools: while South Carolina was one of the original 13 colonies, "and has, therefore, both a star and a stripe in the flag," South Carolina ranked near the bottom of the nation in educational performance. Swearingen called for a statewide literacy effort so that, by the 1920 census, the state would "show what our public schools have accomplished during this decade," and move from the second worst state in literacy.[109]

Most interestingly, Swearingen shone an unflattering spotlight on racial issues in South Carolina's schools, arguing that "the social and economic problems of the race are questions to be studied, especially in our schools."[110] In this regard, Swearingen was not necessarily following the national trend. While schools nationwide were working toward assimilating new immigrants, Graham notes, "Little effort was made to assimilate the 10 percent of the population who were of African ancestry. For African Americans...melting pot rules applied differently."[111] Claiming that the high school was "the inspiration of the grammar grades and the foundation of college education," Swearingen noted that 5 percent of white pupils enter high school; however, "barely two-fifths of one percent of the public high school enrollment complete the high school. Such a condition ought not to exist." The roots of this problem were both above and below the high school: the overcrowded elementary schools neither adequately prepared students for high school nor provided motivation for students to attend high school, and the "practices and requirements of our colleges" also kept students from public high schools.[112]

This problem was not limited to South Carolina; nationally, many students were not completing high school, and many leading educators were becoming aware of the problem. Indeed, "between 1890 and 1920 attitudes toward the schooling of teenagers underwent a sea change." In contrast to earlier beliefs, "educators began to emphasize the importance of educational attainment or school persistence." In fact, there was an economic shift in the debate as well: "Their predecessors had bluntly contrasted the prospects of educated and ignorant workers," but during this period "educators now began to assemble evidence to demonstrate that those who persisted in school until sixteen would earn more over the long run than school leavers before that age."[113]

As part and parcel of the secondary schools' dropout problem, Swearingen also took the state to task for its lack of statewide compulsory attendance law. Explaining that the local option had been approved in 230 districts in South Carolina, Swearingen demanded the enactment of a statewide statute. Sympathetic with impoverished families, Swearingen understood it was an "unfortunate necessity" for "some poor children to work for a livelihood"; however, the only exception to the compulsory attendance law would be "defectives and delinquents." Districts without schools would have two years to levy a local tax and build enough schools to come into compliance with the law.[114]

Just as national and international events were tumultuous, citizens of the Palmetto State also had a more local crisis with which they had to deal: the influenza epidemic of 1918. Unfortunately, just as the scalawags and carpetbaggers emerged post-Reconstruction, health-based con artists came out of the woodwork. Newspapers such as *The State* published articles frequently written by local "doctors" advertising "remedies" and giving the public advice on how to fight the epidemic. Interestingly, often the advice was couched in the rhetoric used to describe the events of

World War I that were unfolding simultaneously: "Avoid crowds, coughs, and cowards, but fear neither germs nor Germans! Keep the system in good order, take plenty of exercise in the fresh air and practice cleanliness. Remember a clean mouth, clean skin, and clean bowels are a protecting armor against disease."[115]

The epidemic had a harsh effect on the state's schools. James Haynes, South Carolina state secretary of the State Board of Health, issued a directive effective October 7, 1918, that all schools (pubic and university) close until the epidemic passed. This request came at the behest of the US surgeon general.[116] Schools were not the only public sites affected; churches were closed as well. Indeed, when the blanket quarantine was lifted after three weeks, the State Board of Health chose a Sunday morning to lift it so South Carolinians could return to church as soon as possible. The public schools, colleges, and university opened the Monday after.[117]

The closing of the schools created many issues, not least among these was the issue of teacher pay: should teachers be paid for services during the quarantine? At the outset of the announcement of the quarantine, Swearingen issued a public directive saying yes. "In order to keep up the organization of the schools," he stated in a press release, "trustees should pay in full the salary of any teacher whose classroom work is suspended on account of the influenza quarantine." Swearingen cautioned that South Carolina was already experiencing a teacher shortage; refusing to pay teachers for the time lost would lead to so many teachers not returning that many schools would be unable to reopen.[118]

Swearingen's handling of the influenza epidemic wasn't the only success he experienced during these years. If 1918 was a hallmark year for the nation, with the economy surging in wartime growth and the schools taking note of the *Cardinal Principles* report, James Dreyfuss explains that 1919 proved to be "a hallmark year for Swearingen as many of his labors came to legislative fruition." Indeed, thanks to one act of legislation, the year stands as "one of the most educationally progressive years in the first half of the twentieth century." It was this year that Swearingen saw the Equalizing Act passed by the state legislature, an act that would improve white rural schools in South Carolina.[119]

The Equalizing Act offered complementary matching state funds for schools that met four criteria. The first was that the districts vote an eight-mill tax. The second was that the district maintained at least 25 students per teacher. The third was that the average attendance in the schools was 15 students per day. The fourth was that the district would meet the teacher's salary. These criteria allowed many districts to receive state funds for the first time, allowing for the expansion of buildings and the creation of high schools. In addition, the Equalizing Act provided appropriations for facets of schools that, until this year, were disregarded by the state legislature. Specific appropriations were made for student transportation, allowing districts to bring more students into their schools, and for building improvements, allowing districts to expand school libraries and high schools. Now, for the first time, rural schools were given a means to provide a solid secondary education to their students.

Another significant piece of Swearingen-backed legislation was the new High School Act of 1919. State High School Inspector William Hand detailed the four most significant features of this act. First, it would raise high school teachers' salaries through state aid by $25/month. Second, it provided an allotment to double the salary of any teacher working in a centralized high school, defined as any school serving three or more districts, none of which contain a town of 500 or more persons. Third, the act provided a bonus of $150 to schools of three teachers, and of $300 to schools of four or more full-time high school teachers. Fourth, the state would provide $3/month per pupil tuition for students out of district to enroll in a high school, but only "whenever this outside enrollment causes the number of pupils in attendance to exceed an average of 15 per full-time high school teacher."[120] African American high schools were finally beginning to meet state standards; the Beaufort Negro School applied for state aid under the provisions of the act, the first time an African American high school had applied.

The Beginnings of New Resistance

Manning knew that many of the bills forwarded by him or Swearingen would encounter significant resistance. In sending them before the state legislators, he often included information countering these arguments. However, Manning's term was rapidly drawing to an end, and both he and Swearingen were losing political capital rapidly in the face of new resistance movement. The year 1916 saw the beginnings of a political swing away from progressivism back toward a more conservative base. There was a large turnover in the statehouse: 77 out of 124 state representatives, for example, were serving for the first time, and an additional 27 had only been in office one session. Much of the momentum of Manning's social reform movement had worn out, "and the legislature in 1917 returned to its usual preoccupation with the details of education bills and two long harangues over 'prohibition' legislation." Manning narrowly won reelection, which "seems to indicate that the new legislators did not come pledged to support the Manning program. There was a growing resistance to centralization of power and a constant hammering in the General assembly against 'useless offices,' which was the burden of Blease's complaint against Manning's administration."[121]

For Swearingen, 1918 was an election year, one of the first in which he met with any real formal opposition. Two county superintendents, Black and Knight, made a run against Swearingen in the primary, and lost. The actual race for state superintendent was all but ignored by the media. Swearingen's friend Luceo Gunter described the situation thus: "The paper reports are still giving little attention to any of the candidates except those for the governorship. I think that this is all right for the man that is in."[122] Overall, in spite of most of the top positions in the state up for vote, there existed "little interest or enthusiasm" among the state's voters. In fact, less than 20,000 voters went to the polls. This light turnout was, at least in part, created by an almost unilateral ticket offered to the voters. As reported by *The State*, the Republican Party "put no ticket in the field," which proved "naturally conducive to apathy on the part of the people."[123]

During the campaign Swearingen's nemesis, Cole Blease, once again plagued Swearingen's life. Swearingen's only real opposition was in the Piedmont region. A "Blease candidate," Mr. Rector, actively campaigned against Swearingen. As noted by Swearingen supporter R. E. Hanna, "Rector was in close touch with the Blease leaders." The mill workers of the state offered serious support to candidates such as Blease and his followers. This would be a trend that, while not costing Swearingen the election of 1918, would seriously impact the race four years later. However, Hanna further explained that Rector used a campaign strategy that would also haunt Swearingen in future elections: Rector was pro-Blease in the up-state, but "denied that he was a supporter of Blease" in parts of the state opposed to the former governor.[124]

Swearingen reflected the newly political atmosphere surrounding his work in his 1918 report. In previous years, Swearingen kept politics out of these writings in keeping with his belief that his position was educational and thus apolitical; however, in 1918 Swearingen explained that during that particular election year education was one of "the paramount issues of the campaign." While out campaigning with state legislators, Swearingen noticed that in most whistle stops, "the discussions in every county and on every stump, while emphasizing the progress of recent years, pointed out with still greater emphasis the many unsupplied needs and pressing problems demanding attention." Clearly this was an attempt at reminding the state legislature how effective he had been in the previous years. The arenas in which Swearingen experienced particular success were those impacting historically marginalized populations of the Palmetto State: African Americans, women, and children born in poverty.

Politically, Swearingen understood that the less educated the electorate was, the more likely they would become, to paraphrase both Aristophanes and John Dewey, prey to the demagogue. On one level, Swearingen probably believed that by educating the people of the state, the more likely they would be to see through the bombast of Blease and his followers. Whatever the reason, Swearingen would experience continued success under Manning's successor as governor, Robert Cooper, and would be able to continue his efforts at improving the educational status of the state.

5

Robert Cooper and the Final Battle, 1919–1957

> The trouble with politics is that they never want an honest man in politics.
>
> —*John Eldred Swearingen*[1]

In 1920, South Carolina voted in a new governor; out was Richard Manning, in was Robert Cooper. Both Manning and Cooper were politically and philosophically progressive in their thinking; in keeping with the national and state political trends, both enjoyed a good personal and professional relationship with Swearingen; both made education part of their platforms and devoted much of their time in these endeavors, leading to what can be thought of as Swearingen's glory years. Of course, society as a whole managed some growth during Swearingen's tenure. Attitudes about people with disabilities, for example, were experiencing sea change. Braille print and American Sign Language were moving into the American mainstream. In April 1922, *The State* reported that there was even an all-sign-language version of Shakespeare's *The Merchant of Venice* taking place in New York City. Helen Menken, the lead actress in the production, was raised by two deaf parents; her first language was sign, not verbal. Menken told the story via "the standard symbols and signs of the deaf." She intended the "pretentious production" to be "lightly diverting and extremely interesting to the audience of deaf persons."[2] All of these factors, plus a myriad of others, helped pave the way for Swearingen to commit to improving the schools as a man with disabilities.[3]

Progressivism Continues: Cooper and the GEB

Helping Swearingen continue his work improving the schools was Robert Cooper, born in 1874 in Laurens County, a son of the upstate like

Swearingen. After graduating from Jones High School in Abbeville, he studied abroad. After earning his LLD from the Polytechnic Institute of San German, Puerto Rico, he was admitted to the South Carolina bar in 1898. First elected to the State House of Representatives in 1900, Cooper served one term to 1904, after which he became solicitor of the Eighth Judicial Circuit. He retired in 1912 to resume his private practice. He was married twice, first to Mamie Machen, who passed away in 1914, and then to Dorcas Calmes in 1917.

A supporter of Richard Manning, he rejoined public life and continued much of the progressive work of his predecessor. He expanded state public health services and launched an expansive paving program, paid for with funds raised in his reevaluation of property taxes statewide. He fought for the mill workers, limiting work days to ten hours and a work week of 55 hours. But it was to education that Cooper devoted most of his efforts: seven-month school terms, higher teacher salaries, and compulsory attendance (without local option) all were hallmarks of his terms. However, his second term was marred by an agricultural depression and postwar recession, and public support for a politically progressive agenda quickly waned. After resigning in 1922, Cooper continued his career in public service on the Federal Farm Loan Board, Democratic National Committee, and as district judge in Puerto Rico. Cooper retired in 1947 and died in 1953.

Of those who held office during Swearingen's tenure, the new governor would prove to be the most favorable toward educational issues. Cooper used his first public appearance after announcing his bid for election, a speech delivered to the South Carolina Press Association, to state that education was to be "the paramount issue of the new administration." Cooper argued that the largest deficiency in South Carolina was the problems in education. To remedy this, Cooper announced a platform of a minimum school term of seven months, more vocational education, a uniform standard of efficiency, more money spent on education, and a statewide compulsory attendance law.[4] Swearingen must have been ecstatic with this news, as he had been arguing for the majority of these issues throughout his tenure in office.

The new governor "hit the ground running" in regard to education by publishing a pamphlet formalizing the education plan, titled *An Educational Policy for the State*. Speaking for the entire State Board of Education, of which the governor is ex officio chair, Cooper explained that the board believed "that the people of South Carolina are ready as they never have been before for a forward step in educational progress." Cooper detailed a six-step program to improve South Carolina's education. First, Cooper wanted to strengthen the compulsory attendance law, making it statewide and lengthening the term to seven months for elementary schools and nine months for high schools. Second, Cooper demanded the state hire only competent, trained teachers who would be well-paid for their services.

Third, and most substantive, Cooper wanted a clear delineation between the curricula of the elementary, secondary, and postsecondary schools. Clearly influenced by the *Cardinal Principles* report, Cooper urged schools to implement not only reading, writing, and arithmetic, but also a variety of other coursework: moral living, citizenship, health, industrial/vocational studies, and "cultural studies," including foreign languages, sciences, biography, history, language, and literature. Most interestingly, Cooper declared that it was time "for the State to take a definite stand as to what policy it intends to pursue with reference to the education of the negro." Cooper demanded "a thorough going effort" in order to "do for him [African American students] and for the economic order to which we both belong."[5]

Fourth, Cooper advocated a dual initiative to provide adequate supervision to South Carolina's schools. Cooper advocated making the county superintendents professional positions "and therefore adequate requirements as to scholarship, experience, and professional training should be imposed by law"; Cooper also wanted district trustees elected by the people. The fifth plank of Cooper's educational platform was the implementation of a statewide school sales tax that would support the schools. The sixth and final component was to add these items to the state constitution as amendments.[6]

Swearingen realized that South Carolina would struggle to equalize funding for African American schools. Thus, he recognized the expediency of the funding the GEB could provide within his office and allowed a board-funded position: that of state agent for negro schools. Just as any other agent, this office had to produce an annual accounting and report, the details of which were selected and edited by Swearingen for inclusion in his annual reports to the state legislature. While this position was GEB funded, it is highly unlikely (particularly knowing Swearingen's forthrightness) that he would allow any person not of the same belief as himself to work in his office and publish in his reports for long. The salary and traveling expenses of this new office were paid entirely from funds from the GEB. Although there was much "cooperation with outside agencies" and, more locally, "the attitude of the negro has been appreciative," there were some fiscal and social difficulties in the position. Financially, the position would require money for housing and equipment that the GEB did not provide. Socially, the program would be hampered by "the prejudice that has long hampered the progress of the negro youth."[7]

J. H. Brannon, South Carolina's first state agent for negro schools, reflected what James Anderson describes as the main goal of the GEB's Southern program: "systematizing industrial education where it was practiced; and advocating systematizing industrial education where it was not installed."[8] Brannon detailed establishing African American teacher-training institutes that offered not pedagogy but "several weeks for instruction in the cooking and sewing departments." Brannon lauded the Marion Training School for offering "sewing, cooking, and all kinds of wood work" and detailed the GEB providing $500 to each of five schools "for equipping it with sewing, cooking, and carpentry departments."[9]

There were other examples of Brannon and the GEB favoring the industrial model of education for African Americans. In his first year, 11 teachers were sent to the Tuskegee Institute's summer program and 18 teachers to the summer school at the Hampton Institute.[10] The Jeanes teachers were lauded for their efforts in teaching "simple home industries" and establishing "gardening clubs and other kinds of clubs for the betterment of the school and the neighborhood." The Jeanes teachers also offered summer sessions, teaching "how to can their vegetables and fruits and how to preserve fruits and make jelly" as well as teaching "a number of sewing lessons" and "how to cook." These efforts were subsidized by an infusion of $1,773 from the GEB.[11]

Brannon stated his goals for African American education in this report. "If we are to provide a system of public schools for negroes it is absolutely necessary for us to consider and apply five essentials." Four of these essentials could be held true for any school: good facilities and modern physical equipment, a clearly established length of term,[12] well-trained teachers, and qualified supervision. However, one essential radically differed: that of establishing a program of study "adapted to meet the needs of the children." Brannon explained that academics should not be taught in African American schools, writing, "The school has no time to lose in teaching those things that will not be of service to the children." Instead, he briefly detailed a program of study for all African American schools: "It is the business of the elementary school to teach the children industrial arts, their mother tongue and an interpretation of the things about them. It is the business of the school to make good men and women and competent, intelligent workers of the children."[13]

The tensions between Swearingen and the GEB were truly manifest when, owing to medical reasons, J. H. Brannon had to retire. The esteem placed in him by the GEB was clear as officer B. L. Caldwell described Brannon to one of the board's directors: "Representing the best element of the old regime, he would have been a fine spokesman for the new view on educating the negro as a business proposition and a civic duty."[14] However high the board's opinion of Brannon was, though, this esteem was not shared with Swearingen. In correspondence regarding Brannon's replacement, the negative opinion of the board toward Swearingen was obvious. Writing to Board Director Abraham Flexner, field agent Jackson Davis explained the difficulty with which the pursuit of Brannon's replacement might meet. "You know Mr. Swearingen," Davis reminded Flexner, "and realize that some of the best men in the state do not care to come into his office as it would be difficult for them to get along smoothly with him."[15]

Beyond the efforts supported by the GEB, Swearingen also continued his outspoken efforts to support African American schools in his 1919 report. Swearingen was provided $10,000 in a discretionary fund "for the Betterment of Schools for Negroes." Admitting that this appropriation "provoked much commendation and some criticism," Swearingen predicted that the "use and its effects will probably be closely scrutinized by the lawmakers and taxpayers." However, Swearingen was quick to commend the districts in the state because all of the money from the discretionary fund was matched by local subscriptions; in some cases, "these contributions doubled, trebled, and quadrupled the sum received from the State." This aid was used in a variety of programs: longer school terms, better buildings and equipment, increasing teachers' salaries, adding teachers, and expanding industrial work.[16]

Continued Efforts with Marginalized Populations

In spite of all the challenges faced by the marginalized populations in South Carolina, Swearingen remained optimistic. He genuinely believed once the information became public knowledge, the general populace would do the right thing. With the progressive political trend in the state, he believed the time was right to begin correcting historical inequities. He optimistically, if not naively, explained that even though "five-ninths of our population is colored, the state has been absolutely free from lynchings and race riots." He added that African American soldiers returning from the war were "glad to get back to their homes and their state." Swearingen cited economic reasons for this relative peace: "The agricultural prosperity of the State has brought the colored farmers more money than ever before."[17] It wasn't just Swearingen who was optimistic. In a letter to Abraham Flexner, an unnamed correspondent describes the public lack of racial unrest, in particular in the capital city. "You will be interested to know that a Columbia afternoon paper carried a notice, signed by a joint committee of white and colored preachers, calling on people not to believe the rumors that had been circulated about race friction in Columbia."[18]

Contrary to these public statements, race relations in South Carolina were becoming strained and complex. As previously described, when African American soldiers returned home from war, they expected to be treated as equal citizens, having risked their lives in the defense of the nation. This was not to be. As a result, many African Americans began calling for equal rights. In 1919, a black convention held in Columbia called for better education and representation in school boards, while complaining about segregation and voting restrictions. In May of that year, a race riot broke out in Charleston when white sailors attacked black citizens. In the resulting furor, three African American Charlestonians were dead.[19]

In his annual reports, Swearingen was quick to turn his discussion to a more realistic view of race and education in South Carolina. In Swearingen's view there were "excellent colored schools" that had "been maintained for years" in the cities of Columbia, Florence, Sumter, Marion, Darlington, Newberry, Greenville, and Greenwood. However, Swearingen quickly included a difference: "The contrast between these schools and the negro schools in the country is most striking." Swearingen included this contrast as a means of population description. "This contrast helps to explain the exodus of negroes from the farm. Many are crowding into the towns to secure better school advantages for their children." Using these statements as a foundation, Swearingen argued for a continuance and enlargement of the discretionary apportionment. Relying on the agriculture he loved to create his metaphor, he wrote:

> If illiteracy is ever removed from South Carolina, it must be removed from nearly one-quarter of a million colored adults. It is easier and cheaper to teach the children of these illiterates than to teach their parents. The burden is heavy and the task is hard. School officials and school teachers can and will do their part, if the lawmakers, who have put their hands to the plow, do not turn back.[20]

While GEB funding greatly assisted vocational education in African American schools, African American schools using Smith-Hughes funds to teach agriculture did not grow at the same rate as white schools by 1919. This lack of growth occurred in spite of two factors: the teaching of agriculture rapidly spread through the white high schools, and the GEB tried to supplement it in African American schools. "Lack of trained teachers, school houses, and well organized colored schools have been the most striking handicaps" against African American schools utilizing Smith-Hughes dollars; in fact, only five African American schools taught agriculture under the federal act. These schools included Barnwell

Colored in Barnwell County, Bennettsville School in Marlboro County, Great Branch in Orangeburg County, Cross Anchor in Spartanburg County, and Hickory Grove in York County.[21]

While Swearingen was making efforts to improve the state of African American education, similar efforts were underway in the general population. For example, the first state chapter of the National Association for the Advancement of Colored People (NAACP) in Charleston became active in school affairs in 1920 because of inequities in hiring teachers in predominantly African American schools. Owing to a NAACP-organized effort, African American teachers replaced white teachers in predominantly African American schools in Charleston.[22]

White backlash to these events was swift and multifaceted. Congressman James Byrnes addressed African American soldiers directly, explaining that the war has "in no way changed the attitude of the white man toward the social and political equality of the negro." In addition, the South Carolina Constructive League was formed. While purportedly wanting to "cultivate harmony between the races," the league also stressed that this harmony would in no way change the fact that the state was "dominated by its white citizens." A more violent example of white reaction was the Ku Klux Klan's reemergence. In Greenville, for example, the Klan paraded openly and terrorized African American neighborhoods while also hosting community picnics for their white neighbors, times that offered politicians opportunities to address white voters; in fact, Swearingen's friend J. J. McSwain addressed one such event.[23] The beginnings of this white backlash would exert influence on Swearingen's career. Within two years, the Klan would get directly involved in the unmaking of Swearingen's career, most likely as a result of his efforts in support of African American education.

However focused his efforts were to improve the lot of African Americans in South Carolina, they were not the only marginalized culture for whom Swearingen would make efforts to improve their educational status. The year 1920 was a landmark in terms of benefiting the mill population: Swearingen, coordinating his efforts with Wil Lou Gray, began an innovative effort to combat illiteracy. Capitalizing on the national school extension movement, in August, "Lay-by" schools running for one-month sessions began operating under the slogans, "Not an illiterate in my district September 1st" and "Let South Carolina secede from illiteracy." Teachers were paid an hourly wage, encouraging longer sessions for the students, and incentive awards of 1,000-mile rail tickets were given to those teachers who taught the greatest number of adults. The curriculum would not move above a third-grade level, instead emphasizing beginning reading, writing, and math. The program seemed almost uniquely suited for mill towns. While universal adult education was stressed, it was only for whites, the majority of the mill population.[24]

Table 5.1 Illiterates over the age of ten in South Carolina[25]

Year	White illiterates	African American illiterates	Total illiterates	
			Number	Percentage
1900	54,375	283,883	338,659	35.9
1910	50,242	226,242	276,980	25.7
1920	38,743	181,422	220,667	18.1
1930	36,543	156,065	192,878	11.1

Swearingen was hopeful that the mill population would benefit most from the compulsory attendance law he worked on so diligently to see enacted. Enrollment gain was not the only area affected by the compulsory education law. In the long term, South Carolina experienced a rapid reduction in illiteracy owing to, in large part, the efforts of Wil Lou Gray in the adult schools. While credit is due to Gray, larger credit is due to Swearingen and his efforts to improve schools, raise enrollment, and increase the number of high schools (Table 5.1).

Regardless of the many gains made by Swearingen and, by extension, his agents such as Gray and Brannon, the state still had a long way to go. As his term was moving closer and closer to its conclusion, he and his staff continued to step up their efforts. Swearingen continued pointing out racial inequities in the state's educational system in his 1921 report. Discussing the length of term of schools, Swearingen disdainfully explained that agriculture tended to shorten the length of school terms, except in districts that ran a split session, winter and summer, to account for a seven-month term. Swearingen also explained that the boll weevil's destruction of crops, in particular along the coast, "tended to put children in school earlier this fall." Even that was not enough to overcome the enormous racial inequity facing the schools. He argued that white schools averaged terms of 171 days in towns and 131 days in rural areas, while African American schools averaged terms of 123 days in towns and 70 days in the country.[26]

The 1920 census figures, while improved, were nothing to be happy about. Even though there was a 7.6 percent drop in illiteracy, 6.5 percent of white citizens and 29.3 percent of African American citizens still could not read or write, ranking South Carolina as the forty-seventh of 48 states in literacy.[27] As shocking as this racial discrepancy was, surprisingly, Swearingen did not couch his discussion along racial lines, other than to briefly explain that "whites attend school better than blacks." This, however, was part of a larger comparison, in which Swearingen mentioned several contrasts such as "city children attend school better than country children" and that "education in mill centers is ahead of education in many country districts." In fact, he concluded that "illiteracy has become a rural problem blighting especially our tenant population, regardless of color."[28]

Swearingen's discussion of the illiteracy problem in South Carolina did not look at illiteracy in terms of race, the most obvious necessary discussion, or even economics. Instead, he relied upon a historical and societal argument to phrase his commentary. "South Carolina has been widely advertised as the most backward of all the states in public education," he explained. "Our critics love to point to South Carolina as the birthplace of secession and the home of ignorance. They are blind to the virtues, accomplishments, and spirit of our folk." Swearingen explained that South Carolina's schools were "the most inefficient in the Union," but added that it was a good beginning to the educational campaign. He explained that South Carolina led the nation in three aspects: highest percentage reduction in illiteracy, highest gain in school attendance over the whole population, and highest gain in school attendance for children of compulsory age. Swearingen firmly believed, and made sure he stated outright, that adult education campaigns were good, but were not the solution to South Carolina's illiteracy problem. Instead, he argued that "the public school alone is the single agency through which the removal of illiteracy may be accomplished."[29]

While racial rhetoric did not shape his discussion of the illiteracy problem in South Carolina, Swearingen continued his lament of the poor condition of African American schools in the state. While quick to cite the contributions of philanthropic agencies outside South Carolina and generosity within the state, Swearingen knew those were not nearly enough: "Every handicap clogging the development of our State rests heavily upon the negro. Illiteracy, disease, crime and poverty can not be greatly reduced, much less removed, until literacy, health and industry are given to the blacks. Verily for us, this is the white man's burden."[30]

Using what would be his final opportunity to use the bully pulpit that was his annual reports as a time to reflect on his achievements, Swearingen addressed, in his 1922 report, resistance to funding for African American education that existed in South Carolina. He described the funds contributed by the GEB and to what purpose they were used, the majority of it "given specifically for negro schools." Swearingen also explained that because of this specific purpose, "opposition to these contributions has been noisy and sinister." However, he defended these monies by reminding his audience that it "costs nothing to bring the money into the State and it helped the schools in material equipment and organization."[31]

These comments were in character for Swearingen. While admitting that his work had been "primarily for the white children," Swearingen also explained that he had tried to do what he could for African American students. "Our white folk and black folk must work together if the State is to be health [sic], educated, intelligent, God fearing, self-supporting and self-respecting." He admitted that he had been "criticized severely" for these efforts, but concluded nonetheless that there was still much work to be done: "The negroes have much to learn and much to undertake." In response to his critics, Swearingen simply wrote that he appreciated "the good will of worthy colored men and women."[32] One testament to Swearingen's efforts to assist the African American population came from John Burgess, an African American teacher:

> This letter, together with others and expressions made to you and about you will in a measure express my gratitude to you for the interest you have manifested in the education of the colored people of South Carolina in general and Marion County in particular. I want you to feel that in me you have a friend that will ever cherish your good work...To have been a teacher in South Carolina under you for fifteen years has been a pleasure that I shall never forget. I had looked forward to the day...when I will have the honor of holding a certificate to teach in the high schools of South Carolina signed by the State Superintendent of South Carolina under whom the educational movement of the state was really and truly vitalized.[33]

Accolades and Final Reform Efforts

With Governor Cooper making such a concerted effort to keep education at the forefront of the state's political scene, Swearingen was not content to rest on his laurels in these, the sunset, years of his term. Instead, Swearingen echoed national calls to improve education. Specifically, Swearingen wanted a more stable source of funding; he urged the state legislature to pass a streamlined, statewide school tax. Swearingen also wanted to combat the teacher shortage that South Carolina was on the end of; he urged the legislature to appropriate more funds for better training and higher pay to recruit and retain teachers. Finally, Swearingen wanted a more extensive system of teacher certification, separating teachers by grade level.[34] For Swearingen and his efforts, 1920 marked a significant year; it was the first year that statewide compulsory attendance was mandated. The results of compulsory attendance were both immediate and long term. Immediately, there was a huge rise in enrollment figures for both white and African American schools. Between 1910 and 1920, there was a 31 percent gain in attendance for white students and a 27 percent gain in attendance for African American students.

Another topic worthy of Swearingen's optimism was the number of teachers in South Carolina. Swearingen happily noted that for the first time South Carolina had a body of teachers to be counted in an eight-digit figure (over ten million). In order to continue this trend, though, the state needed to provide "the inducement and compensation to hold in our classrooms the best scholarship and finest personality the State produces." Swearingen recognized that teaching was a profession, even though it was a profession "even yet in process of making."[35] Teachers trained in pedagogical techniques were becoming more and more valued, and there was "a coalescence of professional opinion around a highly unified ideology of what constituted a good teacher and a good preparation program."[36] Swearingen explained with some regret that not all citizens of the state agreed with the notion of teaching as a profession: "Some antiquated folk even assert that there is no such thing as the science of teaching." However, with a note of pride, Swearingen quickly stated that overall the people of the state were beginning to recognize teachers as "more earnest and diligent" while employers who kept children out of school were "responsible for misfits."[37]

Swearingen and Cooper worked swiftly and cooperatively. With no alpha-male conflicts between them, the two managed to put forth a wide variety of bills, including the following:

- An Act to Relieve the School Districts of the State of All Disabilities and Disqualifications of State Aid Resulting from the Influenza Epidemic and Consequent Health Quarantine;
- An Act to Allow State Aid in the High Schools Upon an Average Attendance and Enrollment;
- An Act to Appropriate Funds for the Promotion and Maintenance of Vocational Education in Agricultural Subjects, Industrial Subjects, and Home Economic Subjects;
- An Act to Provide an Equalization Fund in Needy Schools, and to Repeal Certain Acts Relating to the Establishment of Libraries, the Enlargement of Libraries, and the Purchase of Supplementary Readers for Libraries;

- An Act to Establish and Maintain High Schools and to Repeal Act No. 501, Page 875 of the Acts of 1916;
- An Act to Regulate School Attendance of All Children Within Certain Ages; and
- To Establish a Bureau for the Registration and Employment of Teachers and to Make Provision Therefore.

Clearly, the majority of calls Swearingen had been urging during all his years in office were finally becoming heeded. Under Cooper, Swearingen found a sympathetic political voice to make his vision of South Carolina's schools a reality.

Swearingen began to receive accolades for his work in his lifetime. In June 1920, the USC conferred upon him the honorary degree of doctor of laws "for distinguished services to the cause of education." Swearingen accepted the award "in modesty and in humility that the honor is all the more appreciated because it is undeserved." Swearingen used the opportunity to turn the attention back to the schools. In his letter of thanks, Swearingen wrote that "the progress of recent years ought to be nothing more than the beginning of the many fundamental improvements and the too long delayed development that will some day bring to South Carolina an adequate system of education."[38] One year later, J. J. McCain of the English Department at Erskine College wrote to Swearingen, congratulating him on the honorary LLD degree given by Erskine: "I feel that the college honors itself in honoring such men as you and the other on whom at different times it has conferred this degree."[39]

The Swearingen Family

It wasn't just politically that Swearingen was enjoying good times: his personal life was causing great happiness as well. If the ultimate performance of masculinity is fatherhood, Swearingen finally achieved this steppingstone of paternalistic domesticity. Swearingen's first son, John Jr., was born on September 7, 1918, followed by a brother, George Van, on February 21, 1922. To Mary's great happiness, Mary Douglas, called "Dougie" by the family, arrived September 10, 1926. Mary describes her family in, quite literally, flowery terms: "We had our bouquet; we had our hopes for the future; we had our lifetime work laid out for us. From that time on, our whole life's vista radiated from the center of our 'bouquet'."[40]

Swearingen proved to be a devoted husband and father. Coming from a farm background, he was used to a sunrise-to-sunset schedule; as such, when the children were infants, Swearingen would tend to them in the early morning hours to allow Mary extra time to sleep in. Lessons learned at his mother's knees were not lost on the new father; during this time together, Swearingen began the instruction of his children in areas such as recitation of the alphabet, days of the week, and months of the year, as well as elementary math problems. He also followed the oral tradition: he told them stories, secular and biblical, and taught them poems and bits of literature.

In many respects, the Swearingen family was no different than any other middle-class family of the period. As did many families of the period, the Swearingens owned a car—a 1918 Buick sedan recalled with humor and warmth by both Mary and John, Jr. The family nicknamed the car after Alexander the Great's horse: "Buick-cephalous." Swearingen "kept that car until [he] found to get new tires for it you had to send to Akron to get tires, and he decided it was time to trade it in." Mary did all of the family driving until John Jr. earned his driver's license at age 12, when he took over the driving duties. When the family had to stop for gas, Swearingen (who knew the exact contents of his wallet at all times), demonstrating his masculine duty as the breadwinner of the family, would always pay the attendant himself.[41]

One such time proved an excellent example of the positive attitude Swearingen had about his disability—and how much he enjoyed playing with society's misconceptions of what the blind were capable of achieving. During one gasoline stop, as usual, Swearingen paid the attendant himself. The cost was a little less than five dollars, and Swearingen rummaged through his wallet until he came up with a five-dollar bill. As John Jr. recalled with a laugh:

> My father gave the attendant five dollars to pay for it. He brought the change back and gave it to my father. The attendant said, "Mr. Swearingen, how did you know that was a five dollar bill?" My father always had a great sense of humor, so he said to the attendant, "Haven't you ever smelled a five dollar bill? Doesn't it smell different than a one dollar, a ten dollar bill? Drive on, mother." And off we drove.[42]

Life for the family was similar to other families of the period. The children grew up and attended school. Swearingen, the talented academic with the amazing memory, would often help his children with their homework. Recalls son, John:

> I can remember when I was [in] grade school, why, he used to always insist on reviewing my homework with me to make sure I had done it all. I can remember in particular, when we got to cube root, I was having difficulty

even doing the cube root problems on paper. He would do them in his head quicker than I could do them on paper.[43]

The house on Blanding Street had a large backyard that soon became the center for the neighborhood youth. Pick-up games of football and baseball were the norm in the household; Swearingen would attend to the children and "watch" the games as any other parent in the neighborhood might. However, there was one "sport" in which Swearingen was able to surpass all the children of the neighborhood: marbles. Going back to Rotundo's notions of masculine boyhood, Swearingen put on demonstrations for the children of the neighborhood, once winning a game with a single shot.

In spite of Swearingen's familial wealth, he ensured that his children would understand the values of money and working to achieve a goal. His son describes working part-time jobs to help defray college costs. For four summers, John Jr. worked for the cog railway at Mount Washington, Vermont. Living in a bunkhouse with about 30 other college men, he would park cars, wait tables, and even schedule the trains; he earned approximately $150 each summer, about the cost of his year's tuition at university. His brother, George, went to work for the same locale until he was accepted into West Point Academy.[44] While his personal life was flourishing, however, Swearingen's professional life was soon to come to an unplanned end owing to, in no small part, the machinations of his old nemesis, Cole Blease.

Governor Swearingen?

The year 1922 was a year of great turmoil in Swearingen's life as politics encroached in this, his final year in office. Throughout his career, Swearingen was notably apolitical and honest in his office. For example, when an insurance salesman asked him to use his office to get schools to use the insurance representative's company, the salesman was told an abrupt "no." Swearingen prided himself on never taking a bribe or receiving any sort of questionable income while in office. When the salesman threatened to campaign against Swearingen, the state superintendent's reply was direct: "Neither your bribe nor your threat makes any impression on me. When I have to sell my soul for political support, I shall gladly step out."[45] Swearingen's resistance to playing politics took an unfortunately ironic turn in the most tragic but interesting event in Swearingen's life, that of his final campaign in 1922. After 14 years in office, Swearingen had earned both staunch supporters and bitter enemies. As recounted by wife Mary:

> His friends and supporters called him courageous and brave, while the opposition called him blunt and hard-headed. They both may have been right. I am not sure that the word "tact" was a part of Mr. Swearingen's vocabulary. "At best," he said, "tact is usually a method of evasion and confusion—not far removed from lying."[46]

In spite of his lifetime refusal to play politics, in 1922 Swearingen decided to run for governor. His opponents in the governor's race were Thomas G. McLeod, Andrew Bethea, and Cole Blease. The reasons for his decision to try to move up to the Executive Mansion are not entirely clear; his wife doesn't explain other than in vague terms, saying that the decision to run "was urged upon him by many friends and acquaintances...Although Mr. Swearingen had never aspired to that office, endorsements and requests came in such number that he finally decided to enter the race."[47]

Clearly many of these friends and acquaintances were the various superintendents of county districts from across the state. E. C. McCants in Anderson, for example, wrote, "There are persistent rumors hereabout that pressure is being brought to bear on you for the purpose of inducing you to run for governor...this letter is merely to say that, if you do decide to offer for the position, you may command my vote and whatever of influence I may happen to possess."[48] William Banks echoed these sentiments, writing, "Was in Anderson Tuesday, asked a number of people about gubernatorial situation. They seem to think you can win."[49] Letters of support came in from Ridge Spring, Darlington, Bennettsville, Earhardt, Rheems, Inman, Saluda, Colleton County, and Smoaks; Swearingen even heard from a former colleague in Tucson, Arizona, voicing confidence. Many, such as D. B. Lockwood, were supportive of Swearingen mainly because of his opposition to Cole Blease:

> I am confident you will succeed...I think there may be a second race, possibly between yourself and Cole Blease, for there is still a clique who will vote for Blease regardless of what he may do or say. In such case you would undoubtedly be elected, as there are enough voters, who have the welfare of our State at heart, to defeat Blease. Your record is clean; you have no political enemies, but have many well-wishers. I have no "axe to grind"; I want to see you elected, and I will, at every opportunity, do all in my power to advance your candidacy.[50]

Blease's influence in the mills was not to be underestimated. Though J. V. McElveen, superintendent of Easley Schools, confided that "the best element in Easley will vote for you," he admitted that he had "not yet had a chance to look into the situation at the mills here. The mills have always I have learned given Blease a big vote." However, McElveen suggested a campaign strategy of sorts: "When I come back to Pickens County I expect to visit every mill in the county and attempt to secure an influential worker for you in each mill."[51] Some supporters, such as B. F. Gasque of Dillon, cautioned Swearingen to lighten up a bit on his anti-Blease rhetoric, knowing the power amongst the poor, working-class whites that the hated former governor still wielded:

> I am afraid a great many people have forgotten the short comings of Ex-governor Bleeze [sic] and that he will run better than some expect. Bleeze [sic] has gained some ground in this county, but whether we will be able to un do [sic] it or not is a question...Now since you are in the field, I hope you will work through the news papers and create the impression that you are the foremost in the race, and I certainly hope you will not under any circumstances for get yourself and friends and refer to mr. Bleezes [sic] past record in any way. Let...others score Bleeze and you keep quiet and as the old saying is pick up the persimmions which they shake down."[52]

Another piece of campaign advice was to keep the election about Swearingen's perceived strengths: education. Particularly when running against an alpha-male demagogue such as Blease, cautioned B. B. Bishop, secretary of Inman Textile Mills and chairman of the mill school board of trustees, Swearingen needed to stay calm and focused:

> As I wrote you before, as I see it, the people are engaged in ONE BIG BUSINESS of education—all else is subordinate. Every man and woman who have children, whether they concede it or not are conscience [sic] of it, have but one thought, and that is the advancement and welfare of their children, and they now realize that education is the basis of their welfare and advancement...I have a fear that demagogic politicians will discuss non-vital subjects so "LOUDLY"—with so much noice [sic]—that the attention of the people will be pulled away from this very vital subject, and it will be up to you to meet them on their own ground, but, of course, keeping the subject of education uppermost.[53]

Swearingen heeded most of this advice when preparing his campaign. The platform set forth at the beginning of his campaign was as far-reaching: continuing education, lowering taxes, assisting farming, and improving infrastructure. His campaign speech began by playing to his strengths—education:

> For fourteen years the people have allowed me to work as State Superintendent of Education. The modest standards that have been introduced are under fire. The fight for the common schools is on and I prefer to make this fight in the open before all people. Despite the progress of recent years, education is still the chief need of the State. It is the only cure for ignorance as well as the best and safest remedy for poverty and crime.[54]

The remainder of his platform speech took on an ambitious set of issues. First, he tackled the age-old issue of taxes, saying, "The tax system should be adjusted and equalized so as to lighten the burden carried by the small farmer, the small home owner and the small business man... Our tax burden needs to be justly distributed, our taxes fully and impartially collected and our funds economically and constructively expended." He continued in this vein, tapping into rhetoric the common farmer could understand: "Notwithstanding business depression, the ravages of the boll weevil and the uncertainty of the outlook, our people are not ready yet to close our schools and colleges or to pull down our institutions."[55]

The state's infrastructure was next on his agenda: "Second only to education and taxation stand law enforcement, good roads and public health. The carnival of crime should be checked. The investment already made in good roads should be conserved. Further improvements should be made when funds become available." To help achieve these, he argued that "the campaign for public health should be pressed and every public health agency should be strengthened."[56]

Not all of Swearingen's friends and colleagues were in favor of his gubernatorial bid. For example, as early as April 20, S. H. Brown of Conway wrote, encouraging him to stay in the office at which he so excelled:

> I notice that the Co. Supts. have asked you to enter the race for governor... We regard you as the father of our educational system and under your judicious leadership I believe that the education conditions of our State will continue to improve not withstanding the hard times. I hope that you may decide to stay where you are.[57]

Others tried to warn him that the very people encouraging him to run were most likely in opposition to him. The same William Banks who offered his support also included a bit of a warning in his letter, writing,

"Some are unkind enough to say that the county superintendents were not altogether frank in getting you into the gubernatorial race. As I pointed out to Mr. Easterling, there are certain State officials that you must be chary of."[58]

In the vacuum left in the race for state superintendent, many candidates entered the primaries in order to fill a seat that was considered, until then, unchallengeable. From all over the state, candidates such as Jasper Hope, O. D. Seay, and Paul Moore stepped in to fill the void. The impact of women's suffrage was beginning to be felt on this campaign; a Vera Drake announced her candidacy, and there were calls for Wil Lou Gray to run. One correspondent, calling themselves "Interested," wrote to *The State*, asking that since Gray was "fitted by experience and education" (words lifted straight from Swearingen's campaign materials) and had "accomplished nothing short of miracles" in her fight against illiteracy, "what's the matter with Miss Gray?"[59]

Just as the gubernatorial and superintendent's races were locking in, for a variety of reasons, Swearingen withdrew from the race. In the Swearingen family papers, the finale of the governor's race is ascribed to an anonymous note written to Swearingen on June 16. Signed simply "Friend," the author states his or her reason for writing as, "I am your friend and constituent and hate to see you being sacrificed in any such way." The note clarifies that the only reason the county superintendents urged Swearingen to run for governor was that they viewed him as "being too autocratic, and in order to get you out of the office they had a secret meeting and decided to get you to run for Governor."[60] Considering that when first elected Swearingen referred to this group of men as his "brother superintendents," this betrayal would surely sting—and raise enough ire in a perceived affront to his manhood that Swearingen would insist on trying to return to office to prove them wrong once again.

In retrospect, the opposition from the county superintendents should not have come as any surprise to Swearingen. Four years earlier, Swearingen faced opposition in his candidacy for reelection for the first time since his original election—and the opposition, according to employee Luceo Gunter, came in part from the county superintendents. Reporting to Swearingen on a meeting of the county superintendents, Gunter wrote, "As to the political side of the meeting, only your friends ventured to discuss your race with me. But I had a chance to learn from your most intimate friends how matters stood... The only superintendents at the meeting who made no secret of their purpose to oppose you were Black and Knight."[61] Swearingen was clearly paternalistic in his dealings regarding the public schools of the state; many superintendents would have viewed this as an affront to their own masculinity and worked against him accordingly.

Swearingen's former rival alpha-dog Blease was also in part behind the 1918 opposition. As recounted by Swearingen supporter, R. E. Hanna of Cheraw:

> I was in school with Rector and knew of his successful efforts to secure an education against odds and had intended voting for him, but had heard persistent rumors that he was a Blease candidate...I told Rector of this at Chesterfield on yesterday and he evaded the issue in this way—he asserted that while in the Legislature he was a member of the Manning Caucus, but was expecting the Blease-ite vote from the Piedmont section—he denied that he was a supporter of Blease, but the manner in which he evaded the issue satisfied my mind that he is in reality a Belase-ite [sic]. When Blease was making his speech, Rector was in close touch with the Blease leaders.[62]

It wasn't just the notion of having been played a fool by the county superintendents, the high cost, or the lack of political machinery that drove Swearingen from the race. His son John explains that there is another, more insidious reason for his father's withdrawal from the race: Swearingen was told the Ku Klux Klan would oppose him in his bid.[63] While his son did not remember the Klan ever threatening the family or making an appearance at the family's home, two pieces of information appear to corroborate the story. First, the best man at Swearingen's wedding was Congressman J. J. McSwain, who, historian Walter Edgar notes, spoke frequently at Klan rallies. It easily could have been McSwain who was a participant in a story recounted by Mary Swearingen in her husband's memoir: "I remember the night before his withdrawal, a group of men visited him. He had always considered them friends. They urged that he withdraw from the governor's race because the 'cards have been stacked against you.'"[64] Just two pages earlier, Mary also recounts Klan opposition to her husband in terms of his refusal to play politics with his position. "He never considered the political effects of his decisions," she recalled. "When the KKK accused him of giving teacher certificates to Catholics, Jews, and Negroes, he said frankly, 'Of course I do. What do you expect me to do? Break the law to suit prejudice?'"[65]

If McSwain was involved, then it is safe to assume that while the Klan was serious in not supporting Swearingen, it had made no threats to him or his family. It is also safe to assume that it was McSwain who warned Swearingen of the cards being stacked against him. The Klan's bravado may have also arisen from a weakening of Swearingen's progressive type of masculinity. By 1922, the Civil War, Reconstruction, and the concomitant strife were well on their way to myth. The disabled were no longer seen as coequal to masculine war veterans, but rather as simply incomplete men.

In contrast, those who joined the Klan or otherwise worked to continue discrimination in their daily lives perceived themselves as manly and moral, enforcing traditional paternalistic order and law. Aristocrats who questioned white superiority and the need for lynching were effete and socially dangerous. Cole Blease embodied this antebellum traditional notion of Southern manhood. He unequivocally defended lynching because he wished to protect womanly virtues: "Whenever the constitution of my state steps between me and the defense of the virtue of a white woman...then I say to hell with the Constitution!" Blease so relished Klan-style violence that he often celebrated their extra-constitutional means of preserving the status quo with a death dance, a way in which publicly performed masculinity reinforced the performer's manhood while simultaneously ensuring observers of justice.[66]

Publicly, Swearingen released a statement to the press explaining the reasons for his abrupt change. The first reason detailed was "because hundreds of my friends throughout the state have urged me to do so," and the second was "my services to South Carolina would be as valuable and worthy in the state superintendent's office as in the governor's office." Admitting that his gubernatorial bid was "seeking to emphasize the importance of education," Swearingen acknowledged that his efforts were better suited in the superintendent's office, with which he was "familiar with every detail" and could continue to push his agenda, which, by then, was "understood and recognized throughout the state."[67]

Whatever the reason, Swearingen "had hardly done so [entered the governor's race] when he felt he had made a mistake." Swearingen very quickly came to realize, "There was too much money involved, there was too much unrest in the state, he had no political organization, etc." Accordingly, "without blaming any one, without saying he had been overpersuaded, he assumed full credit and full blame for his own political error" and withdrew from the gubernatorial campaign.[68] Swearingen's withdrawal conceded the resurgence of Blease's style of masculinity, but was not the end of the electoral conflict between the two men: he decided to mount a bid for reelection to the state superintendent's office that same year.

What was it that truly caused Swearingen to withdraw from the governor's race? Was it the "mystery note," explaining that he had been made a pawn by the county superintendents? This would have provided the necessary blow to his ego to drive his decision. Was it his competitor, Blease?

While he would appear to be driven all the more to oppose his former adversary, Swearingen was also politically savvy enough to realize that a campaign against Blease might be a losing battle. What happened at that meeting the night before Swearingen's decision to withdraw? Who were those friends mentioned by his wife who paid him a visit that night? What was said? Was it really a veiled Klan threat? With Swearingen's definite pro-African American education stance, this is a reasonable conclusion. However, there is no real evidence to support one version over another.

Regardless of reason, once Swearingen announced he would run for the state superintendent, friends and supporters once again rallied around their candidate; letters and public declarations of support came in piles, as opposed to the trickle that came in during the gubernatorial campaign. With the shift, as explained by supporter T. Gordon Carpenter, "Quite a few of my friends who would not support you because you first announced for gov [sic] say to me now they will support you."[69] Almost all counties in the state sent letters of support, from business leaders to county superintendents alike. It is interesting to notice that by this time, in addition to the support of many schools, Swearingen had earned the support of the very wealthy, privileged society of "aristocrats" that his Uncle Bennie had so railed against years ago. Swearingen earned endorsements from universities, including Clemson University, Erskine College, Greenwood Business College, Presbyterian College, and Winthrop University; he also earned endorsements from businesses, including Farmer's Bank of Edgefield, Home Bank of Barnwell, Port Wentworth Lumber Company, Lydia Cotton Mills, General Merchandise of Cades, Beach-Ihrie Jewelry of Rock Hill, attorney J. A. Weinburg of Manning; V. G. Arnette Merchandise of Cades, Poole & Yarborough Automobiles from Spartanburg, Standard Oil Charleston Branch, Merchants and Planters Bank of Hartsville, the People's Bank of Conway, and the Bank of Williamsburg. In addition, Swearingen received letters of support from the president of the NEA; the Houghton School in Augusta, Georgia; the State Normal School for Women in Farmville, Virginia; the Warenton Baptist Church of Warrenton, Georgia; and friends from as far abroad as Oswego, New York, and Los Angeles, California. Even disenfranchised African Americans wrote letters of support, such as J. R. Palloway and W. F. Martin of Willington, who wrote on September 4, 1922, "We take this method to let you know that we are praying for your reelection. We can't vote, but we are praying that you may be victorious."[70]

It was when Swearingen withdrew from the governor's race and reentered the state superintendent's race in earnest that the proverbial gloves came off in the campaign. In the primaries, Swearingen ran against Jasper Hope, Vera Drake, and Paul Moore; Swearingen and Hope would become the candidates for the final race. Blease and the state superintendent candidate he supported, Jasper Hope, campaigned actively against Swearingen. It was a no-win situation for Swearingen, as described by Swearingen supporter J. B. Rasor. "Blease and Hope, wherever possible, rounded the Bleasites up against you. Hope also rounded up the anti-Bleasites against you wherever possible, stating that you were a Bleasite."[71] Blease and his supporters led a multifaceted smear campaign: they spread rumors about mixed-blood parentage in Swearingen, drummed up religious controversy, and ran a fictional textbook scandal. While neither wife nor son recounted any specifics, Swearingen addressed these rumors in correspondence with friends. Responding to family friend (and wife of a political supporter) Sophie Rasor after the election, Swearingen joked, "I am glad you wrote me about the criticisms, rumors and other charges. They gave us all a laugh. I did not know myself that I had such a fine admixture of blood from all races. I do admit, however, that I am part Dutch, part French, part English, part German, part Scotch, with some ingredients that I ought not to name."[72]

During the campaign, religion was combined with politics against Swearingen: at one point, Blease announced that Swearingen was an anti-protestant Catholic in beliefs. As bluntly explained by friend Harry Calhoun, "They tried to associate you with the 'ROMANS', but the OLD ELDER CHURCH IS GOOD ENOUGH FOR YOU."[73] In his letter to Swearingen, J. B. Rasor described the religious attacks: "They [Blease and Hope] also said you were a Catholic, and the lie that surprised me the most and that I find got circulated around quite a good deal was that you were a Jew."[74] Swearingen supporters quickly released statements to the contrary. C. E. Burts, secretary of education to the General Board of the State Convention of the Baptist Denomination in South Carolina, released a statement in the *Charleston News and Courier* in September, stating that Swearingen was not a Catholic—his family were Baptists, and Swearingen was a member of the First Presbyterian Church in Columbia. His statement was also sent to the Columbia *State and Record*, Greenville *Daily Piedmont*, and Spartanburg *Herald Journal*.[75]

Blease and his supporters, predictably, took this defense with them around the rest of the state. They prominently featured Swearingen's defense of his religion—and described Swearingen's reaction as anti-Catholic rhetoric. There is some evidence that there is some truth to this accusation, however. The principal of the Bennett Public School in Charleston, H. O. Strohecker, wrote some words of caution: "You recall your conversation with Father Fleming on a train several years ago. This has never been mentioned during the campaign but the less said about church the better... 55% of the population is Catholic. I am an Episcopalian and feel the same as you do about the question."⁷⁶ Just what those feelings were, and what that question was, exactly, are still undefined.

A fabricated scandal also challenged Swearingen in the election. The state textbooks were up for readoption in 1922. Whenever a company would contact Swearingen with new texts, he would recommend they send samples to all members of the state board in an attempt to keep them all "in the loop." During Swearingen's tenure, the prices of the textbooks had been secured, via contracts, for ten years without rise. However, those old contracts expired in 1921 and the textbook companies significantly raised the prices of newly adopted books. While he was governor, Blease had no interest in textbook companies or contracts; when one company sent him sample copies of their texts, for example, Blease replied to Longman, Green & Company, "If you desire to send samples of books, that they be sent to State Superintendent of Education J.E. Swearingen, who is secretary of the State Board of Education."⁷⁷ However, with the new higher prices in 1922, many districts felt a serious financial pinch, and Swearingen's opponents blamed him for this raise. While Blease didn't care about such mundane matters while governor, as ex-governor he had rather strong sentiments on the matter—at least in terms of laying blame for the price increases at Swearingen's feet. Much opining was done during the campaign about which textbook company representatives paid what duties to Swearingen to get their new, higher prices in place. Supporter W. O. Tatum advised Swearingen "to make it clear to the people that the change in the school book adoption and the increase in the price of books was not brought about by your office," explaining that "I understand the matter and of course a great many of the people understand it, but some people, otherwise well informed, do not."⁷⁸ Textbook companies, trying to capitalize on the rumors of overcharging, took to advertising that appealed to the public's notions (Figure 5.1).⁷⁹

Making the situation worse were public declarations by former book agents to the state. The men who Swearingen had upset by refusing to "play ball"—accept bribes, perform favors, or anything else—came out of the woodwork, sensing revenge. "I saw in the State of yesterday that you were attacked by a book agt," wrote one anonymous friend. "No we do not need a book agt. for Supt ed [sic]of the State...I am out of politics now, and I am late in the evening, but I see a candidate for a better world than this, but it touched me deeply to see one of my best friends thus attacked."⁸⁰

The fallout from this issue was threefold. First, in a rare bit of professional correspondence that made its way into the Swearingen papers, there is evidence that the scandal caused the office of state superintendent to be audited. The State Bank Examiner's office made a formal request

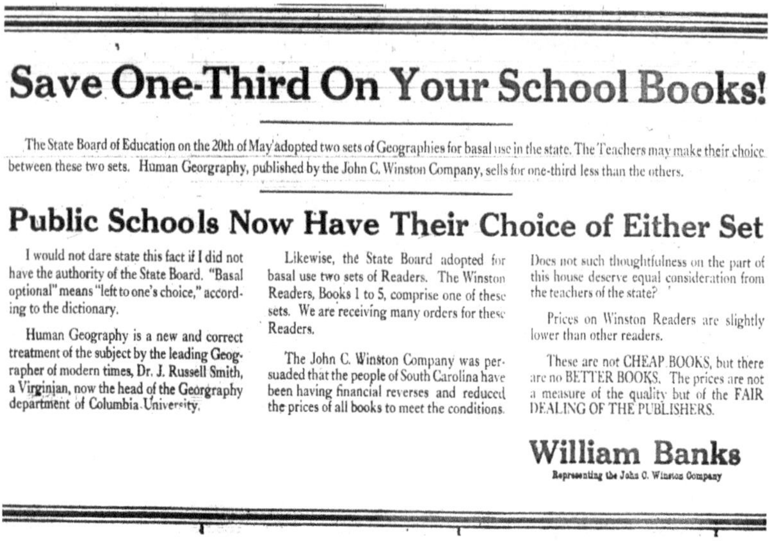

> # Save One-Third On Your School Books!
>
> The State Board of Education on the 20th of May adopted two sets of Geographies for basal use in the state. The Teachers may make their choice between these two sets. Human Geography, published by the John C. Winston Company, sells for one-third less than the others.
>
> ## Public Schools Now Have Their Choice of Either Set
>
> I would not dare state this fact if I did not have the authority of the State Board. "Basal optional" means "left to one's choice," according to the dictionary.
>
> Human Geography is a new and correct treatment of the subject by the leading Geographer of modern times, Dr. J. Russell Smith, a Virginian, now at the head of the Geography department of Columbia University.
>
> Likewise, the State Board adopted for basal use two sets of Readers. The Winston Readers, Books 1 to 5, comprise one of these sets. We are receiving many orders for these Readers.
>
> The John C. Winston Company was persuaded that the people of South Carolina have been having financial reverses and reduced the prices of all books to meet the conditions.
>
> Does not such thoughtfulness on the part of this house deserve equal consideration from the teachers of the state?
>
> Prices on Winston Readers are slightly lower than other readers.
>
> These are not CHEAP BOOKS, but there are no BETTER BOOKS. The prices are not a measure of the quality but of the FAIR DEALING OF THE PUBLISHERS.
>
> ### William Banks
> Representing the John C. Winston Company

Figure 5.1 Textbook advertisement, *The State*

that the financials of the State Superintendent of Education's rolls be audited. The result of the audit was that nothing was noted as to being in arrears—however, the damage had been done.[81] Second, the B. F. Johnson Company filed a temporary restraining order against the entire State Board of Education, forbidding them from ordering any books from Johnson's competitor D. C. Heath Company, "on grounds of alleged irregularity in the handling of the bids for furnishing school books."[82] Third, and most compelling, come Election Day, since the public were led to believe Swearingen was to blame for an increase in textbook costs, legal or otherwise, they did not vote for him.

In addition to the various smears and scandals of the campaign, Blease carried the mill workers' vote as well in spite of Swearingen's campaign tactics of spreading campaign flyers amongst mill owners and workers alike. As explained by Bryant Simon, mill worker politics was a blend of race and gender: male mill workers "interpreted Blease's rhetoric and actions as a defense of their manhood against the forces of industrialization and the reform agenda of the progressives." To these mill workers, the state's political system was broken into two parties: Bleasites and anti-Bleasites. "Casting their vote for Cole Blease," explains Simon, "textile workers pressed their claims of patriarchal privilege and equality with all white men and asserted in the strongest language available to them that the economic and socially mighty did not control everything." Tapping into anti-industrial and antireform sentiment, Blease offered mill workers a defense of their manhood, patriarchal privilege, and white equality.[83]

Going into Election Day, the situation was muddled for Swearingen. One opponent, Hope, was able to indirectly ride Blease's coattails. The other candidate, Drake, earned the votes of the newly enfranchised women of the state. George Cofield, from the Walterboro American Legion, described what was happening to Swearingen:

> As you know this county went for Blease by about 25 votes. An attempt is being made to put certain candidates' names on all Blease tickets. Hope's name being used in that way with our without Hope's knowledge...The Club women of this place endorsed Mrs. Drake in the papers. Now, let me give you the vote of our county, and when I tell you that I was put into office by the Ladies Civic League, you can readily see I ought to be able to help you with the women, and get some of Mrs. Drake's vote. Swearingen, 1055—Drake, 887—Hope, 310—others, 306, total—2558.[84]

Ultimately, Swearingen lost the election. All told, by midnight election night, Swearingen had collected 73,528 votes to Hope's 104,543. Describing the election loss to Sophie Rasor, Swearingen explained that "the cotton mill vote went against me about three to one. This was the strongest element in the opposition, so far as any one class of schools or voters was concerned."[85] His reply to Rasor about his defeat revealed much about his character and his beliefs. When discussing his defeat, Swearingen was apolitical, but extremely democratic: "The people have ordered a change in the State Superintendent's office and I have no regrets, repinings, criminations or recriminations in bowing to their wishes." He continued on in almost gracious terms: "A fellow in public life must quit as well as begin. It is as natural to die politically and otherwise as it is to be born."[86]

Letters of condolence poured in from all over. New York City attorney Pinckney Estes Glantzberg wrote, "I don't know anything that has made me so impatient with my own South Carolina folk than the election of your successor. I met him at Winthrop College and to think he is to take your place fills me with a quiet disgust. However, you have the consolation of knowing that you're the only man who has ever done anything worth while for the schools of South Carolina."[87] Winthrop College's board of trustees adopted the following resolution at their November 21, 1922, meeting:

> Resolved, by the members of the Board now in session: First, that we appreciate his interest in and devotion to the cause of women's education

in the State as represented in Winthrop College. Second, that we extend to him our best wishes for his success and happiness in whatever business he shall engage when he retires from the office now held by him, the duties of which he has discharged efficiently and with great benefit to the State.[88]

When Swearingen was voted out of office, *The State* newspaper ran an article under the headline, "Fought for Schools for Fourteen Years: Swearingen Quits Post With Fine Record of Achievement."[89] The newsletter *South Carolina Education* covered the story under the headline, "Mr. Swearingen's Administration." The newsletter recognized Swearingen for preparing South Carolina to make educational progress. "Much has been accomplished, but there is still work to do," wrote Furman Professor B. J. Wells in the article. "The soil has been well prepared, and good seed have been sown, and are now springing up, bringing forth an improved harvest."[90]

In addition to the published praise, Swearingen received many letters offering condolences and praise. One of the most representative came from J. A. Stoddard, professor of secondary education at the USC, who wrote, "The people of South Carolina will see the retiring of an official whose wholehearted, vigorous, efficient, and constructive service has probably never been equaled, certainly never surpassed, by that of any other public servant…The results of your able service will not be altogether measurable in less than a whole generation."[91] Even the GEB, an organization with which Swearingen exchanged much heated correspondence, was surprised by the election results and supportive of Swearingen after his loss. When notified of the election results, Wallace Buttrick responded with praise for Swearingen, writing, "Your work has been of the highest character, and you have won for yourself a place in the respect of all who are interested in educational progress."[92]

Swearingen handled the loss and transition with his usual intelligence, bluntness, and humor. Writing to Georgia friend W. A. Chapman, Swearingen commented, "On September 12th I was submerged under an avalanche of thirty thousand adverse votes. I have dug out, however, and am able to take nourishment as usual."[93] The only bitterness voiced by Swearingen about the entire disastrous 1922 campaign was about his opponent's platform, not his opponent. In correspondence, he stated that it would be impossible to achieve them all:

> If my successor can carry out all his campaign promises, he will certainly do more than I have been able to accomplish. He said he was going to give cheaper books, better books, fewer books, higher salaries to teachers, longer terms, more high schools, lower taxes, and more economical service.

He promises to secure larger appropriations from the Legislature and more school taxes from the voters, better standardization, more efficient teachers, closer and more professional supervision, to make more personal visits and to strengthen all our institutions of higher learning. The task he has outlined for himself is varied and difficult. I would not like to describe these promises because the word I should have to use would not look well in print.[94]

Mary's memoirs recall little bitterness from either her or her husband about politics generally. "Although he was not a politician as the term is usually interpreted, he firmly believed in the people choosing their leaders and maintained that a leader should be retired when the people so desired. While he admitted that a person could be sacrificed by misunderstanding or by a wave of propaganda, he still insisted that election by the people was the safest plan in the long run."[95]

Swearingen was a man of honor and insisted on leaving a "clean house" for Hope to move into—in a sense, proving himself a more honorable gentleman than Blease was. "In turning over the office to my successor, I wish him a progressive administration, although he will find more problems and more work than he now expects...I mean to turn over the office, however, without a single defect, a single crack in the fence, or a single error." However, his intentions were not entirely noble, as he explained his primary purpose was so that nothing in the transition might "be used against me by way of criticism or further misrepresentation."[96] Swearingen wanted to make sure that this final duty was completed to the best of his ability—that there could be no possibility of anyone accusing him of shirking duty in the face of his electoral loss or of using his disability against him.

Retirement and Legacy

Swearingen left office on January 16, 1923, at noon. Swearingen's legacy began with his work as a teacher. Upon his passing, a former student wrote to Swearingen's widow, expressing just how influential he was: the former student became a teacher of students with disabilities herself, working in St. Augustine, Florida:

> Mr. Swearingen, I think, did more for me during my young life than any other person who influenced me at all. But for his having taught nine years at Cedar Spring, the lives of scores of us would have been so different, so empty, compared to what we all have enjoyed and been able to do after going out from under his wonderful influence...a host of us, regarded

your husband as the greatest mind, the greatest soul with whom God had brought us in touch for good. Eight years of happy tutorage under him enabled me, with May, to give the young folk at our Florida school something slightly akin to his work at Cedar Spring. For thirty-one years we carried on at St. Augustine after our Carolina heritage, and scores too have gone out from the Florida school with the Swearingen blessing upon them. The great influence I hope will never cease![97]

With his background as a teacher, it is little wonder Swearingen was such an outspoken advocate for teachers. One battle, not the least, was over teacher salaries, both African American and white. "I have tried to secure a living wage for teachers," he wrote to friend Sophie Rasor soon after losing the 1922 election. "In my opinion, a competent college graduate is still worth about $100.00 a month, in spite of assertions to the contrary. Many other states are paying even higher salaries to their teachers." Swearingen encouraged further education, though in his characteristically blunt fashion: "For the incompetent folk I have sought to give them an opportunity only to go to school themselves."[98]

When Swearingen began his position, the office of the State Superintendent of Education was housed in the attic of the State House, with a staff of three. By the end of Swearingen's tenure, the office would be moved to an entire floor in a nearby Columbia skyscraper, and the office personnel would be expanded to include several supervisory positions and their respective staff. When Swearingen assumed his official duties, the state superintendent had been a passive position, created by the state constitution but never really showing what power the position could entail. By the end of Swearingen's term, he would redefine the role of the state superintendent into a position that wielded influence over the state legislature and power within the governor's office.

Swearingen also faced the challenge of taking a state that had never truly experienced the common school movement and goad it toward a statewide school system—with the focus being on the secondary schools. During his tenure, the number of high schools grew from a reported 95 public and private institutes to 178 public high schools, of which 14 were Negro.[99] The true measure of the growth of the high school under Swearingen, however, is in the number of schools whose graduates received state diplomas. In the 1908–1909 school year, only eight high schools had a total of 74 students qualify for state diploma. By Swearingen's final year in office, 1921–1922, that number had risen to 94 schools, with 1,606 state graduates.[100] Swearingen was the man who transformed the notion of the high school as an extension of the elementary to a separate, comprehensive whole. He wrote in his 1922 report that "school people everywhere should look to the time when centralized high schools can be so located throughout the country that all country children shall have the opportunity of reaching such schools."[101]

In fact, in the first half of the twentieth century no superintendent had a greater impact on the public schools of the state. His primary area of impact was in funding; Swearingen increased state funding more in pure dollars than any superintendent who held office between 1907 and 1940. When he took office, state spending on white students was $1,148,474, and on black students was $267,250. In 1923, the year after he left office, those amounts had increased to $11,561,850 for whites and $1,400,151 for blacks—net increases of $10,413,376 and $1,132,901 respectively. To put these numbers in perspective, over the next ten years the state increased funding only by $2,855,599 for whites and by $369,717 for blacks. Clearly, specifically for African American students, Swearingen was the staunchest advocate of his time.[102]

While the end of Swearingen's political career was not exclusively by choice, the fact that for the most part he remained distant from politics, was. Swearingen refused offers from friends and supporters to run for federal office. One nonpolitical postretirement option came courtesy of his friend J. J. McSwain, who encouraged Swearingen to take up an academic position. "Incidentally, I want to see you employed there in order that the State may have the benefit of your experience and ability in education," wrote McSwain. "I hope it will be the outgrowth of an enlargement of the pedagogical work of the university."[103] As early as September 1922, McSwain began encouraging Swearingen to apply for an academic position at Furman: "We would all be so happy to have you and Mary in Greenville—The work would be easy (compared with what you have always done) and you should conserve your strength some now." Knowing Swearingen's love of the South Carolina College, though, McSwain kept this option open: "Of course, Carolina may need your services later, but Greenville is a fine place to live—a fine place to raise John and George and to become their future home."[104]

Swearingen was unsure, but it was religious reasons, not professional, that raised doubt in his mind: "In my opinion, Furman University will need a Baptist at the head of its educational department. This professor will have to do much field work in Sunday Schools, Churches and Associations as well as other denominational assemblies. I would greatly enjoy these activities, but I doubt whether a Presbyterian of my type would fit into the picture."[105] After the religious attacks on Swearingen in the 1922 campaign, it is no wonder he wanted to avoid a position in a religious institution.

After a mutual friend, B. J. Wells, was named to the position, Swearingen later wrote to McSwain, confirming that this religious dissention was not his being skittish or making empty excuses for his not pursuing the Furman job: "The University and the State are gainers by this appointment. Being a Baptist, Ben will exactly meet all the requirements, both of the classroom and of the Church."[106] Swearingen also wrote to Wells, congratulating him on the position: "I note with pleasure that you are to return to South Carolina to fill a chair in Furman. We are the gainers by your decision. I congratulate Furman upon securing your services, and I know you are glad to come back to your native heath."[107]

Neither politics nor university life seemed a fit for Swearingen, and, for a short while, he appeared adrift. He even wrote to a former correspondence sparring partner from the GEB, Wallace Buttrick, asking about opportunities: "I prefer to stay in the educational field if circumstances allow. My preparation and experience lie in education. If you can use me in any way or place me I shall greatly appreciate your consideration." Given the generally negative dealings between the two men it is of little surprise that Buttrick's response, while positive, was less than overwhelming:

> You may be sure that we of this office would do anything in our power to secure for you a good position in the educational field. As I have said to you in another letter, your work has been of the highest character, and you have won for yourself a place in the respect of all who are interested in educational progress. I do not now know of any position, but I shall bear it in mind and will talk with my associates about it from time to time.[108]

When Swearingen retired from politics, he chose to live in Columbia but maintained the family farm in Edgefield. He raised his three children in Columbia and vacationed on the family farm. In spite of the years between living on the farm and his return with his own children, Swearingen never lost his uncanny memory of the estate. As recalled by his son:

> There was one time we were out on the farm, and it was mulberry time. We were telling my father that we had found the mulberry trees. "When I was growing up, there used to be a big mulberry tree down here, not too far from the house. I'll take you down and show you where it is." And so we started walking down the road, "Tell me where we are, tell me where we are, tell me where we are." We got down there, I guess it must have been a mile from the house, and he says, "The tree used to be right in there." And he pointed in the direction and by God, there was the biggest damn

mulberry tree I ever saw in my life! And he could direct us right exactly to it without any failure or mishap in getting there. But he just had that ability.[109]

Swearingen's brother, George, tended to both his own and the family farms in Edgefield until his death in 1932. Swearingen's son recalls the family arrangement as: "My Uncle George, my father's younger brother, ran his own property and my father's property, and his twin sister's, and I think there were a couple of cousins'. All together, you had about five thousand acres."[110] George was renowned for the most efficient and productive cotton farm in South Carolina, even winning the title "Cotton King" (Figure 5.2). Under the supervision of his brother, the family farm produced cotton for profit until the Great Depression, when, in response to the declining textile market, Swearingen shifted from selling cotton to selling lumber for profit.

In addition to managing the family farms, Swearingen also spent considerable time serving as a role model for other people with disabilities. As during his teaching career at Cedar Springs, his message was always

Figure 5.2 George Swearingen, South Carolina's "Cotton King"

one of empowerment, of overcoming societal definitions of ability. As recalled by his son John:

> He used to go around to see people who really had serious handicaps...when I used to be able to, was able to drive him around, I used to drive him around to see people like this. And his...I can remember going to the Confederate Home to see people who'd had accidents of one kind or another. His message always was, "Don't let that handicap, don't just sit in a rocking chair waiting for somebody to take care of you. You've got to do something to justify your own existence, or work with whatever you have in the best way you know how to do it."[111]

Swearingen didn't limit his postretirement philanthropy to time. From the time of his teaching career, Swearingen was devoted to giving to those less fortunate. While teaching at Cedar Springs, for example, Swearingen bought new graduation suits for several of his blind students. Even at the height of the Great Depression, Swearingen never lost his generosity of spirit or pocketbook. Nor did he lose his love of toying with public perception of his ability, even when the public in question was begging from him. One such example was recounted by John Jr.:

> At one time, during the Depression days, Mother and Dad were walking down Main Street in Columbia. In those days, Columbia was about 35,000 people. Anyway, there were always a lot of people on the road looking for work or looking for food or trying to get south to spend the winter and that kind of thing. My father never refused giving them something to eat, and it seemed like almost every week we'd have several people come by asking for something, some food. My father would always give them something of whatever we were eating. But anyway, they were walking down Main Street that day, and a beggar on the streets accosted them and said, "Mister, would you please give me a nickel for a cup of coffee?" My father reached in his pocket looking for a coin. About the time he found it, the man looked up on him and says, "Oh, I'm sorry mister, I didn't realize you was afflicted." My father said, "Here, take your money, I'm not afflicted, I just can't see."[112]

Mary echoes Swearingen's generosity in her memoir. When the family farm would have a good crop, Swearingen would donate the extra profits to a local orphanage "or some other cause he wanted to help." For much of their married life, the man who first found Swearingen after his accident—a woodcutter named Aus—would make appearances at the Swearingen home. "His visits usually occurred when his rent was overdue or he needed shoes or clothes," recounts Mary. "He never went away without receiving what he came for."[113]

However happy his family life, the combined love of service to his state and desire for intellectual challenge wouldn't let Swearingen rest easily for long. Less than a decade after his initial retirement, Swearingen again heard the clarion call of public office. Putting aside the "calumnity and slander" of his last political campaign, Swearingen once again turned his sightless eyes to public office and in 1930 attempted another campaign for state superintendent. During the campaign, Swearingen explained that the state superintendent's office of 1929 ran the public schools with a program "almost identical with" the program of Swearingen's administration. He railed against Jasper Hope, his successor, explaining that "no new endeavor or new experiment has been formulated or undertaken. No new activity has been introduced. No special line of growth has been pointed out except in cost and expenditure." This was the principal weakness of the successive administration, according to Swearingen: even though they had not made any improvements or additions, their administration cost more than $5 million more than his budget.[114]

Swearingen attacked his successor again and again, citing inconsistencies with the budget and spending as well as Hope's inability to fulfill campaign promises made eight years previously. For example, Hope promised to reduce the costs of textbooks, blaming Swearingen for the price increases as part of the 1922 attacks. However, as of 1930, the price of textbooks had risen significantly. Swearingen mirrored the campaigns of his uncle Ben Tillman, sounding almost populist as he appealed to the taxpayers: "The promise made to the people has not been redeemed by the present administration and the public schools are not a proper place for juggling and manipulation."[115]

Seven years may not sound very long in a person's life, but it is an eternity in political life. The mill hands still smarted over perceived past injustices explained to them by Blease and his ilk; there were newer faces on the scene for the more privileged classes. The sweeping waves of political progressivism that had so invaded the state in the beginning of the century had crashed on the rocks of the beginnings of the Great Depression; it was low tide for reformers. In spite of Swearingen's powerful platform and literature, the campaign did not pass the primary, and Swearingen again returned to private life. However, it wouldn't take him long before he found another cause, another means to serve his family and beloved state. After his failed campaign, Swearingen began a new campaign: to benefit his dead uncle.

Tillman was extremely helpful to Swearingen during his career. In the beginning, Tillman would offer generalized words of advice on politics, and surely provided some guidance to his nephew about campaigning in the state. While in office Tillman provided tips about pending educational legislation that allowed Swearingen to prepare South Carolina to enact them. While it was a mutually beneficial relationship, Swearingen was personally and professionally indebted to his uncle. Swearingen's respect for his uncle even went so far that Swearingen wanted every child in South Carolina to read his uncle's words. In 1917, his office was putting together a reader on Southern literature for use in South Carolina high schools and, "In recognition of your service to South Carolina and especially of your service to education, I hope to include in the 5th reader an extract of 1,000 words which ought to be interesting to 12-year old boys and girls." Swearingen suggested as examples, "Your speech on the occasion of the laying of the cornerstone at Winthrop College is usable material. Perhaps you would prefer an extract from some other subject or document such as your eulogy on Senator Earle, your first inaugural message to the Legislature or your 'red shirt' speech in Anderson."[116] The last example is notable, of course, because in spite of all the efforts Swearingen made to help African Americans in the state, he would still include one of the more racist speeches—the "Red Shirt speech" of his uncle's history.

Post retirement, Swearingen mainly stayed away from the public eye, only speaking at the occasional gathering such as the Edgefield County Historical Society's Second Annual Meeting, on Friday, December 27, 1940, during which he delivered the "Address on Col. Leroy Hammond." While Swearingen left many memories of himself in the form of pieces of legislation he actively campaigned for, he would leave a permanent monument at the State House; it was not for himself, but to his uncle, Ben Tillman. Swearingen began campaigning for funds to build a statue for his uncle in 1937. By 1939, Swearingen was notified by the tax commissioner that enough money had been generated to build the statue.[117] Dedicated on May 1, 1940, at 11 a.m. the memorial contains a plaque briefly explaining Tillman's educational legacy. The inscription on the monument reflects Swearingen's sense of duty to the state above personal gain: "This monument erected / by the Legislature / the Democratic Party / and / private citizens of / South Carolina."

While Tillman received both a granite monument in the cemetery and a metal statue on the statehouse grounds as legacy, Swearingen and his family would have a lasting legacy not only to South Carolina but to the entire nation. While son George was fulfilling his father's dream of being a cadet at West Point,[118] Swearingen was too ill to come visit. George wrote to his father in 1944, hoping that he was feeling better, but cautioning his father to remain in bed "until you regain your strength."[119] While George was attending West Point, he worked in a variety of roles at the institute including that as lead defense council on a Moot Court Martial (Figure 5.3). Achieving the rank of captain, he eventually moved

Figure 5.3 George Van Swearingen, West Point Graduation

into aviation, later becoming a pilot. Sadly, he would be killed with his entire crew during a training mission near Savannah, Georgia, in 1949.

Swearingen's daughter Mary, called "Doug" by the family, would become a scholar as well as a proud mother herself. A 1945 Phi Beta Kappa graduate of the USC, Mary also earned her master's degree from the institution. Writing a letter of recommendation was Havilah Babcock, then chair of the USC English Department, who described Mary as beautiful, intelligent, and possessed of a radiant personality. She was a well-balanced student, involved in Phi Beta Kappa, a champion swimmer, a diligent student, a dutiful assistant, and a fine dancer. Babcock mentioned that Mary taught Freshman English to war veterans through the university as well. Concluding his letter, Babcock wrote that Mary was "of an excellent family. No family in the State is more respected. Aw heck, she is just a perfect prospect."[120] Mary would go on to study at the University of North Carolina—Chapel Hill and McGill University in Montreal, Quebec, Canada, before becoming a teacher at both USC and Dreher High School (Figure 5.4). Mary wed John Gladden Ehrlich, Jr. in 1948 and had four children: Mary Van, John Gladden, Bruce Swearingen, and Ann Louise. Mary Douglas passed away in 1992.

Figure 5.4 Mary Douglas Swearingen

Swearingen's eldest son, John Jr., would become the most well-known of the three children. From 1934 to 1938, John Jr. attended the USC. Inducted into Phi Beta Kappa in 1938, he graduated magna cum laude with a bachelor's degree of science in chemical engineering. He attended the Carnegie Institution of Technology in Pittsburgh (now Carnegie-Mellon University) from 1938 to 1939, earning a master's degree in chemical engineering and the title Industrial Fellow. He would later be honored with 15 honorary college degrees over his lifetime, including from the USC and Carnegie-Mellon (Figure 5.5).

John Jr. accepted a position with Standard Oil's (now BP-Amoco) research department at Whiting, Indiana, in 1938. Under his work there, he was the coholder of the patent on the catalytic converter. In 1951 he was transferred to Standard Oil's Oklahoma City Branch in Tulsa, Oklahoma, before being promoted to director in 1954, then elected president in 1958. In 1960 he was named president and chief executive officer. John Jr. became company chairman in 1965, a position he filled until he retired on his sixty-fifth birthday in 1983.[121]

During his tenure he became an outspoken opponent of government interference in private industry, streamlined Standard's operations,

Figure 5.5 John E. Swearingen, Jr.

and expanded into 40 nations, eventually becoming decorated by the governments of Egypt, Italy, and Iran. He also directed the exploration of nontraditional fuel resources such as natural gas, coal, and chemicals. As part of the duties of these positions, John Jr. appeared on many television programs to oppose President Carter's plans for solving the fuel crisis, eventually becoming recognized as the national face of "Mr. Big Oil."

In 1984, John Jr., at the request of the Federal Deposit Insurance Corporation, became the chairman of the board of the Continental Bank of Chicago (now Continental Illinois Corporation), which was experiencing financial difficulties. He held this position until 1987, then retired as a board member in 1989. In addition to these positions, John Jr. has held a variety of professional memberships, educational trusteeships, and corporate board positions. In 1965 he was awarded an honorary law degree from the USC, which, in 1987, dedicated its new College of Engineering facility to him—the John E. Swearingen Engineering Center. John, Jr. was inducted into the South Carolina Business Hall of Fame in 1988 and into the National Business Hall of Fame.[122] John Jr. married twice: he divorced his first wife, Rolly George Osterberger, in 1969. Later that year, he married Bonnie Bolding, who would remain with him until his death in September 2007. He had three children: Marcia Lynn, Sarah Katherine, and Linda Sue.

Swearingen's wife, Mary, continued a career in education both after her husband's retirement and after his death. Having worked as a teacher before Swearingen's tenure in office, Mary kept one foot in education by teaching Sunday school at the First Presbyterian Church of Columbia. With the outbreak of World War II, Mary volunteered with the United Service Organizations. Upon Swearingen's retirement Mary attempted to return to the classroom. Ironically, the new teacher certification standards her husband helped to implement prevented her from renewing her certificate; as her son John described, she didn't have enough education classes to resume work as an educator.[123]

However, lack of certification would not keep Mary from the schools for long. Earning a master's degree in social work, Mary worked for the Columbia city schools in a variety of roles, such as chaperone of the swimming team, sponsor of the literature club, and president of the Taylor School Parent Teacher Association. Mary worked as a visiting teacher for Columbia City Schools until 1957. During that time, she coordinated efforts with the Juvenile Court system, the NEA's national and state offices, the National Visiting Teachers Association, and the National Social Workers Organization. She also took time to address a variety of conferences, serving as a panel leader at a discussion of South Carolina school attendance at the 1940 National League to Promote School Attendance's 30th Annual

Figure 5.6 Mary Hough Swearingen, Mother of the Year

Conference held in Philadelphia. She was a member of the Daughters of the American Revolution, United Daughters of the Confederacy, Social Survey Club, and League of Women Voters; she served on the boards of the Young Women's Christian Association and Camp Committees. For all of her outstanding personal and professional contributions, Mary was named South Carolina Mother of the Year in 1962[124] (Figure 5.6). She passed away on July 28, 1978.

The Final Retirement

Plagued by headaches throughout his career as a result of the birdshot left in his head and face from the accident, Swearingen's health began to deteriorate in his later years. As early as the 1940s, his headaches began to become insufferable. One bout with illness, for example, was so severe that Swearingen had to miss George's West Point graduation. Writing home one month before the ceremony, though, George was jokingly reassuring to his father: "Dad I hope you are beginning to heal up now. I am sorry I can't be there to rub that 'rink dink' or at least scratch your head for you. I know you are plenty tired of lying in bed but for goodness sake stay there until you regain your strength."[125] Swearingen honored his son's (and, of course, his doctor's) wishes and stayed home; Mary was issued a base pass on June 3, 1944, to attend George's graduation.

Swearingen's other senses also began to fail him, with the onset of old age. First, his hearing began to suffer; son John had Swearingen fit with a hearing aid, which Swearingen wore when more than one person was visiting him. Eventually, Braille books became too heavy for him to hold. Also, his sense of touch began to deteriorate; he commented often to his wife that Braille magazines were not printed as clearly as they used to be. Soon, he stopped his usual habits; he no longer sat on the porch, listened to the radio, or had anyone read the daily newspaper to him. After a yearlong bout of invalidism, Swearingen passed away in the early morning of September 27, 1957, at the age of 82.

His wife recalls that "those of us who watched with him knew that his gallant journey of seventy years in the dark had ended. He had reached his goal in triumph."[126] Knowing the personal highs and lows Swearingen faced throughout his life garners respect for him and humanizes him to some extent. However great the legacies of his personal life— successful operation of multiple farms, Tillman's monument, and his family's extraordinary achievements—none come close to matching the legacy of him as a leader of education in South Carolina.

6

Conclusion: Not the Windows but the Occupant Looking Through

> Your monument is the lives of the boys and girls of South Carolina that you touched through your administration and made brighter and better for your having served them.
>
> —J. H. Thornwell, 1923[1]

For a man who was adventitiously blind, Swearingen had a clear vision for what he wanted his home state to be and the role that the public schools could play in this. Swearingen understood that the state as a whole could not improve until conditions for all its citizens improved. As recounted by his wife, Mary:

> The layman of today, or even the students of educational progress in our state, can scarcely believe the school system of South Carolina was as inadequate as it was when Mr. Swearingen became State Superintendent of Education fifty years ago...I am today amazed at the status of things as I look back over his reports and recommendations during the first and second decade of the new century. But I must admit that it gives me a feeling of infinite pride to see how he grappled with the situation, determined to correct abuses, to extend opportunities, and to create a worthwhile public school program.[2]

Swearingen wanted to create a world that became blind to differences in race, class, gender, and ability, and knew that the public schools were one battleground from which this condition could arise. Unfortunately, the United States has not become what he envisioned. We do not live in a post-racial United States. Discrimination still exists. People who were marginalized then—working class, people with disabilities, those racialized—remain marginalized today. So why is Swearingen's life still worthy of study? There are two reasons: first, his legacy on the schools of South Carolina; second, the uncanny parallels between the politics of his time, the first two decades of the twentieth century, and what the United States is seeing in our time, the first two decades of the twenty-first century.

Legacy in the State

It didn't take Swearingen long to make a tremendous impact on the schools. In 1911, a scant few years after taking office, Swearingen issued a report analyzing the previous decade's worth of progress in the public schools of South Carolina. Titled "A Decade of Public School Programs in South Carolina," it serves as a thorough review of the first years of Swearingen's tenure combined with the years leading up to his taking office. In it, Swearingen acknowledged that reviewing school progress from year to year, as done in the annual reports, had its uses but that "a comparison covering ten years reveals some significant facts barely recognized by school officers themselves" and that, when viewed in this context, "the progress of the last 10 years furnishes the finest index to the life and spirit of our people." Numerically, in spite of the move toward school consolidation that reduced the total number of schools in the state, the number of districts and teachers grew; districts, "from 1592 to 1901," which was evidence of "a healthy development of community interest in school affairs, and bringing the people into close contact with school administration." The teaching force in the state grew from 3,378 to 4,255; this gain of almost 26 percent was evidence to Swearingen of "consolidation, better buildings, transportation, local taxation and more efficient teachers."[3]

The school term had been extended by an average of three weeks to a minimum length of 24 weeks. Spending increased from per capita $5.82 to $12.62—though that had to be remarked with an asterisk as this was for white students only. The average teacher salary increased from $188.91 to $332.48. Local support grew exponentially as well, as demonstrated by the number of districts levying local mills to support the public schools: from 218 in the year 1901 to 927 ten years later. These local taxes helped support school libraries (1,427 in 1911) and a tremendous growth in the high schools, which grew in number from 95 to 177.[4]

Beyond the numbers, Swearingen's real legacy can be recognized in South Carolina's public schools in the twenty-first century. Items that many districts take for granted, such as transportation of students and state funding per pupil, are legacies of Swearingen's years in office. Swearingen's tenure created several policies that South Carolina implemented since. For example, when an influenza epidemic spread through the state in 1918, closing many of the schools, Swearingen ordered that teachers be paid in full by their districts—whether they worked or not. Whenever a school is closed because of weather or other reasons, it is this precedent that keeps the teachers paid in full.

At the time of this writing, the nation is struggling with alternative certification programs for teachers, such as Teach for America. While seen by some as innovative, Swearingen began a similar program in 1919. Swearingen approved a program giving a "special war emergency certificate" to high school graduates and college graduates in order to fill the classrooms of South Carolina. However, while the current program is a renewable certificate program, Swearingen's was not; he specified that these war certificates would "in no case be renewable."[5]

Swearingen's policies affected politics in South Carolina for years to come. Most notably, Swearingen raised the state's awareness of the need for a solid system of public education. When the Great Depression hit the state, then governor Ira Blackwood responded, in part, by reducing teacher's salaries and decreasing aid to education by 19 percent. He was not reelected; instead came the "Education Governor" Olin Johnson. While in office during the New Deal relief programs, Johnson established a textbook rental system, extended the school term from six to eight months, raised teacher salaries, and required compulsory school attendance laws, removing the local option component, for children between seven and 16 years of age—almost all of which were demands previously voiced by Swearingen.[6]

When leaving office, Swearingen wrote out one final press release that summarized his years in office. Titled "Public Schools of South Carolina During the Administration of J. E. Swearingen 1909–1923," it presents the pithiest yet inclusive summaries of Swearingen's ultimate legacy: the vast improvements in the public schools. Items of note in the report include a casual mention of the resistance to his move to improve schools serving African Americans, as well as his generally positive tone regarding the work of the GEB. It is also interesting both for its dispassionate recounting of the improvements and for its lack of political commentary on the events—something in character for a man who wished to keep politics out of education, even after he had been undone by it:

> The South Carolina Department of Education consisted in 1909 of the state superintendent, one clerk and one stenographer. The office was a small room in the gallery of the State House. This small office was heated

by a grate, and lighted by one window. The scant furniture was in keeping with the cramped quarters.[7]

The educational problem of the state in 1909 demanded a large increase in school funds, the introduction of the policy of direct state appropriation for the public schools, the equalization of school opportunity among the poorer districts, the elevation of school standards, the enrichment of the school curriculum, and the awakening of a widespread popular interest in more efficient education.

The beginning was small. The legislature was asked for $20,000.00 to lengthen the school term and communities unable to run five months. Discussion among the lawmakers was active and acrid. One gray-bearded senator inquired caustically, "How will the State Superintendent of Education use so large a sum?" The appropriation was voted by a majority of one—the presiding officer casting the deciding ballot...the disbursement of the state fund of $20,000.00 proved universally stimulating and satisfactory.

At the 1910 session of the Legislature...The campaign for State aid to schools and for increased local taxation was what was thus launched. It grew rapidly. Within 14 years the legislative appropriation for free schools reached one million and a quarter dollars annually...The net result was a five-fold increase in school revenues, thereby laying the foundation for corresponding improvements along other lines.

The population of South Carolina was 53% Negro and 47% white. The Negroes were one generation removed from slavery. About half of them were illiterate. A state Supervisor of Negro Schools was appointed through the cooperation of the General Education Board of New York. This policy was severely criticized, but it has brought general improvement in the colored schools.

The quality of class room instruction was raised and the high school curriculum broadened. Within a few years the General Education Board contributed to salary and expenses of a full-time high school inspector, in addition to its previous contribution for the professor of secondary education in the university.

Night schools and adult schools for illiterates were organized along the lines of the "Moonlight Schools" of Kentucky. The Legislature appropriated this money to be used in the discretion of the State Superintendent of Education.

The development of the cotton mill industry created in South Carolina a large economic and industrial problem involving also educational and social questions. The Mill population embraced about one-third of the white people of the state. Most of these had left the farm and come the factory in order to earn more money. Each manufacturing locality was in a large measure owned and operated by a corporation. The mill management was usually progressive, but the factory was built and operated to make profits. Word had gone out that mill people did not need and did not wish more than a sixth-grade education. A supervisor of middle schools was appointed. He had no authority but persuasion. The cooperation of mill executives and no operatives was quickly secured. These villages already had the children. They understood the democracy of education, and in a few years the mill schools of South Carolina were among its best. Industrial education was fostered by the prompt acceptance of the Smith-Hughes law. Vocational classes in agriculture, industry and in Home Economics became permanent features of the schools.

A single standard for the examination answer to certification of teachers was secured by the creation of the Board of Examiners for teachers. Licenses were thus adapted to the nature of the work and the qualification of the teacher. Scholarship was stimulated and professional preparation encouraged.

Cooperation with the underlying principle of every improvement. Coercion was never used. The majority in every school community had to be actively enlisted in every step forward. The central administration was given new responsibilities and additional resources, but autocracy and bureaucracy were scrupulously avoided. The results of the program are clearly shown in the census of 1920. The progress of the decade gave South Carolina and improved rating in every educational tabulation, both positive and relative.[8]

John E. Swearingen, Model Politician

Whatever the reasons why Swearingen acted as he did—whether as an attempt to transcend societal notions of disability or to conform to societal notions of masculinity—an aspect of Swearingen's legacy is his role as politician. Swearingen always looked to the greater good first when making decisions about South Carolina's schools. He knew that his decisions could be viewed as unpopular, and that he would take criticism for his views, but he continually voiced his opinions and made the unpopular decisions because they were for the greater good. Also, Swearingen refused to partner with anyone he was in disagreement with, no matter how lucrative the opportunity might be. After rudely refusing a favor of one wealthy individual in the state, Swearingen was told he should not be so bold. "I don't care how much money and influence he has," replied Swearingen. "I have no intention of recommending a high-school building solely for the benefit of his three children."[9] Imagine if politicians today still operated under such noble terms instead of the system of lobbyist-written legislation, scandal, and corruption within which we currently operate in the United States. Surely I am not alone in the assertion that our great nation deserves better.

History is full of such leaders, people who looked to the greater good than popularity or expedience. In Canada, for example, Saskatchewan premier Tommy Douglas took on the entire medical industry and endured the closing of doctors' offices and hospitals in order to implement provincial socialized medicine, providing the blueprint from which a national system was modeled. Soundly reviled during his time, today he is recognized as one of the ten greatest Canadians. It is unfortunate that this aspect of Swearingen's legacy, let alone all the others before and since, is the most ignored. In a nation that is facing such a wide array of challenges—military, social, and political—the elected leaders from both sides of the aisle have seemingly lost this directive. No longer are the ministers of our civil religion willing to step forward and make the difficult decisions, and no longer are the congregants willing to accept that challenging times require challenging decisions, not all of which can be popular or pretty.

Many contemporary thinkers argue that the comparisons are apples and oranges, and that the bloodsport of contemporary politics is far removed from those of Swearingen's time. However, nothing could be farther from the truth. Politics then and now was a sport of the wealthy and devoted, those who could afford to run, and those who have a true passion for it. Beyond that, in both periods the times were a-changing. One hundred years from now, historians will cede that the contemporary reforms and the progressive reforms of the period in which Swearingen lived and worked are similar.

The writing of this work began pre-9/11 and has continued through two political swings in the White House. In the intervening years the times have shifted to see the election of the nation's first African American president and the legalization/decriminalization of marijuana. While racism, sexism, and classism still exist, the nation has turned its eyes to a new civil rights struggle: that of people who are MSGI (minority sex and gender identity, more commonly referred to by the acronym LGBT). Just as the military led efforts domestically to desegregate first internally, then in the schools serving the children of servicemen in 1950, so too did the military lead the movement with the elimination of "Don't Ask, Don't Tell." Since then, there has been an upswing in states' granting the 1,000-plus legal rights associated with marriages and civil unions to MSGI couples, and the worlds of collegiate and professional sports have seen the first openly gay players emerge.

Those who are socially liberal cheer, those who are socially conservative wince. With every swing of the political/philosophical pendulum there is backlash, and this too had great similarities then and now. The far Right had its populist extremists then, as personified by Coleman Blease and Ben Tillman. However, the antics of Blease should not seem overly surprising to anyone who follows contemporary efforts of radicals from the Right wing. Indeed, Blease and many ultraconservatives are both cut from the same alpha-male cloth. Tillman's description of Blease can be used for almost any member of Congress today, who vote to ruin the economy rather than negotiate with someone from the other party: "For Blease is so constituted that unless he is fighting, he thinks himself obscured entirely. He will, therefore, keep the Legislature in hot water as often and as long as he can."[10]

It is sad that more Americans haven't learned their lessons from the past on this front and continue to elect uber-masculine politicians who put machismo before duty. When in 2005 Thomas Frank asked, "What's the Matter With Kansas?"[11] he would probably have found a very sympathetic audience in David English Camack, the scholar who was so aghast at the rhetoric of Blease and his followers. Much of the core of the Tea Party movement is wrapped in the exact same rhetoric used by opponents of progressivism in the 1920s; then, as now, they were essentially movements powered by working-class white men who had been fed masculine rhetoric of reclaiming their country and not allowing any wealthy politicians to tell them what to do. Indeed, those paying attention to Blease's repeated efforts to oust South Carolina College president Mitchell would find direct parallels with the current Congress's equally impossible repeated votes to repeal the Affordable Health Care Act. History has already judged such acts as folly.

Indeed, many who watch far Right-wing rallies would not see a difference from Camack's description: "With glib tongue spouting billingsgate he launched a broadside of invective against his opponents, prodding his coarse deluded admirers to one shrieking yell after another... What could I do to show the people that they were being toyed with? Was there really any use trying to educate a few when the great mass behaved like this?"[12] A level of irony in all this is that this antipolitician argument comes, of course, from other politicians who somehow remain unspoiled by all their sprayed filth. Now, as then, it is demagoguery at its best.

Just as many of today's progressive reform suggestions are either highly contentious or outright rejected, not all of Swearingen's suggestions were well received, and many of his calls went unheeded. While works such as *The Shopping Mall High School* indicted schools for watered-down, too expansive curricula, Swearingen cautioned against this as early as 1913: "Any institution that undertakes to be universal in its province or its function is doomed to break down of its own weight," he warned. He continued in words that are as meaningful in the twenty-first century as they were in 1913:

> We attempt to correct all our shortcomings and to cure all our evils, social, political, and industrial, through the public schools... The school is fast becoming the factotum in our civilization. One set of people demands

that academic degrees be given for swimming and aviation. Another set hopes to reform society by giving high school credit to boys for running errands at home and for pulling weeds out of the front yard. The famous company for extracting sunbeams from cucumbers was not much more quixotic than some of our over-enthusiastic educators. There is a world of difference between a school's linking itself sympathetically to every good community undertaking and its attempting to incorporate into its work everything in which the community might be vitally interested. Whenever a small school undertakes to do a little of everything, to spread itself out over every community enterprise, it becomes very thin.[13]

Swearingen's push for vocational education flies in the face of today's misguided push for all youth in the United States to get a university degree. In his report, Swearingen urged his audience to "accept what ought to be self-evident—that God does not create all boys and girls equal or alike in capacity, in opportunity, in taste, in ambition, or in ideals, and that it is folly for fond parents and obstinate schoolmasters to undertake to disregard the handiwork of the Almighty."[14] To Swearingen, high schools should offer curricula that would benefit all students instead of "slavishly, if not blindly, following the traditions of four centuries ago" and requiring all students to complete a college-preparatory curriculum. The number of professions has grown; the coursework of high schools should concomitantly grow to prepare students for these new careers. The current curriculum, a "veritable medieval mummy," was inadequate for this purpose. Worse, there was a sort of academic snobbery taking place in the high schools—that students attempting to pursue a course of study in the commercial arts were treated as a "pleb" taking "plebian courses" rather than "aristocratic" academic coursework.[15]

Swearingen is probably spinning in his grave at the notion that today many young people are still told that a four-year degree is an appropriate goal for all high school students. From a strictly economic viewpoint, according to the United States Department of Labor, eight of the ten fastest growing occupations in the United States require an associate's degree or less. The only exceptions—biomedical engineers and meeting/convention/event planners—require a bachelor's degree.[16]

Over the last ten years, we have seen the cost of higher education continue to grow at surprising rates.[17] As noted in *The Economist* 40 years ago, in 1970, college tuition at a public university amounted to roughly 4 percent of the average American family's income; in 2010, it amounted to 11 percent, a 300 percent increase versus the CPI between 1990 and 2011.[18]

Student aid has been forced to climb to keep pace with the rising cost of higher education. Over the last ten years, there has been a significant allocation of funds for students attending college—a 185 percent increase in federal grants; a 120 percent increase in federal loans; a 140 percent increase in federal aid; and a 118 percent increase in state, institutional, private, and employer grants. Student aid has become big business: $244 billion total in 2011–2012.[19] In the year 2014, student loan debt surpassed credit card debt for the first time.

Sadly, as noted by Matt Taibbi—a political/economic commentator who seems destined to be recalled as his generation's Hunter S. Thompson—students are not the ones benefitting from this "crushing, life-alteringly huge college debt"; instead, Taibbi argues that two agencies benefit from a system that has become "exploitive and unfair": colleges and universities (and not just the for-profit ones) that have become "little regional empires," and the government, which sponsors a "predatory lending program that makes even the most ruthless private credit-card company seem like a 'Save the Panda' charity."[20]

However, while student aid is expanding, students' ability to repay this aid is not. As median family income stalls and the price of higher education skyrockets, student aid is the bubble keeping the business running. Few observers would seriously maintain that enrollment growth would continue if there was a significant retrenchment in student aid. It is the indirect subsidy that colleges and universities have become addicted to. And, if most long-term economic forecasts for the United States are to be trusted, this bubble will burst soon. That is, both state and federal governments have long-term liabilities (for the federal government—health care, social security, and national defense; for the state governments—health care, state employee pensions, and corrections) that cannot be effectively controlled.

Indeed, Swearingen would agree that the time has come for higher education communities to reflect on where our public higher education institutions are going and how we are serving our students, to have a reckoning. In spite of the trend to elect corporate CEOs as university presidents, our universities are *not* corporations that have to grow or perish. We do not have to admit larger and larger classes of undergraduates. We do not have to preach the myth that a bachelor's degree is the key to success in America. We need to acknowledge that the American dream does not always require a bachelor's degree. Nor should we tell our high school students that everyone deserves one. Millions of young Americans can become happy, productive, gainfully employed citizens if they are only willing—and supported—in finding appropriate postsecondary educational opportunities to develop their skills in ways that both the market and their happiness will accord.

Swearingen's resistance to federal intervention is another commonality in today's debates surrounding movements such as Common Core and the Next Generation Science Standards. Characteristic of the contradictions inherent in much of Swearingen's work, while he was happy to get Smith-Hughes funds into the state, he was also chary of federal involvement. Swearingen also was visionary in regard to the role of the federal government over education, writing, "The formulation of standards for the United States cannot be made by one Federal Board at Washington...ought not to be centralized in one man, or in one set of men. This work cannot be done outside the public schools and the recognized educational agencies of the states. Any law should be carefully scrutinized before it is allowed to give this broad...power to the Federal Commissioner of Education."[21]

Epitaphs and Epilogue

A biographer's words shouldn't be used to end Swearingen's story, but rather those of his contemporaries. Upon Swearingen's election loss, Lee Davis Lodge, president of the historically black Limestone College wrote a fitting epilogue to Swearingen's career:

> Your broad, enlightened, statesmanlike policy, your indefatigable energy, and your devoted patriotism have won the gratitude of many thousands of your fellow citizens, among whom I am glad to be numbered. The history of education in South Carolina will forever bear the marks, deep and impenetrable, of your strenuous struggle for the betterment of the conditions and classes of all our people. Any fair-minded historian will be compelled to award to you a great meed of praise for the masterly ability you have shown in grappling with the difficult problems and the terribly adverse conditions that have confronted you. The courage, wisdom, and success with which you have administered your office deserve and will receive the unstinted praise of all who are competent to judge.[22]

This work opened with the notion that in a state filled with monuments, none existed in honor of Swearingen. At the commemoration of the monument in honor of his Uncle Ben, however, J. H. Thornwell of the Hartsville City Schools wrote to explain otherwise:

> I feel that you have done a splendid work for the State and built for yourself a monument more enduring than any other you could have built. Your

monument is the lives of the boys and girls of South Carolina that you touched through your administration and made brighter and better for your having served them. When our future citizens come to review the past and the persons connected with it, I know that your name will have high rank among those of the State who were real benefactors to mankind.[23]

Indeed, Swearingen's ultimate legacy is a lesson for us all. What if contemporary politicians, from local school board members to those working in the White House, were to appreciate the true legacy of such leaders? What might happen if today's leaders were to take their lead not from exit polls or "random sampling" opinions, but instead follow the example set by the visionless visionary who was John Swearingen? As the principal of the Houghton School in Augusta, Georgia, wrote to Swearingen in 1922, even children born white or sighted could take lessons:

> I always am watching your career with interest, and have been, as when you first entered public life, quietly explaining to people (who do not know you) that you can see more than most of us who have two external eyes. That it is not the windows that count for most but the occupant looking through.[24]

Notes

Introduction

1. Milton, J. (1977). Sonnet XIX: When I consider how my light is spent. In Bush, D. (Ed.), *The portable Milton*. New York: Penguin Books, 223.
2. Further analysis of Swearingen's disability and its impact on his career can be read in Janak, E. (2010). Adventitiously blind, advantageously political: John Eldred Swearingen and social definitions of disability in progressive-era South Carolina. *Vitae Scholasticae, 27*(1), 5–25.
3. Reese, W. J. (1986). *Power and the promise of school reform: Grassroots movements during the progressive era*. Boston, MA: Routledge & Kegan Paul, xix.
4. Flick, A. (2000). Joyce's biographers and the question of biographical truth. In Kirschstein, B. H. (Ed.), *Life writing/Writing lives*. Malabar, FL: Krieger, 95.
5. Swearingen, M. H. (1950). *A gallant journey: Mr. Swearingen and his family*. Columbia: University of South Carolina Press.
6. Dreyfus, J. V. (1997). *John Eldred Swearingen: Superintendent of education in South Carolina 1909–1922*. Columbia, SC: College of Education.
7. Records of his academic achievements and awards stood unbroken from his graduation in 1899 through the 1950s. See Swearingen, *A gallant journey*, 13 and 48.
8. Woodward, C. V. (1968). *The burden of Southern history*. New York, NY: New American Library.
9. Ramsdell, C. W. (1969). Preoccupation with agriculture. In Billington, M. L. (Ed.), *The South: A central theme*. Atlanta, GA: Holt, Rinehart, and Winston, 85.
10. To J. E. Swearingen from G. Swearingen, September 7, 1909, John E. Swearingen Papers, Box 2, Folder 65, Columbia, SC, South Caroliniana Library.
11. Dreyfuss, *John Eldred Swearingen*, 2.
12. Garraty, J. A. (1957). *The nature of biography*. New York, NY: Alfred A. Knopf, 4–6.
13. Maher, J. (2001). Becoming a biographer. In Kirschstein, B. H. (Ed.), *Life writing/Writing lives*. Malabar, FL: Krieger, 61–62. Similar sentiments are

stated in Gittings, R. (1978). *The nature of biography.* Seattle: University of Washington Press, 15.
14. Swearingen, *A gallant journey*, ix.
15. The High School Act of 1909 greatly expanded state aid to the public high schools of South Carolina. Swearingen, J. E. (1909). *High school act nineteen hundred and nine: Information, regulations, suggested courses of study.* Columbia, SC: State Printing Company, 4.
16. For a full description of the Committee of Ten, see Angus, D. & Mirel, J. (1999). *The failed promise of the American high school 1890–1995.* New York, NY: Teacher's College Press, 8–9; Espy, H. G. (1939). *The public secondary school: A critical analysis of secondary education in the United States.* Atlanta, GA: Houghton Mifflin, 50–52; Kandel, P. (1939). *History of secondary education in the United States.* New York, NY: Houghton Mifflin, 473–476; Kliebard, H. M. (1995). *The struggle for the American curriculum 1893–1958.* New York, NY: Routledge, 8–14 and 162; Perkinson, H. J. (1991). *The imperfect panacea: American faith in education, 1865–1990.* New York, NY: McGraw-Hill, 134–138; Powell, A. G. et al. (1985). *The shopping mall high school: Winners and losers in the educational marketplace.* Boston, MA: Houghton Mifflin, 244–245; Ravitch, D. (1995). The search for order and the rejection of conformity: Standards in American education. *Learning from the past: What history teaches us about school reform.* Baltimore, MD: Johns Hopkins University Press, 169–172; Tyack, D. & Cuban, L. (1995). *Tinkering toward utopia: A century of public school reform.* Cambridge: Harvard University Press, 49–52.
17. For a more complete discussion of the importance of agriculture on the Southern mentality, see Ramsdell, Preoccupation with agriculture, 77–90.
18. For a complete discussion on the Smith-Hughes Act, see chapter 4 of this work and Koos, L. V. (1927). *The American secondary school.* Atlanta, GA: Ginn, 300–307.
19. Swearingen, J. E. (1902). Educated labor. *The Bohemian.* Vol. 3, No. 2. Ft. Worth: Bohemia Literary Club.
20. Swearingen, J. E. to Rasor, J. B. (September 18, 1922). John E. Swearingen Papers, Box 3, Folder 90, Columbia, SC.
21. To Editor from J. E. Swearingen, April 14, 1908, John E. Swearingen Papers, Box 2, Folder 58, Columbia, SC.
22. Kirst, M. W. (1995). Who's in charge? Federal, state, and local control. In Ravitch, D. & Vinovskis, M. (Eds.), *Learning from the past: What history teaches us about school reform.* Baltimore, MD: Johns Hopkins University Press, 25.
23. Swearingen, *A gallant journey*, x.
24. Gittings, *The nature of biography*, 42–43.
25. In order, Bederman, G. (1995). *Manliness and civilization: A cultural history of gender and race in the United States 1880–1917.* Chicago, IL: University of Chicago Press, 7; and Oertel, K. T. (Autumn 2002). "The free sons of the north" versus "the myrmidons of border-ruffianism": What makes a man in bleeding Kansas? *Kansas History: A Journal of the Central Plains, 25,* 176.

26. Gittings, *The nature of biography*, 49 and 52.
27. For discussions regarding shortcomings in completing biographical research and means to overcome these, see Berry, T. E. (1967). *The biographer's craft*. New York, NY: The Odyssey Press, 5–6; Bowen, C. D. (1951). *The writing of biography*. Boston, MA: The Writer, 7–11; Edel, L. (1984). *Writing lives: Principia biographica*. New York, NY: W. W. Norton, 93–108; Hedrick, J. (1998). Biography as interdisciplinary art. In Bak, H. & Krabbendam, H. (Eds.), *Writing lives: American biography and autobiography*. Amsterdam: Vu University Press, 162; Kendall, P. (1965). *The art of biography*. New York, NY: W. W. Norton, 17–24; Kirchstein, B. H. (2001). *Life writing/Writing lives*. Malabar, FL: Krieger, 4–6; Meyers, J. (1998). The quest for Bogart. In Bak, H. & Krabbendam, H. (Eds.), *Writing lives: American biography and autobiography*. Amsterdam: Vu University Press, 204–206; Reynolds, K. (1998). Finding facts, telling truths, achieving art. In Kridel, C. (Ed.), *Writing educational biography: Explorations in qualitative research*. New York, NY: Garland, 178–183; Smith, L. M. (1998). On becoming an archivist and biographer. In Kridel, C. (Ed.), *Writing educational biography: Explorations in qualitative research*. New York, NY: Garland, 159–167.
28. Edel, *Writing lives: Principia biographica*, 102–103.
29. Hayes, J. I. (2001). *South Carolina and the New Deal*. Columbia: University of South Carolina Press, 1.

1 South Carolina, Populism, and the "New South," 1865–1908

1. South Carolina as seen by a Yankee by George Fitch (June 14, 1916). Tillman, Benjamin Ryan. Manuscripts—Political Collections. Incoming correspondence: Box 50, Folder 717. Clemson, SC, Special Collections: Robert Muldrow Cooper Library.
2. This refers to the assassinations of two prominent newspaper editors. Both Francis Dawson, of the Charleston *News and Courier*, and N. G. Gonzales, of Columbia's *The State*, were gunned down in broad daylight. In the 1903 case of Gonzales, it occurred in the shadow of the Capital building—and his killer was Lieutenant Governor James Tillman, son of Benjamin Tillman. In both cases, the assassins were acquitted by their respective juries—although the Tillman case was moved to neighboring Lexington County for trial.
3. Best, J. H. (Spring 1996). Education in the forming of the American South. *History of Education Quarterly*, 36(1), 39.
4. Beneke, T. (1997). *Proving manhood: Reflections on men and sexism*. Berkeley: University of California Press, 48.
5. Jackson, R. L. (July 1997). Black "manhood" as xenophobe: An ontological exploration of the Hegelian dialectic. *Journal of Black Studies*, 27(6), 731–750.
6. Cooper, F. R. (2006). Against bipolar black masculinity: Intersectionality, assimilation, identity performance, and hierarchy. *University of California at Davis Law Review*, 39, 853–906.

7. Swearingen, M. H. (1950). *A gallant journey: Mr. Swearingen and his family.* Columbia: University of South Carolina Press, 17.
8. Friend, C. T. & Glover, L. (2001). Rethinking Southern masculinity: An introduction. In Friend, C. T. & Glover, L. (Eds.), *Southern manhood: Perspectives on masculinity in the old south.* Athens: University of Georgia Press, x.
9. Wells, C. A. (2005). *Civil War time: Temporality and identity in America 1861–1865.* Athens: University of Georgia Press, 118.
10. Prather, H. L. (April 1977). The Red Shirt movement in North Carolina. *Journal of Negro History, 62*(2), 175.
11. For more on the relationship between white supremacy groups such as the Red Shirt Riders and masculinity, see the following: Elaine, F. P. (2005). Midnight rangers: Costume and performance in the reconstruction-era Ku Klux Klan. *The Journal of American History, 92*(3), 811–836. Retrieved from http://search.proquest.com/docview/ 224894118?accountid=14793; Nowatzki, R. (1994). Race, rape, lynching, and manhood suffrage: Constructions of white and black masculinity in turn-of-the-century white supremacist literature. *Journal of Men's Studies, 3*(2), 161. Retrieved from http://search.proquest.com/docview/222638884?accountid=14793l; and Pinar, W. F. (2001). *The gender of racial politics and violence in America: Lynching, prison rape, and the crisis of masculinity.* New York, NY: Peter Lang.
12. Cheng, C. (1999). Marginalized masculinities and hegemonic masculinity: An introduction. *Journal of Men's Studies, 7*(3), 166. Retrieved from http://search.proquest.com/docview/222608043?accountid=14793.
13. Franklin, J. H. (1961). *Reconstruction after the Civil War.* Chicago, IL: University of Chicago Press, 53.
14. For further discussion of the New South specifically, and the South during this time period generally, see Cash, W. J. (1941). Of quandary—And the birth of a dream. In *The mind of the South.* Garden City, NY: Doubleday Anchor Books, 185–191; Cooke, J. E. (1960). The new south. In Sheehan, D. & Syrett, H. (Eds.), *Essays in American historiography, papers presented in honor of Allan Nevins.* Baton Rouge: Louisiana State University Press, 50–80; Gaston, P. M. (1967). The "New South." In Link, A. & Rembert, W. P. (Eds.), *Writing Southern history: Essays in historogoraphy in honor of Fletcher M. Green.* Baton Rouge: Louisiana State University Press, 316–336; Ransom, J. C. (1962). Reconstructed but unregenerate. In *I'll take my stand: The south and the agrarian tradition.* New York, NY: Harper Torchbooks, pp. 17–27; and Woodward, C. V. (1968). A Southern critique for the Gilded Age. In *The burden of Southern history.* New York, NY: New American Library, 83–103.
15. Franklin, *Reconstruction after the Civil War*, 52.
16. Gershenberg, I. (Winter 1970). Southern values and public education: A revision. *History of Education Quarterly, 10*(4), 413–414.
17. Ibid., 414–415. For a more detailed study, see Cahill, E. E. & Pieper, H. (First Quarter, 1974). Closing the educational gap: The South versus the United States. *Phylon, 35*(1), 45–53; Urban, W. J. (Summer 1981). History of education: A Southern exposure. *History of Education Quarterly, 21*(2), 131–145.

18. Dreyfus, J. V. (1997). *John Eldred Swearingen: Superintendent of education in South Carolina 1909-1922*. Columbia, SC: College of Education.
19. Mann, H. (January 1841). Introduction. *Common School Journal*, 3(1), 15.
20. Franklin, *Reconstruction after the Civil War*, 110.
21. Dunbar, N. (1986). *Public secondary education in Columbia, SC 1895-1950*. Unpublished doctoral dissertation, University of South Carolina, 27-28.
22. Martin, C. J. (1949). *History and development of Negro education in South Carolina*. Columbia, SC: State Department of Education, 3.
23. Stephens, T. (1994). *An educational shift: Early public high school legislation and the decline of the boarding school in South Carolina*. Paper written for HIST 788, University of South Carolina, 5.
24. Anderson, J. D. (1988). *The education of blacks in the south, 1860-1935*. Chapel Hill: University of North Carolina Press, 8.
25. The Constitution of the State of South Carolina of 1895. Retrieved from http://www.scstatehouse.gov/scconstitution/scconst.php.
26. Edgar, W. B. (1992). *South Carolina in the modern age*. Columbia: University of South Carolina Press, 27.
27. Reese, W. J. (1995). *The origins of the American high school*. New Haven, CT: Yale University Press, 70-71.
28. Statistics cover both white and African American populations. Edgar, *South Carolina in the modern age*, 19.
29. *United States Census Data*. (2002). University of Virginia Census Information. [Online data]. Available FTP: Hostname: virginia.edu Directory: fisher.lib File: cgi-local/censusbin/census/cen.pl.
30. Martin, *History and development of Negro education in South Carolina*, 6.
31. Stephens, *An educational shift: Early public high school legislation and the decline of the boarding school in South Carolina*, 6.
32. Anderson, *The education of blacks in the south, 1860-1935*, 101.
33. Clark, E. C. (1940). *A history of the first hundred years of the high school of Charleston, South Carolina, 1839-1939*. Unpublished master's thesis, University of South Carolina, 51.
34. Hand, W. H. (1906). A plea for high schools. *Thirty-eighth annual report of the South Carolina state superintendent of education*. Columbia, SC: State Printing Company, 67.
35. Kandel, P. (1939). *History of secondary education in the United States*. New York, NY: Houghton Mifflin, 482-483.
36. Perkinson, H. J. (1991). *The imperfect panacea: American faith in education, 1865-1990*. New York, NY: McGraw-Hill, 70.
37. Richardson, J. G. (1980). Variation in date of enactment of compulsory school attendance laws: An empirical inquiry. *Sociology of Education*, 53(3), 155.
38. Koos, L. V. (1927). *The American secondary school*. Atlanta, GA: Ginn, 7.
39. For an explanation of this incident as it pertains to masculine society, see Oertel, K. T. (Autumn 2002). "The free sons of the north" versus "the myrmidons of border-ruffianism": What makes a man in bleeding Kansas? *Kansas History: A Journal of the Central Plains*, 25, 174-189.

40. Peffer, W. A. (1992). *Populism: Its rise and fall*. Lawrence: University Press of Kansas, 72.
41. McCants, E. C. (1927). *History stories and legends of South Carolina*. Dallas, TX: The Southern Publishing Company, 378.
42. Guess, W. H. (1960). *South Carolina: Annals of pride and protest*. New York, NY: Harper, 275.
43. Wallace, D. D. *South Carolina: A short history 1520–1948*. Chapel Hill: University of North Carolina Press, 598–599.
44. Edgar, W. B. (1998). *South Carolina: A history*. Columbia: University of South Carolina Press, 403.
45. Zuczek, R. "Hamburg massacre." In Edgar, W. B. (Ed.) (2006). *The South Carolina encyclopedia*. Columbia: University of South Carolina Press, 415–416.
46. Tillman B. R. to Henderson, D. S. (October 12, 1911). Tillman, Benjamin Ryan. Outgoing correspondence. Box 2, Folder 27.
47. Bradford, W. R. (1954). Twenty-one governors of South Carolina, Tillman to Byrnes (including both): A related tragedy and other matters. Columbia, SC: State Printing Company, 6.
48. Edgar, *South Carolina in the modern age*, 26.
49. Swearingen, J. E. to Swearingen, H. T. (September 21, 1922). John E. Swearingen Papers, Box 4, Folder 91.
50. Photo of John Cloud Swearingen holding twins George and Sophie, courtesy John E. Swearingen, Jr.
51. History of the Swearingen family documented for enrollment in the Roll of Honor in the Confederate States of America Museum, Richmond, Virginia. John E. Swearingen Papers, Box 4, Folder 112.
52. Swearingen, *A gallant journey*, 21.
53. Photo of Anna Tillman Swearingen, courtesy John E. Swearingen, Jr. family scrapbook.
54. *Copy Book*. John E. Swearingen Papers, Legal box, Folder 7.
55. My last opossum hunt. English notebook c. 1895. John E. Swearingen Papers, Legal box.
56. Swearingen, *A gallant journey*, 33.
57. Rotundo, E. A. (1990). Boy culture: Middle class boyhood in nineteenth-century America. In Carnes, M. C. & Griffen, C. (Eds). *Meanings for manhood: Constructions of masculinity in Victorian America*. Chicago, IL: University of Chicago Press, 15–17.
58. Ibid., 21.
59. Similar to Braille, the Point Print method was one of the first methods of making text readable to the visually impaired. However, the method was subject to machinery and regional differences; thus, when the nationally standardized Braille became available, many visually impaired persons and institutions teaching them switched over. Swearingen and his mother learned to correspond using Point Print, and continued to do so even after the introduction of Braille. His wife would learn both Point Print and Braille in order to correspond with him.

60. Why I came to the S. C. College. English notebook c. 1895. John E. Swearingen Papers.
61. First impressions and experiences at college. English notebook c. 1895. John E. Swearingen Papers.
62. Bunch, G. W. to Swearingen, J. E. (July 31, 1895). John E. Swearingen Papers, Box 2, Folder 51.
63. Swearingen, *A gallant journey*, 42.
64. Ibid., 44.
65. School Transcripts/Reports. John E. Swearingen Papers.
66. Photo of Swearingen at South Carolina College, courtesy South Caroliniana Library. John E. Swearingen Papers, Box 4, Folder 103.
67. Dear mother. English notebook c. 1895. John E. Swearingen Papers.
68. Swearingen, M. H. (April 27, 1961). Remarks in presenting the John Eldred Swearingen Papers at the Annual Meeting of the South Caroliniana Society. John E. Swearingen Papers, Box 4, Folder 103.
69. Reconstruction in South Carolina. John E. Swearingen Papers, Box 4, Folder 109.
70. Brunson, M. C. to Swearingen, J. E. (September 1, 1897). John E. Swearingen Papers, Box 2, Folder 51.
71. Worth while folk: The blind school superintendent. (n. d.). John E. Swearingen Papers, Box 4, Folder 112.
72. Swearingen, John E., Jr. (July 30, 2002). Unpublished interview, Saratoga, WY. Tape 1, Side 1.
73. Hollis, D. W. (1956). *University of South Carolina Volume II: College to University*. Columbia: University of South Carolina Press, 185.
74. Swearingen, *A gallant journey*, 45.
75. Rotundo, 22.
76. Joynes, E. S. to Swearingen, J. E. (June 17, 1899). John E. Swearingen Papers, Box 2, Folder 52; and Swearingen, *A gallant journey*, 46. Photo of John E. Swearingen at his graduation from the South Carolina College, courtesy John E. Swearingen, Jr. family scrapbook.
77. Swearingen, J. E. to Swearingen, A. T. (October 28, 1900). John E. Swearingen Papers, Box 2, Folder 54.
78. Address to Fairfield County. (n. d.). John E. Swearingen Papers, Box 4, Folder 108.
79. Ibid.
80. Ibid.
81. Ibid.
82. Ibid.
83. Swearingen, *A gallant journey*, 61.
84. Swearingen, J. E. to Swearingen, A. T. (January 5, 1908). John E. Swearingen Papers, Box 2, Folder 58.
85. Brief sketch. (n. d.). John E. Swearingen Papers, Box 4, Folder 109.
86. Swearingen, J. E. to G. H. (March 30, 1908). John E. Swearingen Papers, Box 2, Folder 58.
87. Friend & Glover, *Southern manhood: Perspectives on masculinity in the old south*, viii.

88. Swearingen, *A gallant journey*, 100.
89. Temporal/historical conversion courtesy the website Measuring Worth. The reason 2012 dollars is the unit of conversion is that this is the most recent year for which the site has data. Taken from: Six ways to compute the relative value of a U.S. dollar amount, 1774 to present. *Measuring worth: A service for calculating relative worth over time.* http://www.measuringworth.com/uscompare/.
90. Worth while folk.
91. Ibid.
92. Swearingen, J. E. (May 1908). Untitled campaign speech. John E. Swearingen Papers, Box 2, Folder 58.
93. Ibid.
94. Ibid.
95. Photo courtesy South Caroliniana Library.
96. Beneke, 42.
97. Swearingen, J. E. (April 14, 1908). John E. Swearingen Papers, Box 2, Folder 58.
98. From John E. Swearingen: Candidate for State Superintendent of Education. (1908). John E. Swearingen Papers, Legal Box, Folder 9.
99. Ibid.
100. Ibid.
101. Ibid.
102. Swearingen, J. E. to Bunch, G. (September 9, 1908). Swearingen, John E. Papers. Box 2, Folder 58.
103. McSwain, J. J. (n. d.). Swearingen, John E. Papers. Box 2, Folder 58.
104. Graham, S. H. to Swearingen, J. E. (August 12, 1908). Swearingen, John E. Papers. Box 2, Folder 58.

2 Fighting the Good Fight, 1907–1915

1. Joyner, J. Y., Whitfield, H. L., & Mynders, S. A. (1904). Address to the people of the south. *Thirty-sixth annual report of the South Carolina state superintendent of education.* Columbia, SC: State Printing Company, 35–42.
2. Ibid.
3. Ibid., 37.
4. Ibid., 40–41.
5. Ibid., 42.
6. *Thirty-eighth annual report of the South Carolina state superintendent of education.* (1906). Columbia, SC: State Printing Company, 8.
7. Ibid., 53.
8. Ibid., 54.
9. *Thirty-ninth annual report of the South Carolina state superintendent of education.* (1907). Columbia, SC: State Printing Company, 75–76.
10. Ibid.

11. *Fortieth annual report of the South Carolina state superintendent of education.* (1908). Columbia, SC: State Printing Company, 16.
12. Ibid., 87–90.
13. Ibid., 17.
14. Ibid., 35.
15. Ibid., 38.
16. Ibid., 92.
17. Ibid., 44.
18. Ibid., 94–95.
19. Ibid., 31.
20. Swearingen, John E., Jr. (July 30, 2002). Unpublished interview, Saratoga, WY. Tape 1 Side 1.
21. Worth while folk. John E. Swearingen Papers, Box 4, Folder 103.
22. Beneke, T. (1997). *Proving manhood: Reflections on men and sexism.* Berkeley: University of California Press, 40.
23. Swearingen, M. H. (1950). *A gallant journey: Mr. Swearingen and his family.* Columbia: University of South Carolina Press, 116–117.
24. Ibid., 119.
25. *Forty-first annual report of the South Carolina state superintendent of education.* (1909). Columbia, SC: State Printing Company, 16.
26. Ibid.,17.
27. Ibid., 25–26.
28. Ibid., 8.
29. Ibid., 90. For further details on funding inequities along color lines, see Anderson, J. D. (1988). Chapter 6: The Black public high school and the reproduction of caste in the urban South 1880–1935. *The education of Blacks in the South 1860–1935.* Chapel Hill: University of North Carolina Press.
30. *Forty-first annual report of the South Carolina state superintendent of education*, 9.
31. John E. Swearingen Papers. (January 19, 1909). Box 2, Folder 59. SCL.
32. In order: George Swearingen to John E. Swearingen. (March 4, 1909). John E. Swearingen Papers, Box 2, Folder 59. SCL; George Swearingen to John E. Swearingen. (March 9, 1909). John E. Swearingen Papers, Box 2, Folder 59. SCL.
33. The only other person to learn Point Print or Braille for Swearingen was his wife; the story is detailed in chapter 3.
34. Swearingen, John E. to Dr. Mitchell. (September 2, 1909). John E. Swearingen Papers, Box 2, Folders 59 and 63.
35. Swearingen, J. E. to Wharton, Miss L. (September 2, 1909). John E. Swearingen Papers, Box 2, Folder 63.
36. Swearingen, J. E. to Dr. Thomas, A. J. S. (September 2, 1909). John E. Swearingen Papers, Box 2, Folder 63.
37. Wells, B. J. to Swearingen, J. E. (August 28, 1909). John E. Swearingen Papers, Box 2, Folder 60.
38. Swearingen, J. E. (September 2, 1909). John E. Swearingen Papers, Box 2, Folder 59.

39. Mabry, T. O. to Swearingen, J. E. (April 19, 1909). John E. Swearingen Papers, Box 2, Folder 59.
40. *Forty-second annual report of the South Carolina state superintendent of education*. (1910). Columbia, SC: State Printing Company, 88.
41. Swearingen, *A gallant journey*, 120.
42. Ibid., 120–121.
43. Ibid.
44. Edgar, W. B. (1992). *South Carolina in the modern age*. Columbia: University of South Carolina Press, 40.
45. Testi, A. (March 1995).The gender of reform politics: Theodore Roosevelt and the culture of masculinity. *The Journal of American History, 81*(4), 1513 and 1517.
46. Houchins, J. F. Progressive politics, or why no. 3. (December 21, 1911). *The Standard*. Holley, New York.
47. Papers of Gov. Coleman L. Blease, Box 12, School Textbooks Folder. Miscellaneous Papers, Governor's Papers Collection, South Carolina Repository of History and Archives.
48. Rogers, G. C. & Taylor, C. J. (1994). *A South Carolina chronology 1497–1992*. Columbia: University of South Carolina Press, 121–122.
49. Edgar, W. B. (1998). *South Carolina: A history*. Columbia: University of South Carolina Press, 463.
50. Ibid., 467.
51. In order: J. E. Swearingen to Martin Ansel. (April 15, 1910); Martin Ansel to J. E. Swearingen. (March 8, 1910). Martin F. Ansel Papers. General correspondence, Box 4. Columbia, SC, South Carolina Repository of History and Archives.
52. Norva Kemp, personal secretary to Martin Ansel, to John E. Swearingen. (January 23, 1909). Martin F. Ansel Papers. General correspondence, Box 4. Columbia, SC, South Carolina Repository of History and Archives.
53. Martin F. Ansel Papers. General correspondence, Box 4. (November 10, 1909). John E. Swearingen to Martin Ansel. Columbia, SC, South Carolina Repository of History and Archives; and (November 11, 1909). Martin Ansel to John E. Swearingen. Columbia, SC, South Carolina Repository of History and Archives
54. Biebel, C. D. (1976). Private foundations and public policy: The case of secondary education during the Great Depression. *History of Education Quarterly, 16*(1), 3–4. For a more detailed description of the GEB's efforts in vocational-only funding, see also Anderson, E. & Moss, A. A. (1999). Chapter 4: The general education board's choices. *Dangerous donations: Northern philanthropy and southern black education, 1902–1930*. Columbia: University of Missouri Press, 85–107.
55. Anderson, J. D. (1978). Northern foundations and the shaping of Southern Black rural education 1902–1935. *History of Education Quarterly, 18*(4), 373.
56. *General Education Board*. Series I—Appropriations. Subseries I: States. Sleepy Hollow, NY: Rockefeller Archive Center.

57. Collins, E. to Buttrick, W. (September 13, 1904). *General Education Board Archives.* (1993). Series 1: Appropriations; Subseries 1; The Early Southern Program. [Voorhees Normal and Industrial School 1902–1957] Folder 1110.
58. Stinson, R. to Thomas, J. (March 19, 1917). *General Education Board Archives.* (1993). Series 1: Appropriations; Subseries 1; The Early Southern Program.
59. Bonner, R. R. to Peabody, G. F. (November 17, 1902). *General Education Board Archives.* Series 1: Appropriations; Subseries 1; The Early Southern Program. [Mayesville Educational & Industrial School 1902–1919], Folder 1129.
60. *General Education Board Archives.* (1993). Series 1: Appropriations; Subseries 1; The Early Southern Program.
61. Biebel, Private foundations and public policy, 22–23.
62. Leverenz, D. (2003). *Paternalism incorporated: Fables of American fatherhood 1865–1940.* Ithaca, NY: Cornell University Press, 3.
63. Anderson, Northern foundations and the shaping of Southern Black rural education 1902–1935, 383.
64. Williamson, J. (1984). *The crucible of race: Black-White relations in the American South since Emancipation.* New York, NY: Oxford University Press, 2.
65. Swearingen, J. E. to Buttrick, W. (January 29, 1921). *General Education Board Archives.* (1993). Series 1: Appropriations; Subseries 1; The Early Southern Program. [Supervisor of Rural Schools—White, 1912–1927]. New York, NY: Rockefeller University.
66. Swearingen, J. E. to Flexner, A. (April 11, 1921*). General Education Board Archives.* (1993). Series 1: Appropriations; Subseries 1; The Early Southern Program. [State Agent for Secondary Education 1919–1926]. New York, NY: Rockefeller University.
67. Swearingen, J. E. to Flexner, A. (June 9, 1921). *General Education Board Archives.* (1993). Series 1: Appropriations; Subseries 1; The Early Southern Program. [Supervisor of Rural Schools—Negro, 1917–1952]. New York, NY: Rockefeller University.
68. Swearingen, J. E. to Flexner, A. (June 13, 1918). Box 615, Folder 6503. *General Education Board.* Series I—Appropriations. Subseries iv—Higher Education. Sleepy Hollow, NY: Rockefeller Archive Center.
69. Flexner, A. to Swearingen, J. E. (June 17, 1918). Box 615, Folder 6503. *General Education Board.* Series I—Appropriations. Subseries iv—Higher Education. Sleepy Hollow, NY: Rockefeller Archive Center.
70. Swearingen, J. E. to Flexner, A. (June 24, 1918). Box 615, Folder 6503. *General Education Board.* Series I—Appropriations. Subseries iv—Higher Education. Sleepy Hollow, NY: Rockefeller Archive Center.
71. Reese, W. J. (2011). *America's public schools: From the common school to "no child left behind."* Baltimore, MD: The Johns Hopkins University Press, 121–122.
72. Rogers & Taylor, *A South Carolina chronology*, 121–122.
73. Swearingen, J. E. to Tillman, B. R. (December 31, 1915). Tillman, Benjamin Ryan. Incoming correspondence. Manuscripts—Political Collections. Box 44, Folder 676.

74. Swearingen, J. E. to Blease, C. L. (February 17, 1914). Coleman Livingston Blease (1911–1915). Miscellaneous papers. Letters to State Officials. Governor's Papers, Box 14.
75. Blease, C. L. to Swearingen, J. E. (February 18, 1914). Coleman Livingston Blease (1911–1915). Miscellaneous papers. Letters to State Officials. Governor's Papers, Box 14.
76. *Forty-fourth annual report of the South Carolina state superintendent of education.* (1912). Columbia, SC: State Printing Company, 11.
77. Ibid., 12–13.
78. Link, W. A. (1992). *The paradox of Southern progressivism, 1880–1930.* Chapel Hill: University of North Carolina Press, 11.
79. *Forty-fifth annual report of the South Carolina state superintendent of education.* (1913). Columbia, SC: State Printing Company, 17.
80. Anderson, *The education of Blacks in the South,* 197. The South is a unique study of African American education, because as late as 1930, up to 80 percent of the African American population in the United States lived in Southern States. Nationally, by 1910 only 2.8 percent of African American students were enrolled in high schools, compared to 10.1 percent of white students. For further discussion of this matter, see Angus, D. & Mirel, J. (1999). *The failed promise of the American high school 1890–1935.* New York, NY: New York Teacher's Press, 40.
81. Swearingen, J. E. to Blease, C. L. (November 24, 1913). Coleman Livingston Blease (1911–1915). Letters to State Officials 1912–1914. Governor's Papers, Box 14.
82. *Forty-fifth annual report of the South Carolina state superintendent of education,* 37.
83. Reese, *America's public schools,* 149.
84. Tyack, D. (1974). *The one best system: A history of American urban education.* Cambridge: Harvard University Press, 62.
85. *Forty-fifth annual report of the South Carolina state superintendent of education,* 38–39.
86. Tyack, *The one best system,* 63–64. For a further discussion of the feminization of the teaching corps and male reaction to this, see Aspinwall, K. & Drummond, M. J. (1989). Socialized into teaching. In DeLyon, H. & Migniuolo, F. W. (Eds.), *Women teachers: Issues and experiences.* Philadelphia, PA: Milton Keyes Press; Clifford, G. J. (1991). Daughters into teachers: Educational and demographic influences on the transformation of teaching into "women's work" in America. In Prentice, A. & Theobald, M. R. (Eds.), *Women who taught: Perspectives on the history of women and teaching.* Toronto: University of Toronto Press; Oram, A. (1989). A master should not serve under a mistress: Women teachers and men teachers 1900–1970. In Acker, S. (Ed.), *Teachers, gender, and careers.* New York, NY: Falmer Press; Perlmann, J. & Margo, R. A. (2001). *Women's work? American schoolteachers 1650–1920.* Chicago, IL: University of Chicago Press, 34–70; and Weiler, K. (1989). Women's history and the history of women teachers. *Journal of Education, 171*(3), 9–30.

3 Political Triptych: Swearingen, Blease, and Tillman, 1911–1915

1. Edgar, W. B. (1998). *South Carolina: A history*. Columbia: University of South Carolina Press, 473–474; Bradford, W. R. (1954). *Twenty-one governors of South Carolina, Tillman to Byrnes (including both): A related tragedy and other matters*. Columbia, NY: State Printing Company, 20.
2. Camak, D. E. (1960). *Human gold from Southern hills: Not a novel but a romance of facts*. Greer, SC: Published privately by the author, 136–139.
3. Edgar, W. B. (1992). *South Carolina in the modern age*. Columbia: University of South Carolina Press, 41.
4. Ibid., 33.
5. Wallace, D. D. (1961). *South Carolina: A short history 1520–1948*. Chapel Hill: University of North Carolina Press, 661–662.
6. Oertel, K. T. (Autumn 2002). "The free sons of the north" versus "the myrmidons of border-ruffianism": What makes a man in bleeding Kansas? *Kansas History: A Journal of the Central Plains, 25*, 174.
7. Edgar, *South Carolina in the modern age*, 34.
8. Simon, B. (1998). *A fabric of defeat: The politics of South Carolina millhands, 1910–1948*. Chapel Hill: University of North Carolina Press, 67.
9. Burnside, R. D. (1964). Racism in the administrations of Governor Cole Blease. *The Proceedings of the South Carolina Historical Association*, 50.
10. Ibid., 51.
11. Blocker, J. S. Jr. (Spring 2006). Race, sex and riot: The Sprigfield, Ohio race riots of 1904 and 1906 and the sources of anti-Black violence in the Lower Midwest. *Ohio Valley History, 6*(1), 29.
12. Negro rapist was lynched after confessing his crime, 1.
13. Ibid.
14. Prosser, A. C. to Blease, C. L. (September 6, 1913). Coleman Livingston Blease. General correspondence. Governor's Papers, Box 16.
15. Blease, C. L. to Prosser, A. C. (September 6, 1913). Coleman Livingston Blease. General correspondence. Governor's Papers, Box 16.
16. Darnell, Mrs. J. B. to Blease, C.L. (December 18 1914). Coleman Livingston Blease. General correspondence. Governor's Papers, Box 16.
17. Blease, C. L. to Darnell, J. B. (December 18, 1914). Coleman Livingston Blease. General correspondence. Governor's Papers, Box 16.
18. Blease, C. L. to Bond, O. J. (September 30, 1911). Coleman Livingston Blease (1911–1915). Letters to State Officials 1910–1912. Governor's Papers, Box 2513.
19. Bond, O. J. to Blease, C. L. (October 1, 1911). Coleman Livingston Blease (1911–1915). Letters to State Officials 1910–1912. Governor's Papers, Box 2513.
20. Blease, C. L. to Bond, O. J. (October 3, 1911). Coleman Livingston Blease (1911–1915). Letters to State Officials 1910–1912. Governor's Papers, Box 2513.
21. Blease, C. L. to Watson, E. J. (December 15, 1911). Coleman Livingston Blease (1911–1915). Letters to State Officials 1910–1912. Governor's Papers, Box 2513.

22. Watson, E. J. to Blease, C. L. (December 15, 1911). Coleman Livingston Blease (1911–1915). Letters to State Officials 1910–1912. Governor's Papers, Box 2513.
23. Blease, C. L. to Hospital Commission (January 16, 1914). Coleman Livingston Blease (1911–1915). Letters to State Officials 1913–1914. Governor's Papers, Box 14.
24. Blease, C. L. to Mitchum, H. (November 27, 1913). Coleman Livingston Blease (1911–1915). Letters to State Officials 1913–1914. Governor's Papers, Box 14.
25. Richardson, H. W. to Blease, C. L. (August 1, 1913). Coleman Livingston Blease (1911–1915). Letters to State Officials 1913–1914. Governor's Papers, Box 14.
26. Blease, C. L. to Bobley, J. C. (January 5, 1915). Coleman Livingston Blease. General Correspondence. Governor's Papers, Box 16.
27. Blease, C. L. to Blease, A. H. (January 5, 1915). Coleman Livingston Blease. General Correspondence. Governor's Papers, Box 16.
28. Tillman and Blease. (August 30, 1914). *The New York Times*, 14.
29. Blease, C. L. to Tillman, B. R. (May 22, 1911). Tillman, Benjamin Ryan. Incoming correspondence. Box 19, Folder 290.
30. Blease, C. L. to Progressive Farmer. (October 11, 1911). Coleman Livingston Blease. General correspondence. Governor's Papers, Box 16.
31. Blease, C. L. to Tillman, B. R. (October 14, 1911). Tillman, Benjamin Ryan. Incoming correspondence. Box 20, Folder 295.
32. Tillman, B. R. to Blease, C. L. (October 15, 1911). Tillman, Benjamin Ryan. Outgoing correspondence. Box 2, Folder 27.
33. Tillman, B. R. to Glenn, W. H. (September 25, 1911). Tillman, Benjamin Ryan. Outgoing correspondence. Box 2, Folder 24.
34. Tillman, B. R. to Green, L. (October 10, 1911). Tillman, Benjamin Ryan. Outgoing correspondence. Box 2, Folder 24.
35. Tillman, B. R. to Coleman, W. L. (August 26, 1912). Tillman, Benjamin Ryan. Outgoing correspondence. Box 4, Folder 68.
36. Tillman on Blease. (August 24, 1912). *The Anderson Daily Mail*. Anderson, SC, 1.
37. McSwain, J. J. to Tillman, B. R. (September 1, 1912). Tillman, Benjamin Ryan. Incoming correspondence. Box 21, Folder 310.
38. Tillman, B. R. to McSwain, J. J. (September 4, 1912). Tillman, Benjamin Ryan. Outgoing correspondence. Box 4, Folder 69.
39. Tillman, B. R. to Patton, C. (August 26, 1912). Box 4, Folder 69.
40. Tillman, B. R. to. Wilson, W. (September 22, 1913). Tillman, Benjamin Ryan. Personal unfiled correspondence. Box 13, Folder 172.
41. Tillman, B. R. to Bussey, G. W. (August 30, 1912). Tillman, Benjamin Ryan. Outgoing correspondence. Box 4, Folder 68.
42. Tillman, B. R. to Anderson, J. G. (August 30, 1912). Tillman, Benjamin Ryan. Outgoing correspondence. Box 4, Folder 68.
43. Tillman, B. R. to Lewis, A. (August 30, 1912). Tillman, Benjamin Ryan. Outgoing correspondence. Box 4, Folder 68.

44. Tillman, B. R. to Muckley, F. (September 4, 1912). Tillman, Benjamin Ryan. Outgoing correspondence. Box 4, Folder 68.
45. Blease, C. L. to campaign staff. (September 1912). Coleman Livingston Blease (1911–1915). General correspondence. Governor's Papers, Box 15.
46. Greene, J. E. to Blease, C. L. (May 11, 1914). Coleman Livingston Blease (1911–1915). General correspondence. Governor's Papers, Box 16.
47. Blease, C. L. to Tillman, B. R. (August 29, 1912). Tillman, Benjamin Ryan. Incoming correspondence. Box 20, Folder 301.
48. Tillman, B. R. to Wofford, C. C. (September 4, 1912). Tillman, Benjamin Ryan. Outgoing correspondence. Box 4, Folder 68.
49. Tillman, B. R. to Glenn, W. H. (August 30, 1912). Tillman, Benjamin Ryan. Outgoing correspondence. Box 4, Folder 68.
50. Source of the text: *Journal of the house of representatives of the general assembly of the state of South Carolina.* (1913). Columbia, SC: Gonzales and Bryan, 194–195 and 199.
51. Swearingen, J. E. to Tillman, B. R. (January 16, 1913). Tillman, Benjamin Ryan. Incoming correspondence. Manuscripts—Political Collections. Box 22, Folder 328.
52. Tillman, B. R. to Swearingen, J. E. (January 17, 1913). Tillman, Benjamin Ryan. Outgoing correspondence. Manuscripts—Political Collections. Box 8, Folder 88.
53. *Journal of the house of representatives of the general assembly of the state of South Carolina*, 203–205.
54. Ibid., 211.
55. Blease, C. L. to Johnson, D. B. (January 14, 1914). Coleman Livingston Blease (1911–1915). Letters to State Officials 1912–1914. Governor's Papers, Box 14.
56. Blease, C. L. to McReynolds, J. C. (September 20, 1913).Coleman Livingston Blease (1911–1915). Miscellaneous, 1911–1914. Governor's Papers, Box 15.
57. Blease, C. L. to Tillman, H. (January 14, 1914). Tillman, Benjamin Ryan. Incoming correspondence. Box 32, Folder 409.
58. Tillman, B. R. to Hardin, P. L. (January 12, 1913). Tillman, Benjamin Ryan. Outgoing correspondence. Manuscripts—Political Collections. Box 5, Folder 87.
59. Blease, C. L. to Price, W. (July 17, 1911). Coleman L. Blease, General correspondence. Governor's Papers, Box 16.
60. Blease, C. L. to Swearingen, J. E. (June 23, 1911). Coleman L. Blease, Letters, State Officials (1910–1912). Governor's Papers, Box 13.
61. The professors cited, professors at the South Carolina college, were also employees of the State Department of Education. Swearingen, J. E. to Rowland, A. (December 27, 1911). Papers of Gov. Coleman L. Blease, Letters, State Officials. Governor's Papers Collection. Box 13.
62. Hollis, D. W. (1956). *University of South Carolina Volume II: College to university.* Columbia: University of South Carolina Press, 251–252.
63. Ibid., 253–254.
64. Ibid., 260.
65. Ibid.

66. Swearingen, J. E. to Cox, A. H. (November 11, 1913). Coleman Livingston Blease (1911-1915). Miscellaneous papers. Letters to State Officials. Governor's Papers, Box 14.
67. Swearingen, J. E. to Blease, C. L. (November 24, 1913). Coleman Livingston Blease (1911-1915). Miscellaneous papers. Letters to State Officials. Governor's Papers, Box 14.
68. Blease, C. L. to Swearingen, J. E. (December 23, 1913). Coleman Livingston Blease (1911-1915). Miscellaneous papers. Letters to State Officials. Governor's Papers, Box 14.
69. Swearingen, J. E. to Blease, C. (December 24, 1913). Coleman Livingston Blease (1911-1915). Miscellaneous papers. Letters to State Officials. Box 14. Governor's Papers. Columbia, SC, South Carolina Repository of History and Archives.
70. Smythe, A. T. to Tillman, B. R. (March 17, 1914). Tillman, Benjamin Ryan. Incoming correspondence. Manuscripts—Political Collections. Clemson, SC, Special Collections: Robert Muldrow Cooper Library.
71. Swearingen, J. E. to Blease, C. (January 27, 1914) Coleman Livingston Blease (1911-1915). Miscellaneous papers. Letters to State Officials. Governor's Papers, Box 14.
72. Blease, C. to Swearingen, J. E. (January 29, 1914). Coleman Livingston Blease (1911-1915). Miscellaneous papers. Letters to State Officials. Governor's Papers, Box 14.
73. Simon, *A fabric of defeat*, 5.
74. Ibid., 29.
75. Ibid., 26.
76. Wallace, *South Carolina: A short history*, 661-662.
77. Roosevelt, F. D. to Blease, C. L. (October 15, 1914). Coleman Livingston Blease (1911-1915). Miscellaneous Letters 1911-1914. Governor's Papers, Box 15.
78. Blease, C. L. to Roosevelt, F. D. (October 23, 1914). Coleman Livingston Blease (1911-1915). Miscellaneous Letters 1911-1914. Governor's Papers, Box 15.
79. Wallace, *South Carolina: A short history*, 662-663.
80. Edgar, *South Carolina in the modern age*, 41-42.
81. Blease, C. L. (August 24, 1914). Coleman Livingston Blease (1911-1915). Letters to State Officials 1912-1914. Governor's Papers, Box 14.
82. Tillman, B. R. to. Swearingen, J. E. (November 18, 1913). Tillman, Benjamin Ryan. Outgoing correspondence. Manuscripts—Political Collections. Box 8, Folder 164.
83. Swearingen, J. E. to Tillman, B. R. (December 4, 1913). Tillman, Benjamin Ryan. Incoming correspondence. Manuscripts—Political Collections. Box 31, Folder 479.
84. Wallace, *South Carolina: A short history*, 664-665.
85. William of Hohenzollern was Kaiser of Prussia at the outbreak of World War I. Tillman's biblical reference was to how the nation of Israel under Moses conquered the land of Bashan under the rule of king Og. It is likely Tillman was describing the people of South Carolina as being the people of Bashan, with Blease being their Og. Article reference: Tillman and Blease. (August 30, 1914). *The New York Times*, 14.

86. Edgar, *South Carolina: A history*, 664.
87. Tillman, B. R. to Spartanburg Journal, et al. (December 31, 1915). Tillman, Benjamin Ryan. Outgoing Correspondence. Manuscripts—Political Collections. Box 14, Folder 283.
88. Worth while folk: The blind school superintendent. (n. d.). John E. Swearingen Papers, Box 4, Folder 112.
89. Ibid.
90. *Forty-third annual report of the South Carolina state superintendent of education.* (1911). Columbia, SC: State Printing Company, 160.
91. Source of tabular data: Ibid., 156–157. For a detailed list of accreditation requirements, see Koos, L. V. (1927). *The American secondary school.* Atlanta, GA: Ginn, 742–745.
92. Kandel, P. (1939). *History of secondary education in the United States.* New York, NY: Houghton Mifflin, 468–471.
93. Krug, E. A. (1969). *The shaping of the American high school 1880–1920.* Madison, WI: University of Milwaukee Press, 308.
94. *Forty-third annual report of the South Carolina state superintendent of education*, 24.
95. Ibid.
96. Ibid., 25–26.
97. Ibid., 69–70.
98. Ibid., 131–137.
99. To be eligible for a diploma, students had to complete 14 or more standard units of instruction. *Forty-third annual report of the South Carolina state superintendent of education*, 136.
100. *Forty-third annual report of the South Carolina state superintendent of education*, 77–78.
101. Tyack, D. (1974). *The one best system: A history of American urban education.* Cambridge: Harvard University Press, 160.
102. *Forty-fifth annual report of the South Carolina state superintendent of education.* (1913). Columbia, SC: State Printing Company, 34.
103. Tyack, *The one best system*, 144.
104. Fall teacher's examination: Will be held here tomorrow at the court house. (October 5, 1911). *The Anderson Daily Mail.* Anderson, SC, 4.
105. Swearingen, J. E. to Cox, A. H. (n. d.). Papers of Governor Coleman L. Blease, Letters, State Officials 1913–1914. Governor's Papers Collection. Box 14.
106. *Forty-fifth annual report of the South Carolina state superintendent of education,* 106–107.

4 Swept Up in Progressivism, 1915–1919

1. Rogers, G. C. & Taylor, C. J. (1994). *A South Carolina chronology 1497–1992.* Columbia: University of South Carolina Press, 122–123.
2. Burts, R. M. (1974). *Richard Irvine Manning and the Progressive movement in South Carolina.* Columbia: University of South Carolina Press, 95.

3. Swearingen, J. E. to Manning, R. I. (February 17, 1915). Manning, Richard Irvine (1915-1919). General correspondence. Box 51. Governor's Papers. Columbia, SC, South Carolina Repository of History and Archives.
4. Rogers & Taylor, *A South Carolina chronology*, 122-123.
5. Dreyfus, J. V. (1997). *John Eldred Swearingen: Superintendent of education in South Carolina 1909-1922*. Columbia, SC: College of Education, 9.
6. Fletcher, J. G. (1962). Education, past and present. In *I'll take my stand: The south and the agrarian tradition*. New York, NY: Harper Torchbooks, 118-119.
7. *Forty-seventh annual report of the South Carolina state superintendent of education*. (1915). Columbia, SC: State Printing Company, 22.
8. *Forty-eighth annual report of the South Carolina state superintendent of education*. (1916). Columbia, SC: State Printing Company, 13.
9. Swearingen, J. E. to Manning, R. I. (February 25, 1916). Manning, Richard Irvine (1915-1919). General correspondence. Box 51. Governor's Papers.
10. *Forty-eighth annual report of the South Carolina state superintendent of education*, 18.
11. Tyack, D. (1974). *The one best system: A history of American urban education*. Cambridge: Harvard University Press, 184. For further discussion of the need for and effects of compulsory education, see Kett, J. F. (1995). School leaving. In Ravitch, D. & Vinovskis, M. (Eds.), *Learning from the past: What history teaches us about school reform*. Baltimore, MD: Johns Hopkins University Press, 268-271; Perkinson, H. J. (1991). *The imperfect panacea: American faith in education, 1865-1990*. New York, NY: McGraw-Hill, 69-70; Richardson, J. G. (1980). Variation in date of enactment of compulsory school attendance laws: An empirical study. *Sociology of Education, 53*, 153-163; and Simon, B. (1998). *A fabric of defeat: The politics of South Carolina millhands, 1910-1948*. Chapel Hill: University of North Carolina Press, 29-30 and 76.
12. Source of table data: Richardson, J. G., Variation in date of enactment of compulsory school attendance laws, 157.
13. *Forty-sixth annual report of the South Carolina state superintendent of education*. (1914). Columbia, SC: State Printing Company, 19-20.
14. Ibid., 20.
15. Ibid., 21.
16. Ibid., 22-23.
17. Ibid., 26.
18. Ibid., 41 & 44.
19. Ibid., 15-16.
20. Swearingen, J. E. to Spencer, C. E., et al. (June 30, 1914). Coleman Livingston Blease (1911-1915). Letters to State Officials 1913-1914. Governor's Papers. Box 14.
21. Source of tabular data: *Forty-sixth annual report of the South Carolina state superintendent of education*, 168-169.
22. Burts, *Richard Irvine Manning and the Progressive movement in South Carolina*, 95.

23. Ibid, 147.
24. *Forty-seventh annual report of the South Carolina state superintendent of education*, 21.
25. Anderson, J. D. (1988). *The education of blacks in the south 1860–1935*. Chapel Hill: University of North Carolina Press, 36.
26. *Fiftieth annual report of the South Carolina state superintendent of education*. (1917). Columbia, SC: State Printing Company, 16.
27. Thomson, J. W. to Swearingen, J. E. (April 19, 1909). John E. Swearingen Papers, Box 2, Folder 60.
28. Swearingen, M. H. (1950). *A gallant journey: Mr. Swearingen and his family*. Columbia: University of South Carolina Press, 91.
29. Ibid.
30. Ibid., 94.
31. Swearingen, J. E. to Hough, Mary. (March 10, 1914). John E. Swearingen Papers, Box 2, Folder 67.
32. Swearingen, *A gallant journey*, 96.
33. Ibid., 95.
34. Swearingen, G. to Hough, M. (April 14, 1916). John E. Swearingen Papers, Box 2, Folder 67.
35. In addition to knowing Swearingen via his work as a congressman, McSwain was also Mary's high school teacher and superintendent. McSwain, J. J. to Swearingen, J. E. (May 4, 1916). John E. Swearingen Papers, Box 2, Folder 67.
36. Tillman, B. R. to Swearingen, J. E. (May 17, 1916). John E. Swearingen Papers, Box 2, Folder 59.
37. Swearingen, *A gallant journey*, 97. Bridal photo of Mary Hough Swearingen courtesy of John E. Swearingen, Jr.
38. Swearingen, *A gallant journey*, 126.
39. Ibid, 98.
40. The site of the house has now become a complex of medical offices; the whereabouts of the contents of the house are unknown at this time. Description of the house at the time of John Jr.'s birth: Swearingen, *A gallant journey*, 133.
41. Swearingen, John E., Jr. (July 30, 2002). Unpublished interview, Saratoga, WY. Tape 1, Side 1.
42. Swearingen, *A gallant journey*, 117.
43. Swearingen, John E., Jr. (July 30, 2002). Unpublished interview, Saratoga, WY.
44. Swearingen, *A gallant journey*, 117.
45. Ibid., 123.
46. Ibid., 126.
47. Ibid., 127–128.
48. Marsh, M. (1990). Suburban men and masculine domesticity, 1870–1915. In Carnes, M. C. & Griffen, C. (Eds.), *Meanings for manhood: Constructions of masculinity in Victorian America*. Chicago, IL: University of Chicago Press, 117. This notion of the new family roles is detailed in Mintz, S. & Kellogg,

S. (1988). Chapter VI: The rise of the compassionate family, 1900–1930. *Domestic revolutions: A social history of American family life.* New York, NY: The Free Press.
49. Swearingen, John E., Jr. (July 30, 2002). Unpublished interview, Saratoga, WY
50. Swearingen, J. E. to Tillman, B. R. (June 3, 1912). Tillman, Benjamin Ryan. Incoming correspondence. Manuscripts—Political Collections. Box 20, Folder 301.
51. Beginning her career working with mill children, then expanding to work up a series of "opportunity schools," Dr. Wil Lou Gray (1883–1984) became an institution in the state of South Carolina; many programs and entire schools are named in her honor. For her own views on her life, see Gray, W. L. (1939). *Stop, look, and read my history.* Columbia, SC: State Printing Company. For others' take on her life, see Ayers, D. (1988). *Let my people learn: The biography of Dr. Wil Lou Gray.* Greenwood, SC: Attic Press; Montgomery, M. (1963). *South Carolina's Wil Lou Gray: Pioneer in adult education, crusader, modern model.* Columbia, SC: Vogue Press; Smith, G. M. (2000). *The opportunity schools and the founder Wil Lou Gray.* West Columbia, SC: Wil Lou Gray Opportunity School.
52. Source of tabular data: *Forty-eighth annual report of the South Carolina state superintendent of education*, 116.
53. *Forty-seventh annual report of the South Carolina state superintendent of education.* (1915). Columbia, SC: State Printing Company, 26.
54. Anderson, *The education of blacks in the south*, 150 & 178.
55. *Forty-third annual report of the South Carolina state superintendent of education.* (1911). Columbia, SC: State Printing Company, 97–98.
56. Ibid., 99.
57. Krug, E. A. (1969). *The shaping of the American high school 1880–1920.* Madison, WI: University of Milwaukee Press, 200.
58. Kandel, P. (1939). *History of secondary education in the United States.* New York, NY: Houghton Mifflin, 100.
59. *Forty-third annual report of the state superintendent of education*, 102.
60. Ibid., 103.
61. Ravitch, D. (2000). *Left back: A century of failed school reforms.* New York, NY: Simon & Schuster, 65–66 & 94.
62. Koos, L. V. (1927). *The American secondary school.* Atlanta, GA: Ginn, 298–299.
63. Perkinson, *The imperfect panacea*, 142–143.
64. Tyack, *The one best system*, 189.
65. Wooster, M. M. (1994). *Angry classrooms, vacant minds: What's happened to our high schools?* San Francisco, CA: Pacific Research Institute for Public Policy, 7–9.
66. National Vocational Education (Smith-Hughes) Act. *College of Agriculture and Life Sciences, North Carolina State University.* http://www.cals.ncsu.edu/agexed/sac/smithugh.html, 1.

67. Ibid.
68. Ibid., 2.
69. Ibid.
70. *Forty-third annual report of the state superintendent of education*, 12–13.
71. *Fifty-first annual report of the South Carolina state superintendent of education*. (1918). Columbia, SC: State Printing Company, 12.
72. Counts, G. S. (1922). *The selective character of American secondary education*. Chicago, IL: University of Chicago Press, 141.
73. Ibid., 141–148. This conclusion is also discussed in Angus, D. & Mirel, J. (1999). *The failed promise of the American high school 1890–1995*. New York, NY: New York Teacher's Press, 32–44; Fuller, B. Youth job structure and school enrollment 1890–1920. *Sociology of Education*, 56(3), 145–156; Labaree, D. F. (April 1987). *Shaping the role of the public high school: Past patterns and present implications*. Paper presented at the annual meeting of the American Educational Research Association; and Powell, A. G., Farrar, E., & Cohen, D. K. (1985). *The shopping mall high school: Winners and losers in the educational marketplace*. Boston, MA: Houghton Mifflin, 245–251.
74. Blease, C. L. to Oliver, R. S. (July 20, 1911).Coleman Livingston Blease (1911–1915). Miscellaneous, 1911–1914. Governor's Papers. Box 15.
75. Swearingen, J. E. to Tillman, B. R. (February 4, 1918). Tillman, Benjamin Ryan. Incoming correspondence. Manuscripts—Political Collections. Box 63, Folder 959.
76. Edgar, W. B. (1998). *South Carolina: A history*. Columbia: University of South Carolina Press, 476–479.
77. Sedlak, M. W. (1995). Attitudes, choices, and behavior: School delivery of health and social services. In Ravitch, D. & Vinovskis, M. (Eds.), *Learning from the past: What history teaches us about school reform*. Baltimore, MD: Johns Hopkins University Press, 68.
78. Angus & Mirel, *The failed promise of the American high school*, 34 & 47–48.
79. Tyack, *The one best system*, 204–205.
80. *Fifty-first annual report of the South Carolina state superintendent of education*, 7.
81. Ibid.
82. Government helps to supply teachers: Federal board of education established to render free service in present shortage. (October 20, 1918). *The State*. Columbia, SC, 22.
83. Kluger, R. (1977). *Simple justice: Brown v. Board of Education and Black America's struggle for equality*. New York, NY: Vintage Books, 100.
84. Hemphill, J. C. (November 3, 1918). Southern Negro's status after war. *The State*. Columbia, SC, 22.
85. Ibid.
86. Richardson, R. (2007). *Black masculinity and the U.S. South: From Uncle Tom to gangsta*. Athens: University of Georgia Press, 77.
87. Ibid., 76–77.

234 NOTES

88. Dana, R. to Buttrick, W. (February 1, 1916). *General Education Board Archives* (1903). Series 1. Appropriations; Subseries 1; The Early Southern Program. [Mayesville Educational & Industrial School 1902–1919].
89. *Fiftieth annual report of the state superintendent of education*, 24.
90. Angus & Mirel, *The failed promise of the American high school*, 14
91. Bureau of Education, Department of the Interior. (1918). *Bulletin No. 35: Cardinal principles of secondary education: A report of the commission on the reorganization of secondary education, appointed by the National Education Association.* Washington, DC: Government Printing Office, 5.
92. Ibid., 9.
93. Graham, P. A. (1995). Assimilation, adjustment, and access: An antiquarian view of American education. In Ravitch, D. & Vinovskis, M. (Eds.), *Learning from the past: What history teaches us about school reform*. Baltimore, MD: Johns Hopkins University Press, 10.
94. Kett, *Learning from the past*, 269–270.
95. Bureau of Education, *Bulletin No. 35*, 11.
96. Ibid., 12.
97. Ibid., 13–15.
98. *Fifty-third annual report of the South Carolina state superintendent of education.* (1920). Columbia, SC: State Printing Company, 22.
99. Lockwood, C. M. (1938). *Organization and development of the South Carolina High School League*. Unpublished master's thesis, University of South Carolina, 7.
100. Rogers & Taylor, *A South Carolina chronology*, 124.
101. For a detailed account of the sexism practiced by Wilson while president of Harvard, see Bohan, C. H. (2001). *Go to the sources: Lucy Maynard Salmon and the teaching of history*. New York, NY: Peter Lang.
102. Appeal for suffrage voiced by president (October 1, 1918). *The State.* Columbia: SC, 1.
103. Bederman, G. (1995). *Manliness and civilization: A cultural history of gender and race in the United States 1880–1917.* Chicago, IL: University of Chicago Press, 13.
104. Reese, W. J. (1986). *Power and the promise of school reform: Grassroots movements during the progressive era.* Boston, MA: Routledge & Kegan Paul, 31.
105. Dreyfus, *John Eldred Swearingen*, 42.
106. These acts were specifically designed to prepare South Carolina to comply with the Smith-Hughes Act. *Fiftieth annual report of the South Carolina state superintendent of education*, 12.
107. *Fiftieth annual report of the South Carolina state superintendent of education*, 12–13.
108. Ibid., 13–14.
109. *Fifty-first annual report of the South Carolina state superintendent of education*, 8.
110. Ibid.
111. Graham, "Assimilation, adjustment, and access," 12.

112. *Fifty-first annual report of the South Carolina state superintendent of education*, 21.
113. Kett, *Learning from the past*, 269.
114. *Fifty-first annual report of the South Carolina state superintendent of education*, 25.
115. Bowers, L. W. (November 10, 1918). How to fight Spanish influenza. *The State*. Columbia: SC, 9.
116. Advises closing of all schools. (October 7, 1918). *The State*. Columbia: SC, 1.
117. Schools to start classes Monday. (October 31, 1918). *The State*. Columbia: SC, 9.
118. Pay should continue. (October 9, 1918). *The State*. Columbia: SC, 10.
119. Dreyfus, *John Eldred Swearingen*, 17.
120. *Fifty-second annual report of the South Carolina state superintendent of education*. (1919). Columbia: State Printing Company, 120.
121. Burts, *Richard Irvine Manning and the Progressive movement in South Carolina*, 146.
122. Gunter, L. to Swearingen, J. E. (June 29, 1918). John E. Swearingen Papers, Box 3, Folder 68.
123. General election lacks in interest: Practically no oppostion to democratic nominees. (November 6, 1918). *The State*. Columbia: SC, 10.
124. Hanna, R. E. to Swearingen, J. E. (August 1, 1918). John E. Swearingen Papers, Box 3, Folder 68.

5   Robert Cooper and the Final Battle, 1919–1957

1. Swearingen, J. E., Jr. (July 30, 2002). Unpublished interview, Saratoga, WY. Tape 1, Side 2.
2. To present play in sign language: Helen Menken plans to attempt mute Portia. (April 2, 1922). *The State*. Columbia, SC. 2.
3. For more on Swearingen as a disabled man, see Janak, E. (2010). Adventitiously blind, advantageously political: John Eldred Swearingen and social definitions of disability in Progressive-Era South Carolina. *Vitae Scholasticae, 27*(1), 5–25; reprinted in Morice, L. C. & Puchner, L. (2014). *Life stories: Exploring issues in educational history through biography*. Charlotte, NC: Information Age, 85–106.
4. Cooper on education. (October 29, 1918). *The State*. Columbia, SC, 9.
5. Cooper, R. (1919). *An educational policy for the state*. State Agencies File. Governor's Papers. Columbia, SC, South Carolina Repository of History and Archives.
6. Ibid.
7. *Fifty-first annual report of the South Carolina state superintendent of education* (1918). Columbia, SC: State Printing Company, 41.
8. Anderson, J. D. (1978). Northern foundations and the shaping of Southern Black rural education 1902–1935. *History of Education Quarterly, 18*(4), 383.

9. *Fifty-first annual report of the South Carolina state superintendent of education*, 97.
10. Anderson details the relationship between the Hampton and Tuskeegee Institutes in his work *The Education of Blacks in the South*. Tuskeegee was founded using Hampton as a model; both institutions were strongly influenced by Booker T. Washington's model of industrial education.
11. *Fifty-first annual report of the South Carolina state superintendent of education*, 97–98.
12. Brannon advocated a five-month term for African American schools, divided around "the needs of the farm," compared to the seven- to ten-month term in place for white schools.
13. *Fifty-first annual report of the South Carolina state superintendent of education*, 100–101.
14. Caldwell, B. L. to Davis, W. (May 18, 1919). *General Education Board Archives*. (1993). Series 1: Appropriations; Subseries 1; The Early Southern Program. [Supervisor of Rural Schools—Negro, 1917–1952].
15. Davis, W. to Flexner, A. (August 25, 1919). *General Education Board Archives*. (1993). Series 1: Appropriations; Subseries 1; The Early Southern Program. [Supervisor of Rural Schools—Negro, 1917–1952].
16. *Fifty-first annual report of the South Carolina state superintendent of education*, 17.
17. Ibid., 18.
18. Anonymous to Flexner, A. (August 4, 1919). *General Education Board Archives*. (1993). Series 1: Appropriations; Subseries 1; The Early Southern Program. [Supervisor of Rural Schools—Negro, 1917–1952].
19. Edgar, W. B. (1998). *South Carolina: A history*. Columbia: University of South Carolina Press, 481.
20. *Fifty-second annual report of the South Carolina state superintendent of education*. (1919). Columbia, SC: State Printing Company, 18.
21. Ibid., 84.
22. Rogers, G. C. & Taylor, C. J. (1994). *A South Carolina chronology 1497–1992*. Columbia: University of South Carolina Press, 123.
23. Edgar, *South Carolina: A history*, 484.
24. Gray, W. L. & Swearingen, J. E. (1920). *Midsummer drive against illiteracy for white schools*. Office of State Superintendent of Education, State of South Carolina, 11. For more on similar state-supported efforts nationwide, see Reese, W. J. (1986). Vacation schools, playgrounds, and educational extension. *Power and the promise of school reform: Grassroots movements during the progressive era*. Boston, MA: Routledge & Kegan Paul, 148–176.
25. Sources of table data: *Fifty-third annual report of the South Carolina state superintendent of education*, 22; and *1930 United States Census Data*. (2002). University of Virginia Census Information. [Online data]. Available FTP: Hostname: virginia.edu Directory: fisher.lib File: cgi-local/censusbin/census/cen.pl
26. *Fifty-fourth annual report of the South Carolina state superintendent of education*. (1921). Columbia, SC: State Printing Company, 19.

27. Ibid., 34.
28. Ibid.
29. Ibid.
30. Ibid., 36.
31. *Fifty-fifth annual report of the South Carolina state superintendent of education*. (1922). Columbia, SC: State Printing Company, 26–27.
32. Swearingen, J. E. to Burgess, J. P. (September 18, 1922). John E. Swearingen Papers, Box 3, Folder 89.
33. Burgess, J. R. to Swearingen, J. E. (September 16, 1922). John E. Swearingen Papers, Box 3, Folder 88.
34. Dreyfus, J. V. (1997). *John Eldred Swearingen: Superintendent of education in South Carolina 1909–1922*. Columbia, SC: College of Education, 18.
35. *Fifty-fifth annual report of the South Carolina state superintendent of education*, 15.
36. Angus, D. (2001). *Professionalism and the public good: A brief history of teacher certification*. Washington, DC: Thomas B. Fordham Foundation, 12.
37. *Fifty-fourth annual report of the South Carolina state superintendent of education*, 15.
38. Swearingen, J. E. to Currell, W. S. (June 14, 1920). John E. Swearingen Papers, Box 3, Folder 68.
39. McCain, J. J. to Swearingen, J. E. (June 8, 1921). John E. Swearingen Papers, Box 2, Folder 68.
40. Swearingen, M. H. (1950). *A gallant journey: Mr. Swearingen and his family*. Columbia: University of South Carolina Press, 134.
41. While Mary recalls the car being called "Buick-cephalous" in her memoir, John Jr. simply calls it "Bucephalous" in his interviews. Sources: Swearingen, John E., Jr. (July 30, 2002). Unpublished interview, Tape 1, Side 1; and Swearingen, *A gallant journey*, 154–160.
42. Swearingen, John E., Jr. (July 30, 2002). Unpublished interview, Tape 1, Side 1.
43. Ibid. Tape 1, Side 2.
44. Ibid.
45. Swearingen, *A gallant journey*, 113.
46. Ibid., 112.
47. Ibid., 113.
48. McCants, E. C. to Swearingen, J. E. (March 31, 1922). Swearingen Papers, Box 2, Folder 70.
49. Banks, W. to Swearingen, J. E. ("Thursday night," May 1922). Swearingen Papers, Box 2, Folder 70.
50. Lockwood, D. B. to Swearingen, J. E. (June 12, 1922). John E. Swearingen Papers, Box 3, Folder 71.
51. McElveen, J. V. to Swearingen, J. E. (June 4, 1922). John E. Swearingen Papers, Box 3, Folder 71.
52. Gasque, B. F. to Swearingen, J. E. (June 7, 1922). John E. Swearingen Papers, Box 3, Folder 71.
53. Bishop, B. B. to Swearingen, J. E. (June 6, 1922). John E. Swearingen Papers, Box 3, Folder 71.

238 NOTES

54. Untitled campaign speech. (n.d.). John E. Swearingen Papers, Box 3, Folder 70
55. Ibid.
56. Ibid.
57. Brown, S. H. to Swearingen, J. E. (April 20, 1922). John E. Swearingen Papers, Box 3, Folder 70.
58. Banks, W. to Swearingen, J. E. ("Thursday night," May 1922). Swearingen Papers, Box 2, Folder 70.
59. The tone of the letter and the details known of Gray's work in education suggest Swearingen was the "Interested" who wrote this letter; it would be characteristic of him to try and bring in someone he knew was eminently qualified regardless of sex. However, all evidence is circumstantial; there was no draft of such a letter in Swearingen's papers. "Interested." Suggests Miss Gray: Correspondent commends for state office. (May 26, 1922). *The State*. Columbia, SC, 2.
60. "Friend" to Swearingen, J. E. (June 16, 1922). John E. Swearingen Papers, Box 3, Folder 71.
61. Gunter, L. to Swearingen, J. E. (June 29, 1918). John E. Swearingen Papers, Box 2, Folder 63.
62. Hanna, R. E. to Swearingen. J. E. (August 1, 1918). Swearingen Papers, Box 2, Folder 68.
63. Swearingen, John E., Jr. (July 30, 2002). Unpublished interview; and Swearingen, John E., Jr. (November 1, 2002). Unpublished interview, Chicago, IL.
64. Swearingen, *A gallant journey*, 114.
65. Ibid., 112.
66. Simon, B. (February 1996). The appeal of Cole Blease of South Carolina: Race, class, and sex in the New South. *The Journal of Southern History, 62*(1), 82–83.
67. Swearingen leaves race for governor: Quits gubernatorial contest to offer for succeed himself as superintendent of education. (June 18, 1922). *The State*. Columbia, SC, 13.
68. Swearingen, *A gallant journey*, 113.
69. Carpenter, T. G. to Swearingen, J. E. (September 1, 1922). Swearingen Papers, Box 3, Folder 79.
70. Palloway, J. R. &. Martin, W. F. to Swearingen, J. E. (September 4, 1922). John E. Swearingen Papers, Box 3, Folder 89.
71. Rasor, J. B. to Swearingen, J. E. (September 16, 1922). John E. Swearingen Papers, Box 3, Folder 89.
72. Swearingen, J. E. to Rasor, S. (September 1922). John E. Swearingen Papers, Box 3, Folder 90.
73. Calhoun, H. to Swearingen, J. E. (September 1, 1922). Swearingen Papers, Box 3, Folder 79.
74. Rasor, J. B. to Swearingen, J. E. (September 16, 1922). John E. Swearingen Papers, Box 3, Folder 89.

75. Jones, Charles A. to Editor, *Charleston News and Courier*. (September 4, 1922). John E. Swearingen Papers, Box 3, Folder 83.
76. Strohecker, H. O. to Swearingen, J. E. (September 9, 1922). John E. Swearingen Papers, Box 3, Folder 83.
77. Blease, C. L. to Longman, Green & Co. (April 3, 1914). Coleman Livingston Blease. Miscellaneous papers. Letters to State Officials. Governor's Papers, Box 12 "textbook orders."
78. Swearingen followed this advice, releasing a one-page flyer to be printed in the newspapers. Tatum, W. O. to Swearingen, J. E. (June 19, 1922). John E. Swearingen Papers, Box 3, Folder 72.
79. Advertisement June 27, 1922. *The State*. Columbia, SC.
80. "I am truly yours" to Swearingen, J. E. (June 28, 1922). John E. Swearingen Papers, Box 3, Folder 76.
81. Moorman, J. J., CPA to Bradley, W. W., State Bank Examiner. (September 9, 1922). John E. Swearingen Papers, Box 3, Folder 83.
82. The school book case will be heard Monday: Publishing house seeking an injunction against the State Board of Education. (September 30, 1911). *The Anderson Daily Mail*. Anderson, SC, 6.
83. Simon, B. (1998). *A fabric of defeat: The politics of South Carolina millhands, 1910–1948*. Chapel Hill: University of North Carolina Press, 34.
84. Cofield, G. to Swearingen, J. E. (September 5, 1922). John E. Swearingen Papers, Box 3, Folder 79.
85. Swearingen, J. E. to Rasor, S. (September 1922). John E. Swearingen Papers, Box 3, Folder 90.
86. Swearingen, J. E. to Rasor, S. (September 19, 1922). John E. Swearingen Papers, Box 3, Folder 90.
87. Glantzberg, P. E. to Swearingen, J. E. (December 7, 1922). John E. Swearingen Papers, Box 4, Folder 94.
88. Resolution adopted by the Winthrop Board of Trustees (November 21, 1922). John E. Swearingen Papers, Box 4, Folder 94.
89. Kohn, A. (January 1923). Fought for schools for fourteen years: Swearingen quits post with fine record of achievement. *The State*. Columbia, SC.
90. Wells, B. J. (December 15, 1922). Mr. Swearingen's administration. *South Carolina Education, 4* (3), 2.
91. Stoddard, J. A. to Swearingen, J. E. (January 15, 1923). John E. Swearingen Papers, Box 4, Folder 95.
92. Buttrick, W. to Swearingen, J. E. (November 10, 1922).). John E. Swearingen Papers, Box 4, Folder 93.
93. Swearingen, J. E. to Chapman, H. R. (September 16, 1922). John E. Swearingen Papers, Box 3, Folder 87.
94. Swearingen, J. E. to Rasor, J. B. (September 18, 1922). John E. Swearingen Papers, Box 3, Folder 89.
95. Swearingen, *A gallant journey*, 119.
96. Ibid.

240 NOTES

97. Beaty, W. & Beaty, M. to Swearingen, M. H. (January 1, 1959). John E. Swearingen Papers, Box 4, Folder 102.
98. Swearingen, J. E. to Rasor, S. (September 19, 1922). John E. Swearingen Papers, Box 3, Folder 90.
99. In order, *Fortieth annual report of the South Carolina state superintendent of education.* (1908). Columbia, SC: State Printing Company, 9; and *Fifty-fifth annual report of the South Carolina state superintendent of education*, 165.
100. Chief Superintendent of Secondary Education, High School Graduation Records, Box 1, Folder 1, and Box 2, Columbia, SC, South Carolina Department of Archives and History.
101. *Fifty-fifth annual report of the South Carolina state superintendent of education*, 125.
102. Dreyfus, *John Eldred Swearingen*, 12–13.
103. McSwain, J. J. to Swearingen, J. E. (December 13, 1922). John E. Swearingen Papers, Box 4, Folder 94.
104. McSwain J. J. to Swearingen, J. E. (September 17, 1922). Swearingen Papers, Box 3, Folder 88.
105. Swearingen, J. E. to McSwain J.J. (September 19, 1922). Swearingen Papers, Box 3, Folder 89.
106. Swearingen, J. E. to McSwain J.J. (September 23, 1922). Swearingen Papers, Box 4, Folder 91.
107. Swearingen, J. E. to Wells, B.J. (September 23, 1922). Swearingen Papers, Box 4, Folder 91.
108. Swearingen J. E. to Buttrick W. W. (November 7, 1922), and Buttrick, W. W. to Swearingen, J. E. (November 10, 1922). John E. Swearingen Papers, Box 4, Folder 93.
109. Swearingen, John E., Jr. (July 30, 2002). Unpublished interview, Tape 1, Side 2.
110. Ibid. Photo of George as "Cotton King" courtesy John E. Swearingen, Jr.
111. Swearingen, John E., Jr. (July 30, 2002). Unpublished interview, Tape 1, Side 1.
112. Ibid.
113. Swearingen, *A gallant journey*, 147.
114. J. E. Swearingen: Candidate for State Superintendent of Education. John E. Swearingen Papers, Box 4, Folder 96. Columbia: SCL.
115. Ibid.
116. Swearingen, J. E. to Tillman, B. R. (July 13, 1917). Tillman, Benjamin Ryan. Incoming correspondence. Manuscripts—Political Collections. Box 57, Folder 901.
117. Richards, J. G. to Swearingen, J. E. (September 5, 1939). John E. Swearingen Papers, Box 4, Folder 97.
118. Photo of George Van Swearingen at West Point graduation courtesy John E. Swearingen, Jr.
119. Swearingen, G. V. to Swearingen, J. E. (May 2, 1944). John E. Swearingen Papers, Box 4, Folder 100.

120. Mary Swearingen, engagement portrait. Photo courtesy John E. Swearingen, Jr. Text source: Babcock, H. to Noys, R. (April 9, 1946). John E. Swearingen Papers, Box 4, Folder 102.
121. Photo courtesy John E. Swearingen, Jr.
122. John Jr.'s autobiography details his extraordinary life. Swearingen, J. & DiBona, C. J. (2004). *Think ahead: A memoir.* Columbia: University of South Carolina Press.
123. Swearingen, John E., Jr. (November 1, 2002). Unpublished interview. Photo courtesy John E. Swearingen, Jr.
124. Columbian: Mrs. Swearingen is state mother. (March 21, 1962). *The State.* Columbia, SC, 1-A-2-A.
125. Swearingen G. to Swearingen, J. E. (May 2, 1944). John E. Swearingen Papers, Box 4, Folder 100.
126. While Swearingen was 82 years old upon death, he had been blind for 70 of those years. Swearingen, *A gallant journey,* 221.

6 Conclusion: Not the Windows but the Occupant Looking Through

1. Thornwell, J. H. to Swearingen, J. E. (January 23, 1923). John E. Swearingen Papers, Box 4, Folder 95.
2. Swearingen, M. H. (1950). *A gallant journey: Mr. Swearingen and his family.* Columbia: University of South Carolina Press, 107.
3. Swearingen, J. E. (1911). A decade of public school programs in South Carolina. John E. Swearingen Papers, Box 3.
4. Ibid.
5. *Fifty-second annual report of the South Carolina state superintendent of education.* (1919). Columbia, SC: State Printing Company, 12.
6. Hayes, J. I. (2001). *South Carolina and the New Deal.* Columbia: University of South Carolina Press, 188–190.
7. Photo from the Gallery at the State House, Columbia, South Carolina circa 2003, courtesy the author.
8. Public schools of South Carolina during the administration of J. E. Swearingen 1909–1923. John E. Swearingen Papers, Box 4, Folder 95.
9. Swearingen, *A gallant journey,* 113.
10. Tillman, B. R. to Swearingen, J. E. (January 17, 1913). Tillman, Benjamin Ryan. Outgoing correspondence. Manuscripts—Political Collections. Box 8, Folder 88.
11. Frank, T. (2005). *What's the matter with Kansas? How conservatives won the heart of America.* New York, NY: Holt.
12. Camak, D. E. (1960). *Human gold from Southern hills: Not a novel but a romance of facts.* Greer, SC: Published privately by the author, 136–139.
13. *Forty-fifth annual report of the South Carolina state superintendent of education.* (1913). Columbia, SC: State Printing Company, 106–107.

14. *Forty-third annual report of the South Carolina state superintendent of education.* (1911), Columbia, SC: State Printing Company, 97-98.
15. Ibid., 99.
16. Bureau of Labor Statistics. Fastest growing occupations. *United States Department of Labor occupational outlook handbook.* Retrieved from http://www.bls.gov/ooh/fastest-growing.htm.
17. Baum, S. & Ma, J. (2012). Trends in student aid 2012. *College Board Advocacy and Policy Center.* Retrieved from http://trends.collegeboard.org/student-aid.
18. Taibbi, M. (August 29, 2013). The college loan scandal. *Rolling Stone,* 1190, 36.
19. The college-cost calamity. (August 4, 2012). *The Economist.* Retrieved from http://www.economist.com/node/21559936, para 10.
20. Taibbi, The college loan scandal, 36.
21. Swearingen, J. E. to Riggs, W. M. (December 2, 1915). Tillman, Benjamin Ryan. Incoming correspondence. Manuscripts—Political Collections. Box 44, folder 664.
22. Lodge, L. D. to Swearingen, J. E. (January 23, 1923). John E. Swearingen Papers, Box 4, Folder 92.
23. Thornwell, J. H. to Swearingen, J. E. (January 23, 1923). John E. Swearingen Papers, Box 4, Folder 95.
24. Spears, J. T. to Swearingen, J. E. (June 19, 1922). John E. Swearingen Papers, Box 3, Folder 73.

References

Advises closing of all schools. (October 7, 1918). *The State.* Columbia, SC. 1.
Alley, J. P. (April 4, 1922). Hambone's meditations [serial comic]. *The State.* Columbia, SC. 4.
Anderson, E. & Moss, A. A. (1999). *Dangerous donations: Northern philanthropy and southern black education, 1902-1930.* Columbia: University of Missouri Press.
Anderson, J. D. (1978). Northern foundations and the shaping of Southern Black rural education 1902-1935. *History of Education Quarterly, 18*(4), 371–398.
Anderson, J. D. (1988). *The education of blacks in the south, 1860-1935.* Chapel Hill: University of North Carolina Press.
Angus, D. (2001). *Professionalism and the public good: A brief history of teacher certification.* Washington, DC: Thomas B. Fordham Foundation.
Angus, D. & Mirel, J. (1999). *The failed promise of the American high school 1890–1995.* New York, NY: New York Teacher's Press.
Ansel, Martin F. (1907-1911). General correspondence. Governor's Papers. Columbia, SC, South Carolina Repository of History and Archives.
Ansel, Martin F. (1907-1911). Miscellaneous papers. Governor's Papers. Columbia, SC, South Carolina Repository of History and Archives.
Aspinwall, K. & Drummond, M. J. (1989). Socialized into teaching. In DeLyon, H. & Migniuolo, F. W. (Eds.). *Women teachers: Issues and experiences.* Philadelphia, PA: Milton Keyes.
Ayers, D. (1988). *Let my people learn: The biography of Dr. Wil Lou Gray.* Greenwood, SC: Attic Press.
Baum, S. & Ma, J. (2012). Trends in student aid 2012. *College Board Advocacy and Policy Center.* Retrieved from http://trends.collegeboard.org/student-aid.
Bederman, G. (1995). *Manliness and civilization: A cultural history of gender and race in the United States 1880-1917.* Chicago, IL: University of Chicago Press.
Beneke, T. (1997). *Proving manhood: Reflections on men and sexism.* Berkeley: University of California Press.
Berry, T. E. (1967). *The biographer's craft.* New York, NY: The Odyssey Press.
Best, J. H. (Spring, 1996). Education in the forming of the American South. *History of Education Quarterly, 36*(1), 39–51.
Biebel, C. D. (1976). Private foundations and public policy: The case of secondary education during the Great Depression. *History of Education Quarterly, 16*(1), 3–34.

Blease, Coleman Livingston. (1911–1915). General correspondence. Governor's Papers. Columbia, SC, South Carolina Repository of History and Archives.
Blease, Coleman Livingston. (1911–1915). Letters to State Officials (1910–1912). Governor's Papers. Columbia, SC, South Carolina Repository of History and Archives.
Blease, Coleman Livingston. (1911–1915). Letters to State Officials (1913–1914). Governor's Papers. Columbia, SC, South Carolina Repository of History and Archives.
Blease, Coleman Livingston. (1911–1915). Miscellaneous papers. Governor's Papers. Columbia, SC, South Carolina Repository of History and Archives.
Blocker, J. S., Jr. (Spring 2006). Race, sex and riot: The Sprigfield, Ohio race riots of 1904 and 1906 and the sources of anti-Black violence in the Lower Midwest. *Ohio Valley History*, 6(1), 27–45.
Bohan, C. H. (2001). *Go to the sources: Lucy Maynard Salmon and the teaching of history*. New York, NY: Peter Lang.
Bowen, C. D. (1951). *The writing of biography*. Boston, MA: The Writer.
Bowers, L. W. (November 10, 1918). How to fight Spanish influenza. *The State*. Columbia, SC. 9.
Bradford, W. R. (1954). *Twenty-one governors of South Carolina, Tillman to Byrnes (including both): A related tragedy and other matters*. Columbia, SC: State Printing Company.
Burnside, R. D. (1964). Racism in the administrations of Governor Cole Blease. *The Proceedings of the South Carolina Historical Association*, 43–57.
Bureau of Education, Department of the Interior. (1918). *Bulletin No. 35: Cardinal principles of secondary education: A report of the commission on the reorganization of secondary education, appointed by the National Education Association*. Washington, DC: Government Printing Office.
Bureau of Labor Statistics. (March 29, 2012). Fastest growing occupations. *United States Department of Labor occupational outlook handbook*. Retrieved from http://www.bls.gov/ooh/fastest-growing.htm.
Burts, R. M. (1974). *Richard Irvine Manning and the Progressive movement in South Carolina*. Columbia: University of South Carolina Press.
Cahill, E. E. & Pieper, H. (First Quarter, 1974). Closing the educational gap: The South versus the United States. *Phylon*, 35(1), 45–53.
Camak, D. E. (1960). *Human gold from Southern hills: Not a novel but a romance of facts*. Greer, SC: Published privately by the author.
Cash, W. J. (1941). Of quandary—And the birth of a dream. In *The mind of the South*. Garden City, NY: Doubleday Anchor Books.
Cheng, C. (1999). Marginalized masculinities and hegemonic masculinity: An introduction. *Journal of Men's Studies*, 7(3), 295. Retrieved from http://search.proquest.com/docview/222608043?accountid=14793.
Clark, E. C. (1940). *A history of the first hundred years of the high school of Charleston, South Carolina, 1839–1939*. Unpublished master's thesis, University of South Carolina.

Clifford, G. J. (1991). Daughters into teachers: Educational and demographic influences on the transformation of teaching into 'women's work' in America. In Prentice, A. & Theobald, M. R. (Eds.). *Women who taught:Perspectives on the history of women and teaching.* Toronto: University of Toronto Press.

The college-cost calamity. (August 4, 2012). *The Economist.* Retrieved from http://www.economist.com/node/21559936.

Columbian: Mrs. Swearingen is state mother. (March 21, 1962). *The State.* Columbia, SC. 1-A-2-A.

The Constitution of the State of South Carolina of 1895. Retrieved from http://www.scstate house.gov/scconstitution/scconst.php.

Cooke, J. E. (1960). The new south. In Sheehan, D. & Syrett, H. (Eds.). *Essays in American historiography, papers presented in honor of Allan Nevins.* Baton Rouge: Louisiana State University Press.

Cooper, F. R. (2006). Against bipolar black masculinity: Intersectionality, assimilation, identity performance, and hierarchy. *University of California at Davis Law Review,* 39, 853–906.

Cooper on education. (October 29, 1918). *The State.* Columbia, SC. 9.

Cooper, R. (1919). *An educational policy for the state.* Columbia, SC: State Printing Company.

Counts, G. S. (1922). *The selective character of American secondary education.* Chicago, IL: University of Chicago Press.

Dunbar, N. (1986). *Public secondary education in Columbia, SC 1895–1950.* Unpublished doctoral dissertation, University of South Carolina.

Dreyfus, J. V. (1997). *John Eldred Swearingen: Superintendent of education in South Carolina 1909–1922.* Columbia, SC: College of Education.

Edel, L. (1984). *Writing lives: Principia biographica.* New York: W. W. Norton.

Edgar, W. B. (1998). *South Carolina: A history.* Columbia: University of South Carolina Press.

Edgar, W. B. (Ed.). (2006). *The South Carolina encyclopedia.* Columbia: University of South Carolina Press.

Edgar, W. B. (1992). *South Carolina in the modern age.* Columbia: University of South Carolina Press.

Elaine, F. P. (2005). Midnight rangers: Costume and performance in the reconstruction-era Ku Klux Klan. *The Journal of American History,* 92(3), 811–836. Retrieved from http://search.proquest.com/docview/224894118?accountid=1 4793.

Espy, H. G. (1939). *The public secondary school: A critical analysis of secondary education in the United States.* Atlanta, GA: Houghton Mifflin.

Fall teacher's examination: Will be held here tomorrow at the court house. (October 5, 1911). *The Anderson Daily Mail.* Anderson, SC. 4.

Fletcher, J. G. (1962). Education, past and present. In *I'll take my stand: The south and the agrarian tradition.* New York, NY: Harper Torchbooks.

Fiftieth annual report of the South Carolina state superintendent of education. (1917). Columbia, SC: State Printing Company.

Fifty-first annual report of the South Carolina state superintendent of education. (1918). Columbia, SC: State Printing Company.
Fifty-second annual report of the South Carolina state superintendent of education. (1919). Columbia, SC: State Printing Company.
Fifty-third annual report of the South Carolina state superintendent of education. (1920). Columbia, SC: State Printing Company.
Fifty-fourth annual report of the South Carolina state superintendent of education. (1921). Columbia, SC: State Printing Company.
Fifty-fifth annual report of the South Carolina state superintendent of education. (1922). Columbia, SC: State Printing Company.
Flick, A. (2000). Joyce's biographers and the question of biographical truth. In Kirschstein, B. H. (Ed.). *Life writing/Writing lives.* Malabar, FL: Krieger.
Fortieth annual report of the South Carolina state superintendent of education. (1908). Columbia, SC: State Printing Company.
Forty-first annual report of the South Carolina state superintendent of education. (1909). Columbia, SC: State Printing Company.
Forty-second annual report of the South Carolina state superintendent of education. (1910). Columbia, SC: State Printing Company.
Forty-third annual report of the South Carolina state superintendent of education. (1911). Columbia, SC: State Printing Company.
Forty-fourth annual report of the South Carolina state superintendent of education. (1912). Columbia, SC: State Printing Company.
Forty-fifth annual report of the South Carolina state superintendent of education. (1913). Columbia, SC: State Printing Company.
Forty-sixth annual report of the South Carolina state superintendent of education. (1914). Columbia, SC: State Printing Company.
Forty-seventh annual report of the South Carolina state superintendent of education. (1915). Columbia, SC: State Printing Company.
Forty-eighth annual report of the South Carolina state superintendent of education. (1916). Columbia, SC: State Printing Company.
Frank, T. (2005). *What's the matter with Kansas? How conservatives won the heart of America.* New York, NY: Holt.
Franklin, J. H. (1961). *Reconstruction after the Civil War.* Chicago, IL: University of Chicago Press.
Friend, C. T. & Glover, L. (2001). Rethinking Southern masculinity: An introduction. In Friend, C. T. & Glover, L. (Eds.). *Southern manhood: Perspectives on masculinity in the old south.* Athens: University of Georgia Press.
Fuller, B. (1983). Youth job structure and school enrollment 1890–1920. *Sociology of Education, 56*(3), 145–156.
Gaston, P. M. (1967). The "New South." In Link, A. & Rembert, W. P. (Eds.). *Writing Southern history: Essays in historogoraphy in honor of Fletcher M. Green.* Baton Rouge: Louisiana State University Press.
Garraty, J. A. (1957). *The nature of biography.* New York, NY: Alfred A. Knopf.
General Education Board Archives. (1993). Series 1: Appropriations; Subseries 1; The Early Southern Program. [Bettis Academy 1902–1948]. New York, NY: Rockefeller University.

General Education Board Archives. (1993). Series 1: Appropriations; Subseries 1; The Early Southern Program. [Columbia Public Schools 1923–1925]. New York, NY: Rockefeller University.
General Education Board Archives. (1993). Series 1: Appropriations; Subseries 1; The Early Southern Program. [Mayesville Educational & Industrial School 1902–1919]. New York, NY: Rockefeller University.
General Education Board Archives. (1993). Series 1: Appropriations; Subseries 1; The Early Southern Program. [State Agent for Secondary Education 1919–1926]. New York, NY: Rockefeller University.
General Education Board Archives. (1993). Series 1: Appropriations; Subseries 1; The Early Southern Program. [Supervisor of Rural Schools—Negro, 1917–1952]. New York, NY: Rockefeller University.
General Education Board Archives. (1993). Series 1: Appropriations; Subseries 1; The Early Southern Program. [Supervisor of Rural Schools—White, 1912–1927]. New York, NY: Rockefeller University.
General Education Board Archives. (1993). Series 1: Appropriations; Subseries 1; The Early Southern Program. [Voorhees Normal and Industrial School 1902–1957]. New York, NY: Rockefeller University.
General Education Board. Series I—Appropriations. Subseries i: States. Sleepy Hollow, NY: Rockefeller Archive Center.
General Education Board. Series I—Appropriations. Subseries iv—Higher Education. Sleepy Hollow, NY: Rockefeller Archive Center.
General election lacks in interest: Practically no oppostion to democratic nominees. (November 6, 1918). *The State*. Columbia, SC. 10.
Gershenberg, I. (Winter, 1970). Southern values and public education: A revision. *History of Education Quarterly, 10*(4), 413–422.
Gittings, R. (1978). *The nature of biography*. Seattle: University of Washington Press.
Government helps to supply teachers: Federal board of education established to render free service in present shortage. (October 20, 1918). *The State*. Columbia, SC. 22.
Graham, P. A. (1995). Assimilation, adjustment, and access: An antiquarian view of American education. In Ravitch, D. & Vinovskis, M. (Eds.). *Learning from the past: What history teaches us about school reform*. Baltimore, MD: Johns Hopkins University Press.
Gray, W. L. (1939). *Stop, look, and read my history*. Columbia, SC: State Printing Company.
Gray, W. L. & Swearingen, J. E. (1920). *Midsummer drive against illiteracy for white schools*. Office of State Superintendent of Education, State of South Carolina.
Guess, W. H. (1960). *South Carolina: Annals of pride and protest*. New York, NY: Harper.
Hand, W. H. (1906). A plea for high schools. *Thirty-eighth annual report of the South Carolina state superintendent of education*. Columbia, SC: State Printing Company.
Hayes, J. I. (2001). *South Carolina and the New Deal*. Columbia: University of South Carolina Press.

Hedrick, J. D. (1998). Biography as interdisciplinary art. In Bak, H. & Krabbendam, H. (Eds.), *Writing lives: American biography and autobiography*. Amsterdam: Vu University Press.

Hemphill, J. C. (November 3, 1918). Southern negro's status after war: Reconstruction era following close of world conflict to demand section's best thought for proper solution. *The State*. Columbia, SC. 22.

Hollis, D. W. (1956). *University of South Carolina Volume II: College to University*. Columbia: University of South Carolina Press.

Houchins, J. F. Progressive politics, or why no. 3. (December 21, 1911). *The Standard*. Holley, New York."Interested." Suggests Miss Gray: Correspondent commends for state office. (May 26, 1922). *The State*. Columbia, SC. 2.

Jackson, R. L. (July 1997). Black 'manhood' as xenophobe: An ontological exploration of the Hegelian dialectic. *Journal of Black Studies, 27*(6), 731-750.

Janak, E. (2010). "Adventitiously blind, advantageously political: John Eldred Swearingen and social definitions of disability in progressive-era South Carolina." *Vitae Scholasticae, 27*(1), 5-25.

Janak, E. (2014). "Adventitiously blind, advantageously political: John Eldred Swearingen and social definitions of disability in progressive-era South Carolina." In Morice, L. C. and& Puchner, L. *Life stories: Exploring issues in educational history through biography*. Charlotte, NC: Information Age Publishing, 85-106.

Janak, E. & Moran, P. (2010). Unlikely crusader: John Eldred Swearingen and African-American education in South Carolina. *Educational Studies, 46*(2), 224-249.

Journal of the house of representatives of the general assembly of the state of South Carolina. (1913). Columbia, SC: Gonzales and Bryan.

Kandel, P. (1939). *History of secondary education in the United States*. New York, NY: Houghton Mifflin.

Kantrowitz, S. (2000). *Ben Tillman and the reconstruction of white supremacy*. Chapel Hill: University of North Carolina Press.

Kendall, P. (1965). *The art of biography*. New York: W. W. Norton.

Kett, J. F. (1995). School leaving: Dead end or detour? In Ravitch, D. & Vinovskis, M. (Eds.). *Learning from the past: What history teaches us about school reform*. Baltimore, MD: Johns Hopkins University Press.

Kirchstein, B. H. (2001). *Life writing/Writing lives*. Malabar, FL: Krieger.

Kirst, M. W. (1995). Who's in charge? Federal, state, and local control. In Ravitch, D. & Vinovskis, M. (Eds.). *Learning from the past: What history teaches us about school reform*. Baltimore, MD: Johns Hopkins University Press.

Kliebard, H. M. (1995). *The struggle for the American curriculum 1893-1958*. New York, NY: Routledge.

Kluger, R. (1977). *Simple justice: Brown v. Board of Education and Black America's struggle for equality*. New York, NY: Vintage Books.

Kohn, A. (January 1923). Fought for schools for fourteen years: Swearingen quits post with fine record of achievement. *The State*. Columbia, SC. 1.

Koos, L. V. (1927). *The American secondary school*. Atlanta, GA: Ginn.

Krug, E. A. (1969). *The shaping of the American high school 1880–1920*. Madison, WI: University of Milwaukee Press.

Labaree, D. F. (April 1987). *Shaping the role of the public high school: Past patterns and present implications*. Paper presented at the annual meeting of the American Educational Research Association.

Leverenz, D. (2003). *Paternalism incorporated: Fables of American fatherhood 1865–1940*. Ithaca, NY: Cornell University Press.

Link, W. A. (1992). *The paradox of Southern progressivism, 1880–1930*. Chapel Hill: University of North Carolina Press.

Lockwood, C. M. (1938). *Organization and development of the South Carolina High School League*. Unpublished master's thesis, University of South Carolina.

Maher, J. (2001). Becoming a biographer. In Kirschstein, B. H. (Ed.). *Life writing/Writing lives*. Malabar, FL: Krieger.

Mann, H. (January 1841). Introduction. *Common School Journal, 3*(1), 1–16.

Manning, R. I. (1915–1919). General correspondence. Governor's Papers. Columbia, SC: South Carolina Repository of History and Archives.

Marsh, M. (1990). Suburban men and masculine domesticity, 1870–1915. In Carnes, M. C. & Griffen, C. (Eds.). *Meanings for manhood: Constructions of masculinity in Victorian America*. Chicago, IL: University of Chicago Press.

Martin, C. J. (1949). *History and development of negro education in South Carolina*. Columbia, SC: State Department of Education.

McCants, E. C. (1927). *History stories and legends of South Carolina*. Dallas, TX: The Southern Publishing Company.

Meyers, J. (1998). The quest for Bogart. In Bak, H. & Krabbendam, H. (Eds.). *Writing lives: American biography and autobiography*. Amsterdam: Vu University Press.

Milton, J. (1977). Sonnet XIX: When I consider how my light is spent. In Bush, D. (ed.). *The portable Milton*. New York: Penguin Books.

Mintz, S. & Kellogg, S. (1988). *Domestic revolutions: A social history of American family life*. New York, NY: Free Press.

National Vocational Education (Smith-Hughes) Act. *College of Agriculture and Life Sciences, North Carolina State University*. Retrieved from http://www.cals.ncsu.edu/agexed/sac/smithugh.html.

Negro rapist was lynched after confessing his crime: Prisoner was taken from officers after an exciting chase through three counties. (October 11, 1911). *The Anderson Daily Mail*. Anderson, SC. 1.

Nowatzki, R. (1994). Race, rape, lynching, and manhood suffrage: Constructions of white and black masculinity in turn-of-the-century white supremacist literature. *Journal of Men's Studies, 3*(2), 161. Retrieved from http://search.proquest.com/docview/222638884?accountid=14793.

Oertel, K. T. (Autumn 2002). "The free sons of the north" versus "the myrmidons of border-ruffianism": What makes a man in bleeding Kansas? *Kansas History: A Journal of the Central Plains, 25*, 174–189.

Oram, A. (1989). A master should not serve under a mistress: Women teachers and men teachers 1900–1970. In Acker, S. (Ed.). *Teachers, gender, and careers*, New York, NY. Falmer Press.

Pay should continue. (October 9, 1918). *The State*. Columbia, SC. 10.

Peffer, W. A. (1992). *Populism: Its rise and fall*. Lawrence: University Press of Kansas.

Perlmann, J. & Margo, R. A. (2001). *Women's work? American schoolteachers 1650–1920*. Chicago, IL: University of Chicago Press.

Perkinson, H. J. (1991). *The imperfect panacea: American faith in education, 1865–1990*. New York, NY: McGraw-Hill.

Pinar, W. F. (2001). *The gender of racial politics and violence in America: Lynching, prison rape, and the crisis of masculinity*. New York: Peter Lang.

Powell, A. G., Farrar, E., & Cohen, D. K. (1985). *The shopping mall high school: Winners and losers in the educational marketplace*. Boston, MA: Houghton Mifflin.

Prather, H. L. (April 1977). The Red Shirt movement in North Carolina. *Journal of Negro History, 62*(2), 174–184.

Ramsdell, C. W. (1969). Preoccupation with agriculture. In Billington, M. L. (Ed.). *The South: A central theme*. Atlanta, GA: Holt, Rinehart, and Winston.

Ransom, J. C. (1962). Reconstructed but unregenerate. In *I'll take my stand: The south and the agrarian tradition*. New York, NY: Harper Torchbooks.

Ravitch, D. (2000). *Left back: A century of failed school reforms*. New York, NY: Simon & Schuster.

Ravitch, D. (1995). The search for order and the rejection of conformity: Standards in American education. In Ravitch, D. & Vinovskis, M. (Eds.). *Learning from the past: What history teaches us about school reform*. Baltimore, MD: Johns Hopkins University Press.

Reese, W. J. (2011). *America's public schools: From the common school to "no child left behind."* Baltimore, MD: Johns Hopkins University Press.

Reese, W. J. (1995). *The origins of the American high school*. New Haven, CT: Yale University Press.

Reese, W. J. (1986). *Power and the promise of school reform: Grassroots movements during the progressive era*. Boston, MA: Routledge & Kegan Paul.

Reynolds, K. (1998). Finding facts, telling truths, achieving art. In Kridel, C. (Ed.). *Writing educational biography: Explorations in qualitative research*. New York: Garland.

Richardson, J. G. (1980). Variation in date of enactment of compulsory school attendance laws: An empirical study. *Sociology of Education, 53*, 153–163.

Richardson, R. (2007). *Black masculinity and the U.S. South: From Uncle Tom to gangsta*. Athens: University of Georgia Press.

Rogers, G. C. & Taylor, C. J. (1994). *A South Carolina chronology 1497–1992*. Columbia: University of South Carolina Press.

Rotundo, E. A. (1990). Boy culture: Middle class boyhood in nineteenth-century America. In Carnes, M. C. & Griffen, C. (Eds.). *Meanings for manhood:*

Constructions of masculinity in Victorian America. Chicago, IL: University of Chicago Press.

Sedlak, M. W. (1995). Attitudes, choices, and behavior: School delivery of health and social services. In Ravitch, D. & Vinovskis, M. (Eds.). *Learning from the past: What history teaches us about school reform.* Baltimore, MD: Johns Hopkins University Press.

Simon, B. (February 1996). "The appeal of Cole Blease of South Carolina: Race, class, and sex in the New South." *The Journal of Southern History, 62*(1), 82–83.

Simon, B. (1998). *A fabric of defeat: The politics of South Carolina millhands, 1910–1948.* Chapel Hill: University of North Carolina Press.

Six ways to compute the relative value of a U.S. dollar amount, 1774 to present. *Measuring worth: A service for calculating relative worth over time.* Retrieved from http://www.measuringworth.com/uscompare/.

Smith, L. M. (1998). On becoming an archivist and biographer. In Kridel, C. (Ed.). *Writing educational biography: Explorations in qualitative research.* New York, NY: Garland.

Smith-Hughes Act of 1917. *Prentice-Hall documents library.* Retrieved October 30, 2002 from http://hcl.chass.ncsu.edu/garson/dye/docs/smith917.htm.

State's school funding ruled okay. (January 9, 2008). Local News Updates: *Wyoming News dot com.* Retrieved from http://www.wyomingnews.com/articles/2008/01/09/local_news_updates/19local_01-09-08.txt.

Stephens, T. (1994). *An educational shift: Early public high school legislation and the decline of the boarding school in South Carolina.* Paper written for HIST 788, University of South Carolina.

Swearingen, J. E. (1902). Educated labor. *The Bohemian.* Vol. 3, No. 2. Ft. Worth, TX: Bohemia Literary Club.

Swearingen, J. E. (1909). *High school act nineteen hundred and nine: Information, regulations, suggested courses of study.* Columbia, SC: State Printing Company.

Swearingen, J. E. Papers. Columbia, SC: South Caroliniana Library.

Swearingen, J. E., Jr. (July 30, 2002). Unpublished interview, Saratoga, WY.

Swearingen, J. E., Jr. (November 1, 2002). Unpublished interview, Chicago, IL.

Swearingen, J. E., Jr. & DiBona, C. J. (2004). *Think ahead: A memoir.* Columbia: University of South Carolina Press.

Swearingen leaves race for governor: Quits gubernatorial contest to offer for succeed himself as superintendent of education. (June 18, 1922). *The State.* Columbia, SC. 13.

Swearingen, M. H. (1950). *A gallant journey: Mr. Swearingen and his family.* Columbia: University of South Carolina Press.

Taibbi, M. (August 29, 2013). The college loan scandal. *Rolling Stone,* 1190, 34–39.

Testi, A. (March 1995).The gender of reform politics: Theodore Roosevelt and the culture of masculinity. *The Journal of American History, 81*(4), 1509–1533.

The school book case will be heard Monday: Publishing house seeking an injunction against the State Board of Education. (September 30, 1911). *The Anderson Daily Mail.* Anderson, SC. 6.

Thirty-sixth annual report of the South Carolina state superintendent of education. (1904). Columbia, SC: State Printing Company.

Thirty-seventh annual report of the South Carolina state superintendent of education. (1905). Columbia, SC: State Printing Company.

Thirty-eighth annual report of the South Carolina state superintendent of education. (1906). Columbia, SC: State Printing Company.

Thirty-ninth annual report of the South Carolina state superintendent of education. (1907). Columbia, SC: State Printing Company.

Tillman and Blease. (August 30, 1914). *The New York Times.* 14.

Tillman on Blease. (August 24, 1912). *The Anderson Daily Mail.* Anderson, SC. 1.

Tillman, Benjamin Ryan. Incoming correspondence. Manuscripts—Political Collections. Clemson, SC: Special Collections: Robert Muldrow Cooper Library.

Tillman, Benjamin Ryan. Outgoing correspondence. Manuscripts—Political Collections. Clemson, SC: Special Collections: Robert Muldrow Cooper Library.

To present play in sign language: Helen Menken plans to attempt mute Portia. (April 2, 1922). *The State.* Columbia, SC. 2.

Tyack, D. (1974). *The one best system: A history of American urban education.* Cambridge: Harvard University Press.

Tyack, D. & Cuban, L. (1995). *Tinkering toward utopia: A century of public school reform.* Cambridge: Harvard University Press.

United States Census Data. (2002). University of Virginia Census Information. [Online data]. Available FTP: Hostname: virginia.edu; Directory: fisher.lib File:cgilocal/censusbin/ census/cen.pl.

Urban, W .J. (Summer 1981). History of education: A Southern exposure. *History of Education Quarterly, 21*(2), 131–145.

Wallace, D. D. (1961). *South Carolina: A short history 1520–1948.* Chapel Hill: University of North Carolina Press.

Weiler, K. (1989). Women's history and the history of women teachers. *Journal of Education, 171*(3), 9–30.

Wells, B. J. (December 15, 1922). Mr. Swearingen's administration. *South Carolina Education, 4*(3), 1–2.

Wells, C. A. (2005). *Civil War time: Temporality and identity in America 1861–1865.* Athens: University of Georgia Press.

Williamson, J. (1984). *The crucible of race: Black-White relations in the American South since Emancipation.* New York, NY: Oxford University Press.

Woodward, C. V. (1968). *The burden of Southern history.* New York, NY: New American Library.

Wooster, M. M. (1994). *Angry classrooms, vacant minds: What's happened to our high schools?* San Francisco, CA: Pacific Research Institute for Public Policy.

Index

Act Fixing the Military Peace Establishment of the United States, 140
Act to Appropriate Sixty Thousand Dollars to the Public Schools of South Carolina, 63
Act to Increase the Average Length of the School Term and to Improve Efficiency of the Public Schools in This State, 61, 65
Adams, Cicero, 33
administrator training, 54, 120, 163
AFL-CIO, 27
African Americans, 18, 72, 148–9
    education, 11, 12, 80–5, 109, 125, 132, 164–6, 224n80
    schools, 20, 58, 62, 65–7, 75–6, 78, 82–4, 90, 111, 118, 129, 130–1, 139, 149, 171, 236n12
    teachers, 20, 84, 131, 167
    vocational education, 143, 144
    voting, 31, 181
agricultural education, 8, 15, 47, 50, 140, 154, 166, 205
Allen University, 91
American Educational Research Journal, 2
American Federation of Labor (AFL), 27, 134
Anderson, J. G., 103
Anderson, James, 23, 78, 131
Ansel, Martin, 13, 73–4, 108, 109
anti-intellectualism, 108, 116
Aristophanes, 160
Ashley, J. W., 92

Association of Colleges and Secondary Schools of the Southern States, 130
Association of Southern Colleges and Preparatory Schools (ASCPS), 117, 118
Association of Superintendents of Public Instruction of the Southern States, 53
B. F. Johnson Company, 184
Babcock, Havilah, 195
Bacon, Thomas, 32
Banks, William, 175, 177
Barnwell Colored School, 166
Beard, W. P., 106
Beaufort Negro School, 158
Bederman, Gail, 10, 153
Beneke, Timothy, 17, 48, 59
Bennettsville School, 167
Best, John Hardin, 16
Bethea, Andrew, 175
Bettis Academy, 76
Biebel, Charles, 75, 77
Bishop, B. B., 176
Blackwood, Ira, 203
Blease, Coleman L. "Coley," 4, 10, 13, 71, 81, 87–91, 93, 175, 176, 179, 180, 206
    masculinity portrayal, 91, 93, 108, 180
    racism, 84, 87, 90, 91–3, 107, 115, 116, 145–6
    Swearingen relationship, 87, 107–15, 159, 179, 182

Blease, Coleman L. "Coley,"—*Continued*
   Tillman relationship, 97–107, 110, 111, 112, 114, 207
   U.S. Senate bids, 113, 114, 116
bond issuances, 56
Bond, O. J., 94
Bourne, Jonathan, 96
Bradford, William, 88
Bradley, Francis W., 7
Brannon, J. H., 164, 165
Brooks, Preston, 26, 91
Brown, S. H., 177
Brunson, Mason C., 41
Bryan, William Jennings, 71
Bunch, George, 38, 41, 51
Burgess, John, 170
Burn, Henry, 58
Burts, C. E., 182
Burts, Robert, 124
Bussey, G. W., 102
Buttrick, Wallace, 78, 79, 80, 186, 190
Byrnes, James, 167

Caldwell, B. L., 164
Calhoun, John C., 16
Camak, David English, 88, 207
Campaign Executive Committee, 55
Cardinal Principles of Secondary Education, 150–2, 153, 157, 163
Carpenter, T. Gordon, 181
Cavendish, Margaret, 3
Chapman, W. A., 186
Cheng, C., 19
Child Labor Law (1916), 124
child labor laws, 25, 127
Citadel, The, 94
Civil War, 17, 18, 22, 32–3
Clemson University, 11, 28, 60, 102, 106, 154
Cleveland, Grover, 29
Coalition of Essential Schools, 8
Cofield, George, 185
College of Charleston, 152
Colored National Farmer's Alliance, 27

Commission to Examine and Revise the School Law of the State and to Recommend Changes in Same, 62
Common Core, 210
Compulsory Attendance Law (1901), 24, 25
Compulsory Attendance Law (1915), 112–13, 123, 126–30, 138, 162–3, 171, 203
Confederacy of Industrial Organizations (CIO), 27
Conference on Country Schools and Country Life, 74
Converse College, 44
Cooley, Rose, 111
Cooper, Dorcas Calmes, 162
Cooper, Frank Rudy, 17
Cooper, Mamie Machen, 162
Cooper, Robert, 13, 155, 160, 161–2, 163, 170
core curriculum movement, 2
Core Knowledge Foundation, 8
Counts, G. S., 144
Cox, A. H., 121
Crewes, Bose, 100
Cross Anchor School, 167
Currell, S. C., 136
curriculum reform, 116, 119, 130, 140, 143, 150, 163, 204

D. C. Heath Company, 184
Davis, Jackson, 165
Dawson, Francis, 215n2
Democratic Party, 18, 73, 97
Dewey, John, 2, 160
disabilities
   nexus with race, class, and masculinity, 4, 13, 29, 48, 137
   societal treatment, 2, 40, 45, 62, 161, 202–2, 205
   Swearingen as model, 3, 11, 44, 46, 68, 107, 173, 187, 191
Douglas, Tommy, 206
Drake, Vera, 178, 181, 185
Dreyfuss, James, 3, 5, 22, 157

dropout rates, 156
dual-path system, 144

Edel, Leon, 12
Edgar, Walter, 30, 31, 71, 91, 179
Edmunds, S. H., 136
elementary education, 57, 61, 63, 126, 147, 156, 163–4
Elmore, E. C., 47
Equalizing Act (1917), 154, 157

Fairfield Chamber of Commerce, 43
Farmer's Alliance and Industrial Union, 27, 28
Farmer's Mutual Benefit Association, 27
Felton, J. B., 60
Ferdinand, Franz, 145
Fletcher, John Gould, 125
Flexner, Abraham, 79–80, 165
Flick, Arend, 3
Florence High School for Negroes, 77
Fourteenth Amendment, 20
Frank, Thomas, 207
Franklin, John Hope, 21
Friend, Craig Thompson, 18, 46

Garraty, James, 5
Gary system, 75
Gasque, B. F., 176
General Education Board (GEB), 5, 6, 12, 75–6, 77, 78, 79, 80, 142, 149, 163, 166, 186, 203
Gershenberg, Irving, 21
Gittings, Robert, 10, 11
Glantzberg, Pinckney Estes, 185
Glenn, W. H., 104
Glover, Lorri, 18, 46
Gong Lum v. Rice, 93
Gonzales, N. G., 215n2
Graded School Act (1912), 154
Graham, Patricia, 151
Graham, S. H., 52
Grant, Ulysses S., 40
Gray, Wil Lou, 138, 167–8, 178, 232n51, 238n59

Great Branch School, 167
Green, Leon, 99
Guignard, Jane Bruce, 80
Gunter, Luceo, 159, 178

Hamburg Massacre, 29, 30
Hampton Institute, 75, 78, 164, 236n10
Hampton, Wade, 40
Hand, William, 24, 56, 57, 63, 67, 84–5, 116, 117, 118, 119, 140–1, 158
Hanna, R. E., 159, 179
Harvard University Committee of Ten, 8
Hayes, Jack Irby, 13–14
Haynes, James, 157
Heath Springs Model School, 76
Heyward, D. C., 55
Hickory Grove School, 167
High School Act (1909), 8, 55–6, 61, 118, 129, 214n15
High School Act (1919), 158
high school standards/accreditation, 56–7, 116–17, 118–19, 130, 150
high schools, 54–8, 63
Hope, Jasper, 178, 181–2, 185, 193
Houchins, J. F., 72
Hough, Columbus Nixon, 132
Hough, Martha Love Chappell, 132
Hughes, Charles Evans, 145
Hutchinson, Lucy, 3
Hyde, Sam, 93

illiteracy, 24, 73, 166, 167–8, 169, 204, 155
immigration, 25, 148, 156
Industrial Revolution, 48
Industrial Workers of the World, 80
influenza epidemic (1918), 156–7, 203
Inter-State Commerce Commission, 97
Irby, John, 28

Jackson, Andrew, 15
Jackson, Ronald, 17

Jackson, Willis, 92
Jeanes teachers, 164
Jennings, Lang D., 113
Jim Crow, 148
Johnson, D. B., 55, 106, 109, 136
Johnson, Olin D., 203
Johnson, W. Lee, 100
Johnstone, Alan, 70
Jones, Ira B., 99, 112
Jones, Soap, 96
Joyce, James, 3
Joyner, J. Y., 53, 54
Joynes, Edward S., 43, 51
Junior Red Cross, 147

Keller, Helen, 38
Kett, Joseph, 151
King, Stephen, 6
Kingsley, Clarence, 150
Kirst, Michael, 10
Kluger, Richard, 148
Knights of Labor, 27
Krug, Edward, 118, 141
Ku Klux Klan, 5, 19, 27, 148, 167, 179–80, 181

labor movement, 3, 25, 27, 80, 112, 143
Laney, George K., 70
lay-by schools, 167
Lee, Robert E., 67
Leverenz, David, 77
Lewis, Anna, 103
Lewis, William, 142
Liberty Loans, 147
Lincoln, Abraham, 40
Link, William, 82
literacy tests, 31
Lockwood, D. B., 175
Lodge, Lee Davis, 210
Longman, Green & Company, 183
Lost Cause mythology, 27
lynching, 71, 90, 91–2, 180

Mabry, T. O., 69
Mackey, T. J., 40
Maher, Jane, 6

Mann, Horace, 2, 22
Manning, Richard I., 13, 115, 121, 123–4, 136, 146, 154, 155, 158–9
Marion, Francis, 15
Marion Training School, 164
Marsh, Margaret, 138
Martin, C. J., 23
Martin, O. B., 46, 54, 55, 56, 57, 58
Martin, V. B., 92
Martin, W. F., 181
masculinity, 17, 26, 36, 71–2
    performances of, 5, 10, 16–17, 19
    white masculinity, 17, 19, 46
    see also Blease, Coleman: masculinity portrayal; Swearingen, John Eldred: performance of masculinity
Masons, 27
Mayesville School, 76
McCants, E. C., 29, 175
McCravey, Ed, 70
McElveen, J. V., 176
McLeod, Thomas G., 175
McSwain, John J., 41, 51, 101, 102, 134, 146, 167, 172, 179, 189, 190, 231n35
Mellichamp, Stiles R., 47
Menken, Helen, 161
Milton, John, 1
Mitchell, Samuel C., 68, 109, 110
Mitchum, Harvey, 96
Moore, Paul, 178, 181
Morgan, J. P., 142
Morrill Act (1862), 140
Morrill Act (1890), 140
Muckley, Ferdinand, 103
Mulwee, Ernest, 93

National Association for the Advancement of Colored People (NAACP), 167
National Association of Manufacturers, 143
National Citizen's Alliance, 27
National Education Association, 85
National Farmer's Alliance, 27

National Vocational Education Act. *See* Smith-Hughes Act
Next Generation Science Standards, 210
noblesse oblige, 21
Northwest Ordinance, 140

Ogden, Robert C., 76
Oliver, Robert Shaw, 145

Palloway, J. R., 181
Patrons of Husbandry (the Grange), 27
Patton, George S., 148
Peabody, George Foster, 76
Peffer, William, 27, 28
People's Party, 26, 27, 97
per-pupil spending, 65, 83, 124, 202, 203
Perkinson, Henry, 25, 142
Perry, James Margery "Miss Jim," 153
Point Print, 37, 68, 133–4, 136, 218n59, 221n33
Pollock, W. P., 113
poor whites, 19, 24, 88, 90, 91, 102, 112
Populism, 5, 19, 25–8
poverty, 21, 54, 116, 159, 169, 177
preparatory courses, 58
prisons, 89, 90
private schools, 19, 24, 111
Progressive Era, 2–3, 10, 31, 71, 72
public education, 22–3, 140, 143
   see also administrator training; African Americans: education; African Americans: schools; *Cardinal Principles Report*; curriculum reform; dual-path system; high school standards/accreditation; high schools; per-pupil spending; rural schools; school term length; teacher salaries; teacher shortages; teacher training/certification; textbooks

race relations, 165–6, 167
racial violence, 19
   see also lynching; Red Shirt Riders
Rasor, J. B., 182
Rasor, Sophie, 182, 185, 188
Reconstruction, 17, 18, 19–20, 22, 29, 40
Rector-Riddle Act (1917), 154
Red Shirt Riders, 18–19, 27, 31
Reese, William J., 80, 85, 153
Republican Party, 19, 159
Richardson, H. W., 96
Richardson, John, 25
Richardson, Riché, 148–9
Riggs, Walter, 136
Riley, H. L., 134
Rivers, Prince, 30
Rockefeller Foundation, 12, 75, 77
Roosevelt, Franklin D., 113
Roosevelt, Theodore, 72, 142, 145
Rosenwald Schools, 75
Rotundo, E. Anthony, 36, 42, 174
Rural School Improvement Association, 130
rural schools, 47, 48, 50, 57–8, 62, 74, 111–12, 119

Saunders, W. O., 106
scholarships, 56
school enrollments, 25, 63, 66, 82, 156
School Garden Academies, 147
school term length, 163, 168, 202, 203, 236n12
schools-miles ratio, 63
Seay, O. D., 178
secondary education movement, 53–4, 63
Sedlak, Michael, 146
segregated schools. *See* African Americans: schools
Sherman, William T., 18, 22
Simon, Bryant, 112, 184
slavery, 18, 20
Smith-Hughes Act (1917), 8, 140, 142, 143, 154, 166, 205, 210
Smith, Charles, 13
Smith, Ellison D. "Cotton Ed," 113, 114

258 INDEX

Smoak-Rector Act, 154
Snyder, Henry, 136
South Carolina Constitution of 1868, 20, 22
South Carolina Constructive League, 167
South Carolina Federation of Colored Women's Clubs, 72
South Carolina High School League, 152
South Carolina Industrial School for Girls, 124
South Carolina Institute for the Insane, 38, 107
South Carolina State Archive, 12
South Carolina State Board of Education, 23, 56, 73, 74, 111, 119, 126
South Carolina State Board of Vocational Training, 154
South Carolina State Department of Education, 1, 12
South Carolina State Highway Department, 124
South Carolina State University, 130
South Carolina Teachers' Association, 59
Spelman College, 84
St. Helena Island Rural School, 77
Stafford Bill (1917), 126
State Board of Law Examiners, 72
Stinson, Ruford, 76
Stoddard, J. A., 186
Strohecker, H. O., 182
Sullivan, Anne, 38
Sumner, Charles, 26, 29, 91
Swearingen, Anna Tillman, 32, 33–4, 37, 43, 68
Swearingen, Arthur "A. S.," 33
Swearingen, Ben "B. T.," 33
Swearingen, Eldred M., 32
Swearingen, George, 35, 68, 134, 191
Swearingen, George Van, 172, 174, 189, 194
Swearingen, James "J. T.," 32
Swearingen, John Cloud, 32, 33–4

Swearingen, John Eldred, 1, 3–4, 70–4, 175–81, 199, 202–5
African American school improvement activism, 2, 5, 6, 11, 65–7, 80–5, 130–1, 132, 138, 149–50, 155–6, 165–70, 189, 203
Blease relationship, 87, 107–15, 159, 179, 182
blindness, 3, 4, 11, 13, 35–41, 47, 48, 50, 51–2, 61, 81, 137
campaign of 1908, 46–8, 50–2
Cedar Springs Institute for the Deaf and Blind of South Carolina, 4, 37, 43, 45–6, 192
early life, 16, 31–2
family businesses, 5, 8, 138
Georgia Academy for the Blind, 4, 36
Manning relationship, 124–5, 130–1
paternalism, 48, 50, 59, 62, 78, 178
performance of masculinity, 16–17, 35, 46, 48, 59, 79, 108, 135, 137, 173, 205
poor whites activism, 2, 6, 9, 107–8, 138–9, 159, 168
racism, 21, 47–8, 80, 81–2, 132
rhetorical skills, 43, 44, 47, 55
South Carolina College, 4, 13, 35, 37–42, 51, 52
state superintendent of education, 2, 4, 9, 59–65
Tillman relationship, 29, 35, 45, 46, 69, 87, 105, 138, 146, 193–4
Swearingen, John Eldred, Jr., 41, 59, 60, 136, 155, 172, 173, 174, 179, 189, 192, 196–7
Swearingen, Mary Douglas "Dougie," 172, 173, 195
Swearingen, Mary Hough, 3, 17, 46, 60, 69–70, 132–8, 179, 187, 189, 192, 198, 201
Swearingen, Moses, 32
Swearingen, Van, 32
Swearingen, William N., 33

Taibbi, Matt, 209
Tate, Mr., 112
Tatum, W. O., 183
taxation, 23, 40, 54, 56, 58, 90, 121, 154–5, 163, 177
Teach for America, 203
teacher salaries, 157, 158, 163, 170, 188, 202, 203
teacher shortages, 123, 147, 157, 170
teacher training/certification, 119, 120, 126, 163, 170–1, 205
teacher-pupil ratio, 63
textbooks, 183–4, 193, 203
textile mill workers, 113–14, 162, 176, 204–5
textile mills, 9, 48, 88, 90, 112
textile workers, 184–5
Thomas, A. J. S., 68
Thomas, Jesse, 76
Thompson, Hugh S., 23
Thomson, J. W., 132
Thorndike, E. L., 141
Thornwell, J. H., 210
Thrift Stamps, 147
Thurmond, J. William, 51
Tillman, Benjamin "Pitchfork Ben," 4, 9, 12, 15, 28–31, 32, 34, 59, 72, 73, 134, 135, 155, 206, 228n85
  African Americans relationship, 11, 19, 29–30, 31, 80–1
  Blease relationship, 97–107, 110, 111, 112, 114, 207
  Senate career, 28, 29, 142, 149
  Swearingen relationship, 29, 35, 45, 46, 69, 87, 105, 138, 146, 193–4
Tillman, Henry, 106
Tillman, James, 215n2
Tillman, Sophia, 34
Toole Act, 126
Tuskegee Institute, 75, 76, 78, 164, 236n10
Tyack, David, 85, 119–20, 127, 147

United Confederate Veterans (Abner Perrin Camp), 33
United States Bureau of Education, 25
United War Work Drive, 147
University of South Carolina (USC), 1, 11, 42, 93, 80, 109
urbanization, 21
US Bureau of Education, 150
US Coast Guard Academy, 140
US Department of Education, 140

vocational education, 140, 141, 142, 143, 144, 154, 166, 205, 208
Voorhees School, 76

Wallace, D. D., 29
War Savings Stamps, 147
Wardlaw, Patterson, 38
Waring, E. P., 58
Washington, Booker T., 131
Washington, George, 32
Waterman, Nixon, 72
Watson, E. J., 94–5
Weinburg, J. A., 181
Wells, B. J., 186, 190
Wharton, Lee, 68
white teachers, 20, 21, 111, 167
Williamson, Joel, 78
Wilson, Woodrow, 71, 102, 115, 143, 145, 153
Winthrop University, 28, 102, 106, 109, 110
Wolfe, C. W., 108
women, 72, 84–5, 152
women's suffrage, 23, 72, 80, 153
Woodward, F. C., 51
World War I, 145–7
Wyche, C. C., 106
Wyche, C. T., 70

Zimmerman telegram, 145
Zuczek, Richard, 30

GPSR Compliance

The European Union's (EU) General Product Safety Regulation (GPSR) is a set of rules that requires consumer products to be safe and our obligations to ensure this.

If you have any concerns about our products, you can contact us on

ProductSafety@springernature.com

In case Publisher is established outside the EU, the EU authorized representative is:

Springer Nature Customer Service Center GmbH
Europaplatz 3
69115 Heidelberg, Germany

www.ingramcontent.com/pod-product-compliance
Lightning Source LLC
LaVergne TN
LVHW051914060526
838200LV00004B/135